TOUCH
WOOD

ɛ

.e loa
a furthe

TOUCH WOOD

The Autobiography of the 1953 Le Mans Winner

DUNCAN HAMILTON
WITH LIONEL SCOTT
ADDITIONAL MATERIAL BY DOUG NYE

JOHN BLAKE

Published by John Blake Publishing Ltd,
3 Bramber Court, 2 Bramber Road,
London W14 9PB, England

www.johnblakepublishing.co.uk

www.facebook.com/Johnblakepub facebook.
twitter.com/johnblakepub twitter

First published in hardback in 1960
Revised edition published in hardback in 1990
This edition published in 2014

ISBN: 978 1 78219 773 7

British Library Cataloguing-in-Publication Data:

A catalogue record for this book is available from the British Library.

Design by www.envydesign.co.uk

Printed and bound in Great Britain by CPI Group (UK) Ltd

1 3 5 7 9 10 8 6 4 2

Papers used by John Blake Publishing are natural, recyclable products
made from wood grown in sustainable forests. The manufacturing processes
conform to the environmental regulations of the country of origin.

Every attempt has been made to contact the relevant copyright-holders,
but some were unobtainable. We would be grateful if the appropriate
people could contact us.

CONTENTS

ACKNOWLEDGEMENTS

Thanks are due to all who have assisted in *Touch Wood!* and this new edition. Illustrations are from the Hamilton archives and include work by Geoffrey Goddard, Guy Griffiths, Jarrotts and Louis Klemantaski.

FOREWORD

Touch Wood may be the best book ever. I would at least put it up there with *The Nöel Coward Diaries* and Errol Flynn's almost unbelievable autobiography *My Wicked, Wicked Ways*.

Hamilton wins the 1953 Twenty-four Hours at Le Mans in a Jaguar C-Type after staying up drinking the whole night before. He'd thought he was disqualified but he wasn't – and he was only told this on the morning of the race at 10am, when he and his co-driver were still in the bar knocking back cognac. With the start of the race only a few hours away, both drivers attempt to sober up, but can't. So they resort to a hair of the dog to stop them feeling nauseous. They miraculously go on to win – so they stay up the whole of Sunday night as well, drinking through until Monday morning.

The next day, Duncan drives to Portugal to take part in the Grand Prix. After leading into the first corner of the race, he crashes into an electricity pylon and has to be taken to hospital for an emergency operation. When he comes to he's in the operating theatre, in semi-darkness, in the company of two nuns and a surgeon whose 2-inch-long cigar is threatening to drop ash into his open chest cavity at any moment.

'Why is it dark in here?' he mumbles.

'Because the pylon you crashed into fed this hospital's electricity,' snaps the surgeon.

'Why aren't I anaesthetised?'

'Because the anaesthetist went to watch the motor race you were in.'

'And what are the nuns doing here?'

'They are to give you as much port as it takes to numb your pain. Or the last rites. Whichever comes first.'

And that's all within a couple of pages. So there you go!

Chris Evans

INTRODUCTION TO THE 1990 EDITION

It is over thirty years now since *Touch Wood* was first published. It had originally been compiled by my father in conjunction with the journalist Lionel Scott, who produced the final manuscript. It was based upon a series of taped conversations between them, in which my father told his story in the way he was wont to do, punctuated by great guffaws of laughter at the amusing episodes, and moments of great gravity in recalling the occasional disaster...

But perhaps above all, *Touch Wood* was enormously strong on my father's after-dinner stories – which really sealed its appeal for motoring enthusiasts worldwide. It captured much of the character and fun of that last great period of gentlemen's motor racing through the 1940s and 1950s which my father had enjoyed so much, and in which he had featured so prominently. At the time of its original publication, in 1960, it just didn't matter if in places it might be less than nit-pickingly accurate – it captured the flavour of a bygone age, in which sporting achievement alone was never enough without much fun along the way.

For this new edition, with the help of Doug Nye, we have decided to present the original text with as little amendment as possible. Consequently we have re-run *Touch Wood* for a 1990s' audience with this modern presentation, and an extra chapter which sketches-in life after the period dealt with by the original book while also reflecting further upon it. The text – as far as seemed sensible – is unaltered from original form.

What follows thus retains all the attitudes and standards of the late-1950s and should be read very much with this in mind. So, touch wood, we hope it will provide an entertaining and informative read, and a fine insight into an action-packed motor sporting life...

Adrian J. Hamilton, Bagshot, November 1990

FOREWORD TO THE 1960 EDITION

When Duncan Hamilton finally hung up his crash helmet, almost the last of the immediate post-war racing drivers retired from the scene. They were a band of enthusiasts different, in many ways, from their modern counterparts. They were unashamedly amateur in their approach to the sport. In the first place they owned the cars they raced and, as often as not, they prepared them themselves. Though the competitive element was strong and they tried hard to win, the race was only the focussing point of the day's activities. There were friends to meet, technical information to exchange, stories to tell and almost certainly a party to be enjoyed. Gradually all this changed, and the fine old racing and sports cars were replaced by modern machinery. Not all drivers managed the transition — not all wanted to. The sport was now more for professionals, and to win you needed to be professional in your approach. Duncan managed the transition, and both as a team driver for Jaguars, H.W.M., Ferrari and others, and as a private owner/driver, he achieved many successes. These successes were due as much to his sportsmanship, courage and determination as to his great skill.

He survived many serious accidents. Few other people, in any pursuit, would have got up, licked their wounds, and returned to the fray with such vigour and sense of purpose.

Some people are a little larger than life; Duncan is one of them. To any of his naval friends the vicissitudes of his career as a racing driver are merely the continuation of a natural sequence of events; conversely, no one who had known him for the last ten or twelve years would express any surprise to learn that his dog once ate a set of documents and so prevented a fleet from sailing for several days. It would seem quite normal for Duncan to own such a dog. And who else but Duncan could be stopped for speeding in the Cromwell Road while on his way to take part in a television programme on road safety?

The more a man travels the more important his home becomes. Duncan has been fortunate in that his wife Angela is just the person to be in his home. Her placid nature, her refusal to fuss, and above all her understanding of his wants and ambitions made his career a possibility.

As I have said, the man is slightly larger than life, but don't take my word for it — read this book and find out for yourself.

Earl Howe London, 1960

CHAPTER ONE

HOW IT ALL BEGAN

One morning in the spring of 1922, a young Irish girl stood looking out of the nursery window of my father's house near Cork. She saw a two-year-old boy who sat in a pram on the upper lawn of the garden below. He was supposed to be resting. Instead, he was trying to propel his pram forward. The pram had large wheels, and reaching over the side he had found that by moving a wheel he could also move the pram. At first his exertions amused the girl. 'He'll soon tire himself out that way', she had thought. She did not know what effect the movement of the pram was having on him. The effect of suddenly finding a mechanism obedient to his will. If he moved the wheel forward the pram moved forward, if he moved it backwards the pram moved backwards, the faster he moved it the faster the pram moved. Chortling with delight he turned the wheels vigorously, till presently, the pram, aided by sloping ground, was heading at increasing speed for the steps which led to the lower lawn.

Suddenly, the girl realized what was happening. She ran downstairs and out into the garden in time to see the pram somersaulting down thirty eight steps to the lawn below. I was unconscious for several hours. The memory of the fall receded with the bump on my head; the thrill of the experience remained. Although elaborate precautions were taken to keep me out of trouble, scarcely a week passed without some minor catastrophe occurring. I would fall down a hole, off a ladder, into a pond, always emerging relatively unscathed but never any the wiser for the experience. Those who had my welfare at heart had a terrible time.

My father's house was a converted monastery and had a large garden; it was all too easy to escape my nurse, who spent most of her time searching frantically in the outhouses and undergrowth terrified of what she might find.

This was also the period which the Irish, with their gift for understatement, refer to as 'The Troubles'. A friend of my father's was shot at our front door, and more than once bullets splattered into the rooms. We slept on mattresses under the windows to avoid the snipers' bullets. I was tied to mine, to prevent me looking for the sniper. My father was a tolerant man and understood why I might take the Vicar's bicycle to pieces while the good man was inside having tea. And, indeed, he helped me put it together again, asking, 'How else can the boy learn?' The Vicar, judging from the look on his face, knew at least one other way.

My father was a fine sportsman. He played all games well, and represented Ireland at both golf and tennis. He also loved good motor cars, and from my earliest days I was allowed to sit in them, turn the steering wheel, fiddle with the gear and brake levers, get down from the seat and push the foot pedals, blow the horn. My nurse cultivated this interest by dumping me in one of the cars whenever she could, knowing that there was a sporting chance that I might still be there when she returned.

Only once do I remember being unhappy in a car and that was on returning from a visit to Kinsale, a seaside town some twelve miles south of Cork. Father had bought some very large lobsters which he had put in a basket in the dicky of his Darracq. There they had rested peacefully enough until we started for home. I was sitting in the dicky alone and, for once, behaving myself, when suddenly, on rounding a corner, the basket rolled over and the floor was covered with crawling lobsters. I was petrified and quite unable to attract my parents' attention, for the hood was up. Fortunately, my leggings protected me from the odd nibble, though when they came off on arriving home they were a sorry commentary on my fortitude in the face of adversity.

When I was six we left Cork to settle in England. Father bought a house in West London where we lived until the war. I went to preparatory school there and found life very similar to what it had been in Ireland. There was still a big garden to play in; father was just as tolerant, and changed his cars just as often. My childhood was a very happy one.

Shortly after my thirteenth birthday father sent me to Brighton College. I was placed in School House under F.O.B. Stoakes, a fine man who was a model of what a good house-master should be. The head boy of the House, who was later to become head boy of the school, was Macdonald Hobley of television fame. It was my misfortune to fag for him, and I soon learnt that he did not possess my father's tolerance. Many an ugly scene was enacted in the prefects' bathroom when I received the consequences of some thoughtless folly. The consequences were often deserved. I remember helping him to paint his study one day. He was very good humoured at the time: laughing, joking, whistling and even bursting into song, as he stood on a chair contentedly painting a shelf. He seemed so affable that I was tempted to test his sense of humour by jogging his elbow at an inopportune moment. As a result Hobley hit the ground, the paint pot and its contents hit Hobley, and after a short intermission Hobley hit Hamilton. Hobley's sense of humour had not been equal to the occasion, but it emerged from the ordeal in better shape than mine.

I was no scholar and, being lazy, applied myself only to the things in which I was interested: shooting, swimming, boxing, rugger. Shooting was a particular favourite of mine, and I strove to achieve a schoolboy ambition: namely, to be a member of the team to win the Ashburton Shield. In 1936 I achieved my ambition, for the school, with myself a member of the team, swept all before them, winning – the Ashburton Shield, the Cottlestone Vase, the Country Life and Public School Bowl. I had the satisfaction also of achieving the highest personal score. No school has succeeded in winning all these trophies in any one year since then. The strange thing about this ambition of mine was that prior to going to Brighton I had not done any shooting at all. Indeed, my only knowledge of the Ashburton had been gleaned from the pages of glossy sporting magazines, with their pictures of presentations and smug looking young men in O.T.C. uniform sitting proudly behind their newly acquired trophy or trophies. I envied them their satisfaction and determined that I would also stare out from the pages of similar periodicals before my schooldays were over.

When I was a very new boy the question of whether I

played cricket or shot had to be decided. Apart from my personal ambition I loathed cricket, so when the Sergeant Major asked if I had done any shooting I said I had. He invited me down to the shooting range with dramatic consequences: not only did I miss the target but the safety butts as well. My shooting days could well have ended there and then but fortunately he attributed this gross inaccuracy to nerves and gave me another chance; six weeks later I was a member of the reserve team.

I played rugger for the 1st Fifteen and dished out and received a quota of black eyes and bloody noses in the boxing ring, representing the school. I also swam for the school.

These achievements came in my later school days but the earlier ones were beset with vicissitudes. To take one at random. The assistant house master of School House was a very kind man named Sam Jaeger who owned a 1935 Morris Cowley of which he was very proud. Now I was interested in this car, and told him so, asking if I might be allowed to clean it for him. He was only too pleased, so every Sunday afternoon I used to wash and leather this Morris, a task which avoided a compulsory six mile walk. One Sunday afternoon I, and a friend who had inveigled poor Jaeger into allowing him to help me, went to clean the car. It was in the garage, but Sam Jaeger could not be found. We looked for him everywhere: his study, the masters' common room, the library, the chapel; but no, he could not be found. This was an unhappy state of affairs, for neither of us felt like a six mile walk. Then my friend reminded me that I had told him I could drive my father's car (as was perfectly true); why then, he went on, could I not back the Morris out of the garage and save us both a long walk.

The point was well made. I got into the Morris and started

5

the engine. So far so good. It ran smoothly, the exhaust gurgling happily. My friend was impressed. I eased the clutch pedal and selected what I thought was reverse gear, then lifted my left foot, simultaneously depressing my right. There was an awful lurch and the car shot, not backwards, but forwards, through the wall in front of me and into the servants' bicycle quarters. It was all very sad really, for though I explained in great detail how this error of judgment had occurred, it was in vain: I had no business to drive the car. My friends would not let me forget the incident and, to impress them with my ability as a driver, I persuaded my father to let me drive his car back to school at the beginning of the next term.

This car was a rather interesting one: a Marmon straight eight, which he had bought from a Miss Carstairs, a famous American sportswoman of the day. A cream two-seater with flowing wings and a dicky, it had a four speed gear box, wire wheels, and an exhaust note of some prominence. I drove this splendid vehicle down the Horsham-Reigate road to Brighton, and with tuck box on the luggage grid and horn blowing, made a spectacular entry into the school grounds. Much blipping of the throttle as I came down through the gears made the exhaust note exploit the echo-making qualities of the old buildings as it reverberated round the clock tower. The car drew up in a well-controlled slide, gravel flying in all directions as I nonchalantly brought it to a halt. The ill-humoured faces which had appeared at the windows made the whole ostentatious operation worthwhile.

The school had an engineering master and a very fine engineering work-shop. I spent all my spare time there (other than that spent in the tuck shop) and it soon became apparent to those who were concerned with my future that it would have to be connected with engineering. As my school days drew to a close my father suggested that the aeroplane industry probably had more to offer a young man starting out in the world than any other branch of engineering and, accordingly, he proposed sending me to the Aeronautical Engineering College at Chelsea and Brooklands. When I left Brighton College it was to go to this establishment.

I had long wanted to own a car of my own, so shortly after leaving school I raised the matter with my father. Knowing that my mother would object to my driving on the open road alone – after certain experiences she had had when travelling as my passenger in the Marmon – I suggested that an old car, which I could strip down and perhaps drive in the garden, would help my education. Father agreed; and after looking around for a day or two we bought an ancient Austin Seven from a scrap merchant for thirty-five shillings. This was an interesting vehicle. The chassis was badly bent; the block was split; and all the tyres were flat. We towed it home as it was and deposited it in the garden, to my mother's horror. From then onwards all my spare time was spent working on this car. Unknown to my parents, I was taking most of the components up to the loft, where I could work happily and in comfort. To do this I enlisted the help of our two Irish maids. They were big strong girls who made light work of the engine and gearbox.

As I learnt more at the Aeronautical College so I was able to do more to my engine. I stripped it down; repaired each component as best I could, and then began reassembling. The chassis was still in the garden but had now been straightened: the help of a heavy roller and two strapping Irish maids, having apparently achieved the impossible.

The time came when the engine was reassembled on the table. I filled the carburettor with petrol and tested the float, then attended to the timing. I turned the fly-wheel authoritatively. The engine had magneto ignition which functioned with surprising efficiency, and this, coupled with the fact that I had fitted the butterfly back to front, led to the engine bursting into life on full throttle. It leapt into the air and fell off the table onto the floor, knocking down the entire ceiling of the recently redecorated bathroom below. This bathroom had walls finished in marble, and the latest luxurious equipment had just been installed. My parents were away at the time and I was able to clear up most of the mess. When I telephoned the news that the bathroom ceiling had fallen down my father's first reaction was to blame the builders; I accepted some responsibility for the damage but omitted certain details. Fortunately, the engine was not damaged, and a few days later it was – with the help of the Irish girls – installed in the chassis.

Gradually the little car began to take shape, until the great day came when it was ready for its first run. The body looked spartan, although the little bucket seat was quite comfortable. But the dashboard, with its clocks and pressure gauges, was reminiscent of the instrument panel of an airliner. When the engine burst into life there was a dynamic intensity about the way the chassis vibrated suggestive of some pending catastrophe. The exhaust note heightened this effect, having the deep throated bellow that delights all boys under fifty, infuriates adults, and causes everyone to shout for some time after the engine has been switched off.

I summoned the household – family and servants – and explained that my car was now ready for the road. I invited them to witness a demonstration that was about to take place in the garden. We all trooped out. The car started on the first turn of the handle. Everyone was impressed. My mother and father smiled at one another and then retreated a few yards so that he could shout something in her ear. I jumped into the car, engaged bottom gear and let in the clutch. The wheels spun furiously, simultaneously removing a layer of top soil from the tennis court and the grin from my father's face. The car rocketed forward down to the bottom of the garden; engine, gearbox and exhaust system producing a crescendo of sound. I changed up on the point of valve bounce and then, almost immediately, had to brake hard and turn left to return to my point of departure. I saw I was cutting things a bit fine but executed a smart 'heel and toe', accepting 'on the limit' driving as a matter of course. Unfortunately, my heel went down to the floor boards and the car passed straight through the garden wall ending upsidedown in the road outside minus both front wheels and with badly bent chassis. I found myself lying on the road beside the engine, my head aching and blood pouring from a badly cut eye. The realization that I had forgotten to connect up the brakes added frustration to grief and anger at the sight of the broken car. However, once the shock had passed, and my injuries had mended, I started rebuilding again.

Aided by my previous experience the car was quickly rebuilt and soon ready for the road. After a satisfactory trial run round the garden I raised the question of being allowed to tax and insure it and take it on the King's Highway. At first my parents demurred, but in the end they reluctantly agreed. My success in getting their consent, if not their blessing, was based on the precept of 'first catch your hare' which I have applied all through my life. If I had asked my father for a car so that I could drive up to Chelsea every day it would have been refused; not for monetary reasons, but simply because he would have felt that the London Passenger Transport Board would do the job more efficiently. Knowing this I first asked for an old car – something I could tinker around with. Once I had the car running well and safely it was easier to make my overtures. Also father was rather proud of his tennis lawn, to say nothing of his garden. My mother was very nervous however and knowing that any semblance of an accident would mean the confiscation of my car I drove carefully.

This sobriety continued for some time until one day a fellow student challenged me to a race round the back streets of Chelsea. This started a series of lunch-time races which greatly alarmed the local residents. Complaints were made, and the police began to interest themselves in our activities. Usually we saw them first, with the result that by the time they joined us we were motoring in line astern at a steady twenty-five miles an hour. One day I was not so lucky. I was travelling faster than the legal limit when in my mirror I saw a police car coming up fast. I executed a smart left turn down a side street only to see the road in front blocked by a large brewer's lorry and trailer. I braked hard, but the road was damp and its wooden blocks very slippery. The wheels locked, and the car sailed on straight for the obstruction. My reactions were equal to the occasion; I ducked, and passed safely below the trailer's tow-bar, leaving behind the startled brewer's men and frustrated police patrol. But they got my number, and although no prosecution followed, some alarming correspondence arrived home. I was on the mat, and my lunch-time racing days were over.

Soon after this my parents went on holiday to Aldeburgh.

I was determined that nothing should spoil their holiday and behaved myself all week. The fates were against me however, for on returning from a gentle drive round Richmond Park on the Saturday afternoon the car caught fire. I just had time to leap out as the flames licked up through the floor boards and a minute later the petrol tank exploded. The fire brigade arrived and trained a hose on my little car, with a jet of water so powerful that it bowled it over and up against a wall where it disintegrated. All this happened only three hundred yards from my home.

When I telephoned my parents that night they would not believe that I was in no way to blame for the disaster. Father said there was sure to be a bill from the fire brigade and that he was very displeased with me. I was to catch the morning train to Aldeburgh and explain myself.

I overslept next morning and the train was leaving when I reached the platform. I had to run like mad to catch it and, failing to notice that it was marked off in sections, got into a carriage going to Felixstowe. The other occupant of the carriage was a talkative old lady who soon revealed that we were not going to Aldeburgh. It quite made her day; one would have thought I would never see my parents again from the fuss she made. We were detached from the main train and after shunting about a bit jogged off down some side track. The poor old soul went on and on, and just when I was wondering how to shut her up, there was an awful bumping and banging and the carriage was off the track and on its side with the old dear on top of me. She is probably still talking about it. I escaped with minor bruises, but had the irritating task of telephoning my parents and telling them of this accident. It was tiresome having to explain how I came to be in a train to Felixstowe.

CHAPTER TWO

BROOKLANDS

Temporarily my motoring days were over. My car had gone to the scrap yard, and father had said there was no prospect of my having another one until I mended my ways. This distressing state of affairs lasted some time, and though I occasionally made tentative suggestions father was adamant: I did not enjoy his confidence.

It was about this time that I began to take an interest in motor racing. I had gone to race meetings at Brooklands with my parents and always enjoyed myself. So did they, but they were busy people and could not go to every meeting.

Not only was Brooklands quite a bicycle ride from London, but the entrance fee to the track was high. I did not have much pocket money, and had dissipated my savings in keeping the car on the road. Pride prevented my asking for extra cash, so I devised a method of getting into the place without paying. I would get up early on a

Saturday morning and bicycle to Brooklands. Opposite the main entrance there lived a charming old lady who let me leave my bicycle in her garden. I would change into my aeronautical overalls, borrow a bucket of water, and then walk past the queue at the main entrance. With a cheery 'mind your backs chums', and water splashing everywhere, I was through the gate and on my way to the pits without a question from anyone.

I would mingle with the mechanics, lending a hand whenever possible, and greatly enjoying myself. After a time I was a recognized figure and would work on the racing cars of complete strangers, making myself useful by changing wheels, cleaning gaskets, topping up radiators, even removing cylinder heads. Sometimes we would work all night; I would telephone my parents and tell them I was staying with a friend in Weybridge; they never found out what I was up to.

Billy Cotton, the dance band leader, was a fine driver of those days. I did a lot of work on his cars and remember his thanking me after an all-night session. When later that day he called me by name and asked me to fetch his goggles from his car I felt I had arrived.

Shortly after this my class at the Aeronautical College was transferred to Brooklands for practical training in aeroplane construction and management. This meant that I would have to travel back and forth between London and Brooklands every day. Mother did not want me to live away from home, and father thought it was too far for me to cycle. He was also pleased with my behaviour of late – knowing nothing of the way I got into Brooklands – and said he would buy me a car. This car was a six-cylinder Wolseley Daytona – quite a fast car in its day. Though I could not appreciate it at the time, I now know that the chassis whipped, the steering was poor, and the brakes – by modern standards – were hopeless. However, I was unaware of its defects and was thrilled to own such a potent and handsome motor car. Unfortunately, I did not have it for long, for a few weeks later I was compelled to take avoiding action at speed on the Kingston by-pass; the car hit the kerb, lost a front wheel and turned over twice. I came out the second time round more shaken than hurt, having landed on the grass verge; the car, however, was a complete wreck.

This was almost too much for my mother, and it was only after much discussion – in which I was helped by the fact that there had been witnesses to say that I was in no way to blame for the accident that she agreed to my having another car.

It was decided that this car was to be less powerful than the Wolseley and was to be driven, if not sedately, at least with controlled enthusiasm. Accordingly, a second-hand Austin Nippy sports two seater was purchased. This little car was fun to drive and travelled quite quickly, too quickly in fact, for despite its pressure-fed crankshaft the engine was not able to withstand the demands made upon it, and one morning the crankshaft, bearings, con-rods and pistons all parted company with a most expensive noise. A short telephone conversation followed, during which I learnt that my motoring days were definitely over for the time being, and that I was to stay in digs near Brooklands.

Apart from the disappointment of not having my own car the new arrangement suited me: it meant I could spend all my spare time in the racing workshops without any reference to home. Previously I had had to account for my movements which, although not difficult, was tiresome.

I was very friendly with the workshop foreman of Thompson & Taylor's, and spent much time watching the construction of the car with which they attacked the Brooklands lap record.

I actually helped to assemble an interesting car Granville Grenfell built. The basis of this car was an E.R.A. chassis, a Mercedes-Benz engine that had once propelled an airship, a Minerva back axle and gearbox, and Lancia independent front suspension. This was the first racing car I drove. One Sunday afternoon, Grenfell's two sons and I took it in turns to drive this monster round the outer circuit while he was out with his wife visiting friends. We returned the car to its garage before he came home and he never knew anything about it until years later.

★ ★ ★

Brooklands boasted a flying club, and when things were quiet round the car workshops I would wander over to the aircraft hangars to see what was going on. I used to badger the members and as a result flew in many different types of aircraft.

Mutt Summers, Vickers' chief test pilot, was a great friend of my father's, and he occasionally took me up himself. Knowing him gave me an entry I did not fail to exploit. When a squadron of R.A.F Ansons visited us I managed to get a flight. I flew also in torpedo bombers; the single engined long distance Wellesley bomber, and such strange aircraft as the Vickers Vildebeeste.

Although I flew a great deal, the opportunity to take over the controls did not come. The club members were enjoying themselves, and one could hardly expect a Service pilot to hand over his aircraft to a youth who had scrounged a flight. However, I took notice of all that occurred, and learned a great deal by watching pilots controlling their planes.

One day I was wandering round the tarmac, helmet in one hand, flying jacket over my shoulders, when a club member who was just about to take-off saw me and asked me if I wanted to join him. I thanked him and we walked to his aircraft. On the way he asked me whether I had my licence, I told him I had. We climbed aboard, I in the front cockpit, he in the back. When we got to the take-off point he said: 'Well old chap, I'll leave it to you. Show me how you do it.'

It was too late to back out now so I took the controls and tried my hand at flying an aeroplane for the first time in my life. The confidence of youth is wonderful; I had watched others do it so often and was so sure I knew exactly what to do that we took off without complication or difficulty. Indeed, when I banked and saw the Brooklands sewage farm disappearing underneath me, I wondered what all the fuss was about – flying was a piece of cake. We flew on for some little time; I did not attempt any manoeuvre, but climbed to four thousand feet and then flew straight and level. My unknown friend then took over and we flew round the Guildford area climbing over some cloud. When he turned for home and the same cloud bank appeared ahead, he asked me if I would like to fly through it. As a student at the Aeronautical College I had done a ground course on aircraft instruments and fully understood them; there was, therefore, no reason why I could not fly on them, or so I thought. We entered this cloud bank at about three thousand feet. A glance at the instruments satisfied me all was well, but on looking up, and seeing nothing save cloud, I lost confidence and tried to fly by the seat of my pants.

Soon all sense of direction, proportion, speed and what have you had left me and we came out of cloud at about one thousand feet in a dreadful spin. I saw Wisley lake rapidly drawing nearer and gladly surrendered the controls to my friend who was screaming through the Gosport tube that I must let go of the control column. He brought us out of that spin at about tree level, and then flew back to Brooklands. He landed the plane, taxied it to its dispersal point and cut the engine; then got out and walked away without saying a word, leaving me sitting in the front cockpit feeling very stupid. Thereafter every time we met on the tarmac he would look the other way; we never renewed our friendship.

I now knew I must fly, and with the help of Mutt Summers eventually persuaded my father to let me take a course of flying instruction at the Brooklands Club. My mother was very much against the idea, but I had my way and was soon doing circuits and bumps round Brooklands.

Though flying was now my first love I had by no means lost interest in fast motor cars; so when a friend of mine, who was the proud owner of a splendid two-seater Delage, suggested we try out certain modifications he had made to the car's front suspension I was very agreeable. He had had the benefit of my advice while making these modifications so the trip was not without a certain personal interest. This car was really fast and passing over the bridge which crossed the aeroplane road at well over the 'ton' a front tyre burst; the car hit the bridge parapet, shed its front wheel, skated along until the axle dug in and then rolled over. My friend was thrown clear; I was not so lucky, I was pitched out on to the concrete and went on fast on my head and face. I was picked up unconscious by Vickers' ambulance and taken to

Weybridge Cottage Hospital. There Doctor Neville Whitehurst, who later became one of the best known pilots in the Air Transport Auxiliary, performed wonders on my damaged face. He covered it with what was known as a Whitehurst varnish, and after a week in hospital and a further six weeks in bed at home I was fit enough to return to Brooklands and my studies.

I had been saving my money for some time. The allowance father paid me – to cover the cost of living in digs and so on – was generous and this, coupled with the pound or two that came my way for services rendered in the pit area, enabled me to buy a 30/98 Vauxhall. This was a splendid car, great fun to drive and quite fast; it served me well, never giving any trouble, until the beginning of the war.

Mother was not in favour of my owning another car, but was overruled by my father who saw that not having a car of my own did not stop me from driving. I think he thought it would be better if I shunted my own car rather than one which belonged to someone else.

One day a film unit came down to Brooklands to shoot a scene for a film starring the late Will Hay. In this film Will played a bus driver who, at some stage in the story, found himself on the Brooklands track whilst a race was in progress. Just to make things more interesting he was going round the wrong way. I arrived on the scene as eight racing cars were being pushed out on to the Vickers' straight. Freddie Dixon's Riley was one of them, so I joined in and helped push it to its position. The cars were started and the usual pandemonium broke loose when eight 'blown' racing engines were 'blipped' as their drivers warmed them up. Dixon's mechanic, who was going to drive the car, beckoned me over and indicated that he wanted me to keep the engine running while he went back into the pits for something. He handed me his helmet and goggles for safe keeping and we exchanged places.

I was in my element, and just to impress the film technicians who were standing about I put on the helmet and goggles. I blipped away until the engine was hot and then switched off. All the other drivers had switched off and were standing around talking; I pushed my goggles up on to my forehead and joined them. We all knew one another and were laughing amongst ourselves at some of the long haired characters with the film unit when suddenly the director shouted: 'All right. Action stations'. All the drivers got into their cars and started up. I looked around for Dixon's mechanic but could not see him. Then I saw the director shouting and pointing in my direction; he obviously thought I was the driver. Obeying a sudden impulse I jumped into the car and was push started by two helpful mechanics. Some character dropped a handkerchief and we all roared off towards the approaching bus. The acceleration of the Riley was sufficient to keep an experienced driver busy, so when my inexperienced foot kicked in second gear (a preselector gear box was fitted) there was an awful lurch, and the goggles were jerked off my forehead and fell over my eyes, blinding me completely. It all happened so quickly that before I realized I was blind the car was rocketing forward in second gear. I lifted my foot off the accelerator and braked hard, simultaneously clearing my vision. I saw the seven other racing cars stopping in front of me but no bus. I turned round and drove back to the pits. The director was standing beside the bus, his smiling features contrasting vividly with the awe-stricken expression on the bus driver's face.

'Wonderful. Absolutely wonderful. You missed that bus by three inches. Could you possibly do it again?' Even if I had said I could, it is by no means certain that the bus driver (who was standing in for Will Hay) would have agreed. He looked as if he badly needed a drink. The arrival of Freddie Dixon's mechanic relieved me of any further responsibility in the matter. He gave me a fearful wigging in front of everyone, and for some days my name was mud in the pit area. He drove the car in the next pukka take and did it very well; nevertheless, I have often felt that the film director wished his cameras had been turning while the dummy run was in progress.

★ ★ ★

One of the ways pre-war flying club members amused themselves was by invading other flying clubs' airfields. To accomplish a successful invasion one had to land an aircraft on a rival club's field without being intercepted by a resident aircraft. An interception consisted of getting the registration number of the invading aircraft. A successful invasion was rewarded by an invitation to breakfast, lunch or dinner depending on the time of day.

The general opinion was that dawn was the best time to attack, so when a friend of mine, Michael Parkhurst, asked me to accompany him on one of these flurries his suggested departure time did not surprise me. We left Brooklands at first light in Michael's own aeroplane and headed for Redhill. It was the first time I had flown so early in the day and remember how impressed I was at the beauty of the early morning sky when viewed from the air. In a matter of minutes – or so it seemed to me, enchanted by the rising sun – Michael announced that Redhill was ahead, and that he could see the home team's aircraft circling the field on the look-out for types like ourselves. We lost height and then came out of the rising sun beneath the circling planes. It looked as if we had got away with it, but behind I saw an opponent bearing down upon us. I told Michael who shoved the stick forward, roared into the airfield and tried to put the plane down at a speed considerably in excess of the manufacturer's recommendations. To further complicate the issue we were travelling down wind. It was obvious to me that we could not land, so I expected him to go round again. He was always an optimist, however, and attempted the landing. We touched down on the airfield all right but immediately proceeded to leave it rather hurriedly by an unusual route through a hedge, leaving our wings on two dismembered oak trees. We were quite unhurt, and had, of course, qualified for a free breakfast. The sausages were particularly fine.

Michael had his leg pulled by everyone. They looked up the phone number of his insurance company and invited him to use the club's telephone; they suggested the police should be told; they asked whether he was insured against damage to agricultural property; in fact they did everything they could to worry the poor fellow, and succeeded.

While Michael was worrying, and I was still eating, another friend of ours, George Lucky, turned up in a three-litre open Bentley. George (who was later killed on a bombing raid to Hamburg) was a member of Redhill's club and his arrival sparked off an incredible day. We lunched and dined at the club; consumed a certain quantity of liquor and, after a rugger match in the bar that evening, climbed into his open Bentley and headed for home, having spent the entire day as the guests of the Redhill club.

George fancied his chances as a driver, and was showing us how well the car would go when, without warning, a lorry drove out of a side turning. George braked hard, but the road was wet and the car spun. We hit the lorry, knocking it over, and cannoned off on to a telegraph pole, which turned us over. I flew out like a rugger ball which has just been passed from the base of the scrum, only there was no fly-half to take me and I landed in a large thorn bush; I was picking out thorns for the next fortnight. Poor George and Michael passed through the large windscreen; George had severe concussion and twenty-eight stitches in his head; Michael broke his arm. Although I was only bruised and pricked I was taken to hospital with my injured friends and detained for observation. This necessitated one of the all too frequent telephone calls which were ageing me almost as much as they were ageing my parents.

★ ★ ★

And so we went to war.

CHAPTER THREE

THE WAR COMES

The summer of 1939 was a time when war was in everyone's mind. People who remembered the Great War were filled with foreboding at current events as they saw how easily Europe could become a battle-ground again. I never considered the matter at all, my mind was full of aeroplanes and racing cars. I read the newspapers, but found the sports pages more interesting than the news columns. As for editorials – well, they were rather like one's mother saying: 'Don't drive too fast dear'. One did not doubt the wisdom of the advice, just considered it superfluous.

The war clouds continued to gather, until at last, a conversation with father made me appreciate how serious the international situation was. Feeling rather ashamed of my previous lack of awareness, I determined to do something positive; so when a friend at the Aeronautical College suggested joining the Auxiliary Air Force I was all for the idea.

Subsequently, nine of us enlisted together. In view of our background we were treated as a special party and put on a shortened course. In no time we had advanced from the theoretical to the practical stage and were doing circuits and bumps, with an instructor, round Gravesend airfield. We felt the choice of name was ideal for a flying training establishment.

All went well until solo flying started. The first two members of our party were unlucky enough to break their aircraft's undercarriages when landing. A long lecture followed during which our attention was drawn to the fact that these training aircraft were valuable: the R.A.F needed them in order to train the thousands of pilots they would require in an emergency. It was all a lot of nonsense really, for no one crashes an aeroplane for the fun of the thing; however, the I/C flying had his say and then sent up numbers three and four. To their credit they took off and landed satisfactorily which did prove that the thing was not impossible. I was number five. The sergeant pilot who was to give me final instructions eyed me cynically for a moment then bade me climb into the plane. His cynicism was based on one of my landings, when he had asked me, 'What do you think you're doing, mate, playing leap-frog?'.

I adjusted the safety straps and ran through the cockpit drill, then turned to my instructor – whose expression had not changed – for a final word of encouragement or advice. He reminded me that the plane would swing very much on take-off unless the throttle was opened very slowly. 'This is a sensitive military aircraft', he said, 'nothing like the civil planes you civilians have been working on'. I did not like the way he said civilian, but this was no moment to be touchy, so I nodded seriously as if in agreement, knowing that my apparent naivety would irritate him. It did, and before jumping down and leaving me to my own devices he shouted in my ear: 'Remember this is a valuable aircraft. We can always get more pilots but aircraft are scarce'.

I opened the throttle very slowly and moved off up the field. The plane gathered speed steadily and did not swing at all. By the time it was half way across I was confident and, pleased with myself, I continued to open the throttle – applying the gentlest pressure – as my speed increased. Then the realization that hedges and trees were approaching rapidly made me apply rather more throttle, but still the wheels stayed on the ground. There was a moment of panic, and in my anguish I banged the throttle fully open and pulled the stick back. The aircraft, as if determined to show its independence, ignored both movements, but instead of going straight on turned sharply at right angles and went through an extension that was being built on to the Mess, demolishing scaffolding, building and aircraft. I was unhurt; but will never forget the face of that sergeant, or my feelings, when I came out from under the demolished scaffolding. I was at a loss for words: he was not. Three days later a letter arrived at home. It said, in effect, 'Your services are no longer required'.

Shortly after this episode war was declared and I had to consider which service to join. The Army did not attract me at all, and since my relations with the R.A.F were somewhat strained I decided to take a look at the Navy. I heard that the Fleet Air Arm was expanding and needed men with aeronautical qualifications, so I wrote to the Admiralty giving details of my education and air engineering experience. This letter evidently found its way into the right office for soon afterwards I appeared before a selection board who, after asking a lot of questions and keeping me waiting on tenterhooks for an hour, informed me that I was in His Majesty's Navy with the rank of Sub-Lieutenant. I was to be employed on air engineering duties with the promise that I could transfer to full flying duties later. I was dumbfounded at my good fortune.

My first appointment was to H.M.S. *Excellent* for training as a naval officer. Whilst on this course I had an experience which convinced me that the Air Arm was the branch of the service best suited to my talents. A friend arranged for me to go in a submarine doing a patrol up the English Channel, I went cheerfully enough but did not enjoy it.

When we dived and I appreciated that we were some forty fathoms down in the Channel a claustrophobic feeling came over me: not only was the accommodation cramped and the air musty, but the thought of the inky blackness surrounding us was blood chilling. The submariners' life was not for me.

The end of my training in H.M.S. *Excellent* coincided with the German invasion of Norway. I was appointed to H.M.S. *Glorious*, at that time already in Norwegian waters. I embarked at Gourock, in company with members of the Norwegian Expeditionary Force. The steamer which was to take us to Narvik had seen better days, and by the time it had taken on a mixed assortment of troops and their equipment – there were even French Alpinists – it was pretty low in the water. We put to sea and, partly to contain my excitement, I went down to the bar for a few pink gins. It must have been very good gin, for I remember having an argument with a rather senior officer as to whether, in the future, aeroplanes would carry coal more cheaply than ships. We never resolved our argument, for a fearful explosion interrupted us; the lights went out and everyone was thrown to the floor. There was the sound of escaping steam and much shouting and then the emergency lights came on. I staggered out of the bar and met the Chief Steward who was standing outside the door with a small grip in his hand. 'This way, sir', he said and led me up on deck and helped me into a waiting lifeboat. I felt rather like a P&O. Liner passenger who was just about to go ashore to buy a souvenir; the only thing missing was a rug to go over my knees. The ship went down very quickly and unfortunately not everyone got off.

For some twelve hours we were pitched and tossed all over the place. It was bitterly cold, and although no one doubted that we would be picked up sooner or later we had, nevertheless, an uncomfortable time. This was my first real taste of war, and I remember thinking how strange it was that one man could just walk out of the bar and into a lifeboat whereas others perished. It did not make sense to me then, for I was young enough to seek logic even in war.

Eventually we were picked up by the cruiser H.M.S. *Curlew*. On stepping aboard the first two people I met were the Jackson brothers who had been in School House with me at Brighton College. All survivors were taken down to the steam room to thaw out and there, with a glass of rum in my hand, I recounted my recent adventures. After they left me to return to their duties I drank some more rum and lay down to have a sleep. I was roused by what appeared to be great activity on the decks above. The next moment there was a tremendous crash and the ship shuddered from stem to stern. In fact, a shell fired by a German Coastal Battery had scored a direct hit on the bridge, crippling us and killing my friends the Jackson brothers. Half-an-hour later we went down and I was back in the water; fortunately, not for long, for another ship picked me up and took me to Norway. The war was going badly for us and the unit I joined had heavy casualties. For a time my luck held, but one day I found myself rather nearer to the centre of an explosion than was good for me and was on my way back to England on a stretcher. I woke up in Haslar Hospital and spent the next five months convalescing from blast injuries; my legs were in a bad way and it was a long time before I could walk.

In the bed next to me was a very nice chap called Philip Sinker who was a Lieutenant R.N.R. He was a survivor from a Q ship in which he had served in the North Atlantic. I learnt that he ran a school in Woking called Hoe Place and, in view of his kindness to me, said that if I ever had a son he would go to Philip's school. Later my son did go to Hoe Place with Philip Sinker looking after him and teaching him the Naval traditions.

★ ★ ★

My first appointment after leaving hospital was to 771 Squadron, Lee-on-Solent. The Squadron Commander was Lieutenant-Commander Jack Keen-Miller who, incidentally, some ten years later, became my daughter's godfather. I shared the squadron office with Jack and Sir George Lewis who was his second in command. George was a partner in the firm of solicitors Lewis and Lewis, who had been legal advisers to the Kings and Queens of England for over four hundred years. He was killed later while flying Admiral Ramsey, then Chief of Naval Staff, and members of his entourage to the Yalta conference. The plane, a Lodestar, crashed and there were no survivors.

771 Squadron was employed on communication and aircraft ferry duties. This meant that a continual stream of

pilots passed through our offices. Some of them were interesting characters like Johnny Wakefield, the racing driver whom I had known at Brooklands before the war. Two others were Lieutenants Ralph Richardson and Laurence Olivier, both now knighted for their services to the world of entertainment. I remember Sir Ralph, not so much as a pilot, but as the driver of a twelve-cylinder Lagonda. To see him set off on a journey was to imagine a car leaving the pits at Le Mans after an enforced stop. What he did with all the time he saved I do not know. He also owned a four-cylinder motor bike and rode this in a similar manner. He lent it to me one day, and in attempting to emulate his take-off I came a fearful cropper and had a head-ache for a week.

Sir Ralph, although a charming person, had a baffling personality. Some of the things he would do were very strange indeed. Before taking off a pilot would come to our office to collect certain necessary data: the registration number of his aircraft, where he was to take it, how he was to return, and so on. Ralph would write all these details on a piece of paper and then carefully check his instructions by reading his notes back to Jack Keen-Miller. Satisfied that all was in order he would then say 'Thank you very much', screw the piece of paper up into a small ball and throw it into the waste paper basket, turn on his heel, open a door and walk straight into a large locker where we kept our parachutes and flying gear. He would emerge from the locker, and without commenting on his error, or betraying any sign of embarrassment, leave in the normal manner through the office door which was next to the locker. The first time this happened we thought it was a joke; when it had occurred half a dozen times the true humour of the situation was apparent.

Laurence Olivier drove an old open Bentley – I think it was a 4-litre. He never put the hood up – indeed I am not sure there was one even in bad weather; but charged about the place enjoying his car and the fresh air. When his wife, Vivien Leigh, came to stay with him, he had to borrow a little Hillman Minx I was using at the time in order to transport her in something like the manner to which she was accustomed.

While I was at Lee-on-Solent the Luftwaffe carried out a very successful sortie. Twelve Heinkel bombers succeeded in destroying nearly every aircraft we had. These aircraft were lined up in rows; none of them were dispersed. The hangars and squadron offices were flattened and it was a long time before the airfield functioned again. George Lewis, who was in the air-watch office, had a miraculous escape when the entire building collapsed around him: he was completely unharmed. Their Lordships at the Admiralty learnt much from this raid, and instructions went out which ensured that no other Naval Air establishment was caught napping similarly.

Shortly after this I was posted to the R.A.F. Station at Felixstowe as Naval Officer in charge of the Fleet Air Arm detachment. I travelled there with Midshipman Hosegood, a young man who was later appointed to the merchant cruiser *Alcantara*. From this ship he flew all over the South American seas in a Seafox. Today he is a well known helicopter test pilot.

Felixstowe was a seaplane base. I had about a dozen Swordfish, half a dozen Seafoxes, and, strangely enough, eight Fokker TW8 seaplanes which had been owned by the Dutch Naval Air Service and had been flown out of Holland when the Germans occupied that country. Another very interesting seaplane was the four-engined Mercury which Air Marshal Bennett, of Pathfinder fame, had flown before the war for Imperial Airways.

My job was to ensure that all these aircraft were fully operational; no easy task, for there was a severe shortage of spare parts.

One day the C.O. sent for me and told me to prepare two of the Fokker TW8s for a mission to occupied territory. The object of the mission was to collect allied agents and bring them back to the U.K. It was likely that the aircraft would be flown by Dutch crews. This was all the information forthcoming at this stage, and it was, of course, top secret. I presumed these aircraft would be going to Holland but could not obtain confirmation: the C.O. had nothing to add to what he had already told me. Indeed, I do not think he knew any more about it than I did.

These Fokkers – although German made – were fitted with American Cyclone engines. All were carefully air tested and the best two put aside and specially prepared for this tricky operation. To help me, I had the services of Dutch Naval personnel who arrived on detachment from their U.K. base. They were followed a day or two later by a Lieutenant-Commander Schaape who informed me that he would be in charge of the operation. He asked me which aircraft I considered the better of the two, and then flew the plane of my choice for about an hour. I went up with him and soon saw that he was a fine pilot. After landing he told me he liked the plane and would use it. He had to return to his unit but said he would be back in a few days' time; we parted the best of friends. When he returned he had two compatriots, Lieutenants Rittie and Vontogran, with him. They were good fellows and we had one or two splendid evenings together.

The balloon barrage at Felixstowe was fixed to buoys in the Channel and was a difficult one to fly in and out of. We had to practise doing this, however, in readiness for our mission, which was, of course, to take place at night. One evening, while we were planning an acclimatization trip, a German bomber which had been bombing Ipswich came down and executed a perfect landing on the mud opposite the Naval Training School at Shotley. The naval party who went out to salvage it were surprised to find no one aboard. It later transpired that the crew had abandoned the aircraft by parachute and that the empty plane had flown on and landed on its own. As a result we collected a virtually undamaged German bomber which was later used by the R.A.F. for training.

Shortly after this incident, I and several friends were having a night out in Ipswich. The inn of our choice was the 'White Horse' and by the time we left to return to Felixstowe in my newly acquired 1927 three-litre Bentley tourer, we were somewhat the worse for wear. As we sped along – the fresh air playing havoc with some people's constitutions – we heard the coastal ack-ack batteries firing and saw what we thought was a German bomber coming down in flames. We cheered like mad, and putting my foot on the accelerator I showed them how a three-litre Bentley could motor. We were doing perhaps seventy miles an hour when, to my great surprise, the car suddenly flew off the road, passed straight through a brick wall, glanced off a tree, came back through another part of the same wall, travelled across the road and into yet another wall where it stopped. I was very shaken but unhurt. I looked round behind me to discover that two of our party were missing. They emerged however, from behind the wall on the other side of the road where they had been deposited. One of them made a fearful fuss because he had broken his little finger but received little sympathy, for we were trying to discover what had happened to the car. The radiator had been cut in two and the block whipped off the crankcase. In fact we had hit a barrage balloon cable. The object we had seen falling in flames was not a plane at all but a balloon shot down by a German bomber. The cable had trailed across the countryside and the Bentley had hit it. If that cable had been two feet higher we would have been decapitated. As it was I kept my head but not my Bentley; it was a complete wreck, and twelve pounds ten was all I could get for it.

There was not much time to lament my loss for only a day later the C.O. sent for me and told me that the special operation was to the Friesian lakes in Holland, where we were to land and pick up Dutch agents. Schaape was there and we straightaway plotted our course, worked out quantities of fuel and rounds of ammunition required and so on, and had the aircraft ready to take off at a few moments' notice. When word came through that it was to be that night we were ready. Unfortunately there was a leak of information; at a local function that evening, someone was heard to say that Schaape and Hamilton would be flying that night. There was an investigation and Schaape subsequently decided to delay the trip. Whether his decision was a sound one or not I do not know, but when we eventually went the Germans undoubtedly knew we were coming: a reception committee was waiting for us on the lake. Our orders were to land on the lake and pick up two men who would be waiting in a rowing boat. We landed on the lake to find, not a rowing boat, but a barge equipped with searchlights and, apparently, every form of automatic weapon. A running fight between the barge and ourselves developed during which both Vontogran and Rittie were wounded. For their part, however, their accurate fire extinguished all the searchlights and Schaape, manipulating his aircraft magnificently, succeeded in turning into the wind and took off over the heads of the Germans, skimming the trees on the edge of the lake. Unfortunately, the agents we had gone to collect were captured and later executed.

Our aircraft was in very bad shape and the journey home was a frightening one. There were bullet holes everywhere; parts of the fuselage looked like a sieve. As soon as we landed she started to sink and we were lucky to get her on to the slipway. Schaape was decorated for his skill and courage in bringing his aircraft home.

I had seen at first-hand how careless talk could cost lives. Admittedly, the 'leak' might have been in Holland, one can never be sure about these things. It might have been better for us to have gone over there on the night originally planned; the Germans might not have had time to prepare such a welcome for us. Only one thing is certain: they knew we were coming and we were lucky to get away with it.

For some time afterwards life seemed rather flat. There was plenty of work to be done and my responsibilities were great; nevertheless, I yearned for adventure. One of the ways I satisfied this need was by going out on night patrols in an M.T.B. The M.T.B. boys were a good crowd, and whether patrolling the Channel on the look-out for Jerry, or the streets of Ipswich in search of 'talent', they were the sort of fellows I liked to be with.

One day, following a night spent patrolling the Channel – during which I had become very wet – my throat was sore. At first I took little notice of it, but after a time it became so painful that I asked the M.O. for something to suck. He gave me some potassium cough sweets. I put one in my mouth and the others in my pocket, and went off to fly in an aircraft we were air testing. Shortly after taking off I smelt burning, and so did the pilot, but a quick routine investigation failed to trace the smell to its source. We presumed it must be a 'short' somewhere and were checking fuses when I saw smoke coming up from around my feet. The pilot decided to land as quickly as possible and made for the nearest suitable water: the mouth of the river Orwell. I then discovered that I was on fire. The whole right hand side of my flying suit was alight and my leg began to burn. Desperately I tried to beat out the flames, at the same time searching frantically for the fire. The pilot put the plane down very quickly, being certain that the whole aircraft would be alight in a matter of minutes. I was now in agony and before we came to rest jumped over the side and into the water. The water was bitterly cold, and I was wondering if it was better to freeze or burn to death when a boat picked me up. When I took off my clothes I discovered the source of the fire: the potassium cough sweets had ignited themselves on a box of matches and had in turn set fire to some letters in my pocket. In due course I applied for a new flying suit, only to be confronted with an Admiralty Order which said that no potassium cough sweets would be carried by flying personnel when airborne, and that their Lordships would not be responsible for resultant damage if they were.

Towards the end of the year I was posted back to Lee-on-Solent and once again joined my old friend Jack Keen-Miller. He had just received some obsolescent Harrow bombers from the R.A.F. and almost the first thing we did was to take one of these monsters up on test. The cockpit of a Harrow was some 18 feet above the ground and it was possible for a man to walk under the spinning propeller of one of its engines without endangering his life. In fact, mechanics who had been working on these Harrows were warned not to take such liberties with other aircraft. At Evanton, an R.A.F. Station in the North of Scotland where there was a Fleet Air Arm detachment, a mechanic who had been working on a Harrow walked straight into the propeller of a Botha and was killed. This incident was made known to us and we briefed our ground crews accordingly. Jack was an ex-Imperial Airways pilot and could fly more or less anything. On our way out to the aircraft we were joined by Sir George Lewis and the three of us squeezed into the front cockpit together. It was a blustery day with much low cloud and the Harrow vibrated from stem to stern. In fact, on looking down the interior of the fuselage, the tail end of the aircraft could be seen wobbling backwards and forwards as if there was a loose connection somewhere. We flew about for a bit, and then George took over the controls and tried to pilot the plane while Jack and I gave him much free advice. Suddenly an aircraft came out of cloud right in front of us; we appeared to drop a wing and the Harrow seemed to shudder even more than usual but that was all. Jack said something about having missed it by inches and told George to look where he was going. Then on glancing down the port wing I noticed that it looked shorter than usual. I mentioned the fact and was told that I was drunk. The laugh was on them, however, for on landing we found that 16 feet of the port wing had been sliced off by the plane we had met coming out of cloud. It had crash landed, fortunately without injury to its crew.

Nothing of very great interest occurred during the next

few months save when the Germans bombed Portsmouth harbour. All duty officers for miles around were called to the harbour to assist in fighting the oil-tank fires. I took a fire engine with trailer, and ordering the regular driver to ring the bell and look after the lights, set off at high speed. Coming into Gosport I took a corner too fast. The fire engine got round all right but the trailer went straight on and made its own personal contribution to the general destruction which was in progress. We went on to the harbour and spent a hazardous night trying to keep the tanks cool so that they would not split, while completely unmolested German dive-bombers came down to one thousand feet and dropped their bombs, when and where they pleased. It was a night I shall never forget.

Although – this incident apart – life was not very exciting, it was quite interesting and we worked hard; nevertheless, when my next posting came through I was an excited man; for my orders were to proceed to the Royal Naval Air Station at Hatston in the Orkneys to join the Home Fleet.

CHAPTER FOUR
THE ORKNEYS

Hatston is situated alongside Scapa Flow, and almost the first thing I saw was the Home fleet at anchor. It was an awe inspiring sight: battleships, cruisers, aircraft carriers, and all the escorting destroyers these giants require. It gave one a feeling of security to see such power, particularly when the war was not going too well for us.

My appointment was as Senior Air Engineering officer at Hatston, and I was responsible for the assembly, preparation and testing of fighter aircraft and torpedo bombers for the Home fleet. Naturally we handled other types of aircraft, but my principal concern was to see that fighting aircraft strength was maintained. The escort forces for our Russian convoys were based here, and they expected their aircraft losses to be made up instantly. All this meant that my unit and I worked very hard indeed. I went with one convoy to Russia in the aircraft carrier H.M.S. *Avenger;* it was a memorable trip. A little later this carrier was sunk while returning to the U.K. from North Africa. All hands – with the exception of seven other ranks – were lost. The senior survivor was a Petty Officer Rowe who subsequently joined my unit.

Although we worked hard there was time for relaxation, and an invitation to join the officers in one of the battleships or cruisers meant an evening during which good alcohol and good company could be enjoyed to the full. We all felt life was short and determined to keep it gay. It was short because one's friends were either lost at sea – Major Nigel Skeene, a great friend of mine, went down in H.M.S. *Avenger* – or were posted to other theatres of war. As soon as a posting came through we celebrated the recipient's departure.

These friendships, although of short duration, were sincere and many of the people I knew then became numbered among my closest friends. People like Tim Seccombe whom I knew at Lee-on-Solent when he was in H.M.S. *Victorious*. Tim turned up at Hatston one day and stayed for a while. It was a period when I enjoyed every evening, and then wondered the next morning if it was worth it. By the time evening came round again the answer was always yes. We lived at a tremendous pace, it is impossible to explain some of the crazy things we did. They just seemed natural at the time. We loved to compete against one another. One visiting officer was able to lick the red hot side of a mess stove without burning his tongue. Another who attempted the feat was unable to eat or drink for several days. The unfortunate officer trying to explain to the Captain why he could not speak properly, or appealing to the M.O. for assistance was thought to be funny. The inability of one side to understand why it was necessary to lick a red hot stove, and the inability of the other to explain why it appeared to be a good idea at the time created just the situation we enjoyed.

I found myself in a similar predicament one night, though not as the result of licking a stove. The junior officers' ante-room had a man-hole in the ceiling. On opening this man-hole we discovered that it was possible, by keeping to the rafters, to walk over the senior officers' anteroom right on to the Captain's quarters where he lived with his wife. The ceilings of the various rooms over which we walked were made of beaver-boarding so it was vital to ensure that you kept to the rafters. Someone suggested a race against a stopwatch. The course was to be from the man-hole, across the senior officers' anteroom, round the chimney stack in the middle of the Captain's quarters, and then back to the manhole by way of the other side of the ceiling. Observers were stationed at various points to ensure that every participant completed the course. After all competitors had completed one timed lap I was lying second. When I went up for my second lap I was determined to capture the record.

Unknown to me, the Captain was entertaining his senior officers and the local Army and R.A.F Commanders. It was a very windy night which accounted for the fact that they had not taken any notice of the odd noises they must have heard above them. When the wind blows in that part of the world it really blows. The circuit was pretty hazardous, for it was pitch dark, and one was dependent on the observers' torches held at each check point. I set off at high speed; the refreshment I had had since making my first run had given me great confidence. Unfortunately, it had also affected my reflexes, and when the observer near the chimney stack allowed his torch to waver I missed the next beam and fell through the ceiling into the Captain's drawing-room where all the bigwigs were taking coffee. I landed on my feet right in front of the Captain and found myself surrounded by Brigadiers, Air Commodores and every senior Naval Officer at Hatston. For a moment there was a stony silence; no one spoke, no one moved. I stood to attention; there was nothing else I could do. The Captain put down his coffee cup and took a cigar out of his mouth. 'Good evening Hamilton', he said. 'Good evening, sir', I replied, and then feeling further conversation would be superfluous executed a smart about turn and walked out of the room leaving a gaping hole in the ceiling and a circle of dumbfounded senior officers behind. The Captain had plenty to say the next morning and stopped my wine bill for a month.

We had a squadron of target towing aircraft at Hatston commanded by a Lieutenant-Commander Goddard. This squadron (781 was its number) gave the fleet its sea to air firing practice, and in doing so had a pretty enthralling time. There was one lovely occasion when Goddard – having been well and truly peppered by Naval Ack-Ack – called up the Admiral on the radio and said: 'We are towing this target, not pushing it'. This remark was translated into Latin and became the Squadron motto. Goddard's experiences towing for the Home Fleet stood him in good stead later on, for in company with Commander Hank Rotherham, the Station Commander, he flew a 'Maryland' to Norway to confirm a report that the Bismark had sailed. They found this great German battleship and were decorated for their skill and courage in doing so.

Another great character was our test pilot Shea Simmons. Shea was a really fine pilot (later in the war he passed the

Boscombe Down Test Pilots course) and he could fly anything. I remember him best, however, as the owner of a Shetland pony which he kept tethered outside the mess. This pony was fond of beer and Shea would bring him in for a pint on most evenings. One morning the pony got loose and, feeling thirsty, went into the mess in search of refreshment. Unable to find anyone in the junior officers' mess he tried next door. In the senior officers' ante-room there sat an admiral in civilian clothes. He was in transit, and while waiting for an aircraft which was coming to pick him up, he sat reading. The pony, having failed to solicit a drink from him, stood on his foot. It was a quarter of an hour before the poor man's cries were heard, for everyone was on duty and the mess servants were working in the kitchens some distance away. There was a fearful row, and both Shea and I had our mess bills stopped for a month. Why I was involved I am not quite sure. It may have been something to do with aiding and abetting!

Although I was sometimes in the Captain's bad books I was very friendly with many of the other officers. One such was Commander Spike Mahoney. He was one of the few officers who had been allowed to bring his wife to Hatston and they often entertained me in the evenings. There were so few women in this part of the word it was good to be able to talk to one occasionally. When their eldest boy Sean was born, Spike asked me to be the boy's godfather. Many years later, after I had married Angela, I returned the compliment: Spike is my boy's godfather.

For me the most disturbing aspect of Hatston was the absence of trees. The Orkney Islands are very exposed, and the hundred-mile-an-hour winds that blow from time to time ensure that no trees stand there. The bleak landscape could be very distressing, and it was easy to get an attack of the blues if one was feeling lonely. Sometimes, particularly after good friends had been posted away, I would walk back to my cabin and sit there trying to read a book while the wind howled outside. I decided I needed companionship, and on my next leave bought a puppy cocker spaniel. He was very small and rather delicate; indeed, I was not sure he would survive the journey north. He made it, however, wrapped in an Irving jacket on my knee as I sat in the nose of an unheated bomber. I called him Lucky, though as events turned out it was not an appropriate name. At first all went well. He sat in a corner of the office I shared with Shea Simmons and behaved himself. He was very popular with the other ranks who were always giving him tit-bits on the side.

We were very busy at this time preparing aircraft for a special convoy which in fact was the August convoy to Malta, though we did not know it at the time. A consignment of American fighter aircraft was delivered to us in packing cases; we had to unpack them, assemble them, air test them and deliver them to the fleet ready for operational duty. This was not easy, and having no previous experience in handling these aircraft we were absolutely dependent on the written instructions accompanying them. Particularly important were the technical flying data which gave details of their flying limitations. Without this information we could not air test them. All this top secret data was contained in one pamphlet. I was studying the document in my office before we flew any of the aircraft – we were, in fact, still assembling them – when I was called out to deal with some trouble or other. I left the pamphlet on my desk where Shea would be sure to see it for I was expecting him to come in and go through it with me. When I came back and it was missing I presumed he had taken it to his quarters. When he came to the office the following morning and asked for the pamphlet I confidently told him that he already had it. When he denied this and added that he had never even seen it I nearly had a fit. I had visions of spies and secret agents as I searched through drawers and cupboards and under chairs and desks. I soon found all that remained of that top secret pamphlet: Lucky's box was surrounded by little pieces of chewed and torn paper.

I was panic stricken. The thought of all those destroyers and cruisers, the four aircraft carriers, to say nothing of dozens of merchant ships, all waiting to put to sea made me feel quite ill. I could not ring the Captain up and say: 'I'm sorry sir, but we'll have to hold up the sailing of the convoy for a day or two, my dog has eaten the flying limitation pamphlet'. While I was wondering what to do, and Shea was talking about courts-martial, the phone rang. It was the captain. 'Tell me Hamilton', he said, 'when will the first aircraft be air tested?' I told him there would be a slight delay and that I would have to phone him back when the position was a little clearer. He accepted this without comment; I do not suppose he knew the destination of the convoy, or of its great importance, any more than I did.

Shea and I got our bush system working and with the help of our American friends – who were flying in to Prestwick daily – we managed to get another flying limitation document in only four days. We tested the aircraft, delivered them, and the convoy sailed. Nevertheless, for four days – while I played for time – thousands of men, destroyers, cruisers, aircraft carriers, and merchant ships laden with vital supplies were kept waiting because a very small dog had eaten a very important document. During this period some of the conversations I had with the Captain were fantastically technical; when I eventually told him we were ready to start delivering the aircraft his enthusiastic 'Good show Hamilton' rather embarrassed me. I kept Lucky with me until I was posted overseas when he had to be left in kennels where, unfortunately, he died of malnutrition.

The day after Pearl Harbour the Captain sent for Shea and myself and told us that the Squadron, with the exception of ourselves and a few other ranks was leaving immediately. We were very puzzled and had to wait a couple of days for an explanation. Then, together with another officer named Galley – who had also been instructed to stay at the last moment – we were summoned to the Captain's quarters where he gave us the exciting and unexpected news that the American fleet would be arriving the following day. We had a tremendous rush getting the hangars, squadron offices and so on ready for them and had to work through the night. However, when their first aircraft from the great carrier *Wasp* flew in we were ready to receive them. They flew in close formation, a most impressive sight. No sooner had they landed than their wings folded up and they parked themselves in tightly packed groups. It was a fine technical exercise perfectly performed; yet we knew – to our cost – that such limited dispersal of aircraft was no longer feasible. One or two well-placed bombs and a whole squadron could be wiped out. I had seen aircraft burn in rows like that when the Luftwaffe had bombed Lee-on-Solent.

These American pilots were very experienced airmen; I believe I am right in saying that not one of them had less than twelve hundred hours flying to his credit. That night I had my first introduction to the great American game of craps and played on until the early hours. The American fleet is a 'dry' fleet and some of these fellows had not had a drink for weeks. As a result there were many casualties. When Shea and I went down to the landing stage – where launches waited to take them back to their ships – to see them off, their departure looked like an evacuation after defeat. The unsteady walk and green face was much in evidence, and the choppy sea was a formidable obstacle to be crossed before their friendly bunks could be reached. Watching the launches as they approached the ships it appeared that many officers were leaning over the side as if looking for fish. If the local fish had any sense they gave those launches a wide berth that morning.

The following Sunday our C.-in-C. entertained the American C.-in-C., the officers from the battleships *South Carolina* and *South Dakota* and the aircraft carrier *Wasp*. During the conversation our C.-in-C. suggested to the American admiral that he might like to see the British and American fleets from the air. The admiral said he would, whereupon the C.-in-C. told me to make the necessary arrangements. The only suitable aircraft we had available was a Boston photographic plane and this was prepared for the flight. Shea Simmons was the pilot and I went as observer. We put the admiral in the perspex nose and briefed him on the drill if any emergency arose, such as the undercarriage refusing to come down or our being hit by Ack-Ack from our own ships. We showed him how to use his parachute, and took off in the early afternoon. We flew through the big balloon barrage that covered Scapa Flow and on out to sea. It was a wonderful sunny day, and the sight of the two fleets below us was the most splendid thing I have ever seen. To witness such sea power was comforting; the beauty of the great fleets in a perfect setting was a vision of perfection. I was so enthralled that I forgot about the admiral, Shea Simmons, the aircraft and everything else. I was, to all intents and purposes, alone in space.

It was necessary for all aircraft flying over the Orkney Isles to maintain wireless silence for the German monitor sets could pick up any radio conversation. Accordingly, all our intercommunication aircraft, such as this Boston, were fitted with the old type Gosport tube which was connected to the ears of the passengers and crew. Before setting off on this trip I had had a very fine lunch: several pints of beer, quite a few pink gins, some wine and, to cap it all, two very large glasses of vintage port. While I stood in my perspex dome enthralled at the sight below me, nature had been dealing with the vast quantity of alcohol I had consumed. Suddenly, she called, and I, with eyes still on the fleet below, reached instinctively for the appropriate tube reserved for this purpose. Unfortunately my hand clasped the Gosport tube which suited admirably until a nasal twang from the aircraft's nose cried out: 'Say boys, it's raining down here'. The poor man was very wet about the ears. I had my leg pulled unmercifully, and was very pleased when my next leave came up three weeks later. While in London I chanced to call on a friend at the Admiralty, and found that the story of my faux pas had preceded me. Even their Lordships knew about it.

The Americans were always training and we flew with them whenever we could. They had many casualties: some flew into high ground, others out to sea on the wrong compass reciprocal and on to Norway where German fighters got them, or they ran out of fuel trying to get back after discovering their mistake. They found flying in and around Scotland a new experience and took some time to adapt themselves. One day Galley and I were flying with their 54th pursuit Squadron commanded by a Lieutenant-Commander Turner. In the exercise the Squadron was to dive-bomb an imaginary submarine.

We took off and flew in close formation for about an hour. Both Galley and I knew how hazardous flying could be in this part of the world and hoped that we would not dive-bomb through cloud. We hoped in vain, for suddenly Turner fired his guns – the signal that he was about to dive – wheeled over and dived through the cloud below him, followed by some thirty-five to forty aircraft. A microphone attached to a gun ring in front of me no longer hung down but stayed suspended at right angles. In other words, the rate of our descent was equal to the gravitational pull of the earth. I became alarmed: not only was there another plane no more than thirty feet behind us, but cloud as thick as this might end on the top of a mountain. I respected their navigation, but they had made mistakes before. Suddenly we broke cloud and my fears were confirmed, for over on our starboard side was an ominous looking mountain. Fortunately the sea was on our port side and we had some two thousand feet in which to come out of our dive. As we skimmed along over the water everyone realized that if Turner had been a little starboard of where he was when we broke cloud the whole squadron would have gone into that mountain. As the pilot of my plane put it 'This is not like flying in Arizona'. Incidentally, we never saw anything of the submarine we were supposed to dive-bomb though apparently they waited for us all afternoon. The Americans were quick to realize that flying conditions round Britain were not to be trifled with.

When Shea Simmons and I finished our time with the Home Fleet – the Orkneys counting as sea time – we went different ways: he to the Empire test pilots' school, and I to the fighter station at Yeovil. From Yeovil I was appointed to Port Reitz near Mombasa in East Africa.

My orders were for me to go out there by sea, sailing through the Mediterranean, and so I had time to condition myself to the extreme heat that was so hard on both men and machines. All types of aircraft were assembled there: Seafires; Hurricanes, Beaufighters, Fulmars, Swordfish, in fact just about every type of aircraft in the Fleet Air Arm. At this time East Africa was being built up against the possible fall of India so that we would have ports for our warships. Mombasa is one of the few ports of the world where a fifty thousand ton ship can come in alongside the quay. From here our carriers operated against the enemy submarines that hunted merchant shipping in the Indian Ocean.

I was now able to do a great deal of flying and it was not long before I had my own personal aircraft: a Seafire Mark 113, M.B.340. I used this Spitfire for visiting the various airfields that came under our control. By this time I had been promoted to Lieutenant-Commander and my appointment covered engineering, test flying and staff duties.

CHAPTER FIVE
AFRICA

The C.O. of the communications squadron at Port Reitz was Commander John Ansell. John and I became very great friends and had some splendid times together, particularly on Friday nights when we would – in naval parlance – go ashore, and consume vast quantities of gin in Mombasa. For the rest of the week we worked pretty hard with only the odd swim in the sea to break the routine. We flew all kinds of aircraft and John was very kind in helping me to become familiar with aircraft I had not previously flown. Many aircraft were stored at Port Reitz for the Eastern Fleet: torpedo bombers and fighters which had to be ready as replacements. Much of our time was spent in air testing them. John had some forty-odd air crews in his Squadron, and in aircraft such as Fulmars and Albacores they flew up and down the East African coast on communication and supply work. We did quite a lot of this sort of work ourselves; indeed, we welcomed it. Life in the tropics could be tedious and boring; it was pleasant to be able to fly up to Nairobi into Tanganyika, or Abyssinia, or Mogadishu, down to Zanzibar and Dar-es-Saalam. Many of these trips we made jointly, many alone. When it was alone I nearly always used my own Seafire M.B. 340.

The heat was so bad that the R.A.F. fixed six months for a tour of duty in this part of the world: the Navy had no such limitation. At certain times of the year it was too hot to consider taking exercise when off duty; you could only amuse yourself on the beach or in the sea. Everyone swam whenever they could simply because you cannot perspire in water.

One Sunday I was lying on the sand after a swim, talking to the Station Commander, Commander I. D. Elliot, when a native messenger came to say that I was to report to the Admiral's H.Q. immediately. I went as I was – in my bathing togs – and on arrival was confronted with the news that my father was dying. He had been admitted to the London Clinic and was expected to die within a week. The Admiralty requested that – operations permitting – I should be given compassionate leave. My C.-in-C. was very kind and said he would do all he could to help, but that an air passage for a man on compassionate leave was dependent on there being a vacancy in an aircraft. Combatants, or anyone on duty, no matter how low their rank, had precedence over an officer on compassionate leave. I asked him whether I might be allowed to fly my Seafire to Cairo and then try to get on a plane going to the U.K. He agreed to this and at dawn the following day I set off for Cairo, long-range tanks having been fitted overnight.

These long-range tanks allowed me to fly as far as Nairobi before refuelling, and this first stage of the journey home was completed without incident and slightly ahead of the schedule I had planned for myself. Unfortunately, shortly after leaving Nairobi I saw that the aircraft's radiator temperature was rising rapidly, and though I pressed on as long as I dared I was eventually forced to land at Kisumu on Lake Victoria, where my worst fears were confirmed when the fitters diagnosed an internal coolant leak as the cause of the trouble. This was the end of my journey in M.B.340: an internal coolant leak meant an engine change, or at least a block change, and there were no spare engines or parts available. To get a new engine or block could take weeks, for unless an aircraft was coming in to Kisumu from a maintenance station (a most unlikely event) the engine or block would have to come by road and rail, and in this part of Africa such routing could take a very long time.

I sent a signal to my station telling them what had happened and then called on the local C.O., a Group Captain, to see if he could help me. He told me he was very short of aircrew and might need a pilot to take a plane to Cairo; if I could fly the aircraft in question – which might be of any size or make – we could probably help one another. Here was the only chance I might have of reaching my father's bedside before he died, so I told the Group Captain that I was fully conversant with all types of service aircraft. He seemed rather surprised but, also, obviously delighted. I had no right to lie to him like this, and knew only too well what a chance I was taking, but argued with my conscience that desperate situations demand desperate remedies.

For thirty-six hours nothing happened. My father was dying and all I could do was walk up and down outside the Group Captain's office praying that he would have an aircraft for me and that I would be able to fly it. When he left his office I hung about round the mess until he went to bed. On his way out he came over to me. 'Sorry we haven't had anything today old man, perhaps tomorrow!' That seemed to be that for the time being so I went to bed. I had not been asleep for more than a few minutes when I was awakened by a messenger who said the duty pilot wanted to see me. I dressed quickly and ran over to the office where I learnt that the pilot of a Dakota, which had just come in from Rhodesia, had malaria. Could I take it on to Khartoum and then to Cairo. I said yes with a fairly easy conscience, for I knew that all these communication aircraft had two pilots and though I had never flown a Dakota it was reasonable to presume that my services would only be required as a second pilot.

I was given the number of the aircraft and went down to the aerodrome to take a look at it. It was dark and the faint nip in the air made me shiver; even the butterflies in my stomach felt it judging from the way they were flapping. I opened the side door and looked down the fuselage; just sufficient light was coming from the crew's compartment for me to see that the aircraft was empty – the inside had been completely stripped. This was better, for clearly no passenger liability would rest on my shoulders. I had anticipated finding the aircraft empty for most of the cargo planes came through at night. I walked up the fuselage to the cockpit and found a South African Second Lieutenant who, I learned, was the second pilot. He seemed almost too willing to accept me as his new skipper, and further questioning revealed that he had just received his wings and had only accomplished one take off in a Dakota. This rather shook me, and it was with great relief that I learnt that he was fully conversant with the technical and theoretical side of flying these planes. He quite understood when I told him that I was a little rusty on flying Dakotas, and said he always marvelled at the way pilots like myself could come back to an aircraft after months of flying other types and, after brushing up their cockpit drill, fly them without difficulty. I dismissed the compliment with a modest shrug of my shoulders and a vague reference to experience, and then suggested we ran through the cockpit drill together. After this I magnaminously suggested he might like to do the night take-off. He was quite overcome and blurted out how decent it was to show such confidence in him. Little did he know that this was the first time I had sat in a Dakota, let alone flown one.

While we had been talking, some bumping and banging had been going on behind which I had presumed was the ground crews loading our cargo; on leaving the cockpit after about three quarters of an hour, I was horrified to see twenty-two sunburnt British soldiers sitting happily on the seats I had unsuspectingly heard being installed. It was too late to do anything about it now: I was too involved to back out; so with a cheery nod to them all I walked down the fuselage and, with the second pilot, went to sign the necessary clearance papers before taking off. These soldiers were going home on leave; I tried to convince myself that I was doing them a service: had I not accepted responsibility for transporting them to Cairo they would have had to wait in Kisumu for days, perhaps weeks.

My deputy executed a perfect take-off. He was very pleased: so was I. Responsibility for the dawn landing rested on my shoulders, and I tried to accept it in good heart. Much concentration, stern determination and a good share of luck allowed me to get the wheels on the ground at the third attempt, and then stop the plane inches from the end of the runway. I have often wondered whether those soldiers appreciated that providence was on their side: my co-pilot certainly did. Nevertheless we made Khartoum and then Cairo without further incident, and by the time I had delivered my charges and said goodbye to the South African Lieutenant I felt I was flying that Dakota rather well.

As might have been expected, no one in Cairo had received the signal my C.-in-C. had sent, indeed the signals officer professed never to have heard of him, let alone to have received a signal from him. Things looked black, but once again luck came to my rescue. after several hours of trying to hitch a lift I ran into an old friend who was able to get me on to a plane going to Castel Benito near Tripoli. We flew through the night arriving in the early morning. Then my troubles began again: the plane was going no further, indeed it was flying back to Cairo later in the day. Eventually I managed to hitch a lift in a troop-carrying Dakota which was bound for Marseilles. There was no seat for me so I settled down in the middle of the companionway near the Elsan. I sat on my baggage and tried to rest but, every time a soldier became air sick or wanted to answer a call of nature I had to stand up to let him get at the Elsan. The flight took an interminable time, and I began to wonder what sort of a headwind we were up against, for I could not believe that a Dakota could stay airborne for so long. It was no good asking the crew, for they were a mixture of French, Polish and Czechoslovakian and spoke very little English. When we arrived it was dark. The airfield was very badly lit. There was no power available to light the runways, only emergency red lights. While making our approach we struck a partially demolished building and lost a wing. The aircraft crashed immediately and broke up on the grass. Unlike everyone else I had no safety straps, and was thrown out through a hole in the side of the fuselage. I suffered bumps and bruises, whereas all the crew and many of the passengers were killed.

The first thing I learnt after explaining who I was and how I came to be travelling in the aircraft was that they could not let me go on to the U.K as I would be required to attend the court of enquiry that would be held on the accident. I explained how imperative it was that I should leave for London as soon as possible, and the Duty Officer was very decent. He pointed out that I was not shown on the flight plan and was in fact additional baggage, also my position in the aircraft did not allow me to know anything of what was happening in the cockpit before the crash. He even went so far as to get me on to a plane going to Hurn near Bournemouth. When we arrived there it was to find the countryside covered with some three inches of snow. This made me rather conspicuous for I was wearing shorts and tropical kit. I felt very cold and ill at ease as I wandered about trying to find out how I could get to London. Suddenly a gentleman in a black coat with a velvet collar, wearing a bowler hat and carrying a rolled umbrella appeared and said he had heard that I was anxious to get to London. I explained my predicament to him while he listened sympathetically. He then asked me, very kindly, whether I would like to travel in his train. Naturally I said yes, and we tootled off to the station in a staff car. Our departure amused the R.A.F. personnel: the sudden appearance of a solemn faced man in dark city clothes accompanied by a naval officer dressed for a tropical safari walking side by side through three inches of snow made a local wit ask: 'Who's taking the mickey out of who?'

We drove to the station and boarded a restaurant car; so far as I could see there were no other carriages attached to the train. My friend sat at one end of the restaurant car, I at the other. Although his manner was courteous, he made no attempt to introduce himself, and it was obvious he intended to pass the time with the pile of papers he drew from a large document case. A very good dinner was served, and I enjoyed the first bottle of Bass I had seen since leaving England.

On arriving in London I hurried (still in tropical kit) to the London Clinic where I learnt that my father had died an hour earlier. after eleven thousand miles I had missed seeing him alive by sixty minutes; sixty minutes that might have been saved on almost any leg of the journey.

After leave in London I went up to Gourock where I joined H.M.S. *Battler*. One week later we sailed to join the Eastern fleet, I with instructions to leave her at Alexandria. Many old friends were on board: the C.O. of the fighter squadron was a chap called Dickie Law whom I had known in earlier service days. His squadron later distinguished itself in the Far East against the Japanese. I don't remember much about the trip except that we played a great deal of poker. From Alexandria I took a train to Cairo, where I was lucky enough to discover a consignment of Spitfires awaiting delivery to Nairobi. I flew one of them down in easy stages and then completed the journey to Mombasa in a Naval transport plane.

It was on reporting to Naval Headquarters the following morning that I met Angela Sanderson for the first time. She was a Second Officer in the Wrens; quite the best looking Wren Officer I had ever seen. Our meeting did not last long, but was long enough to learn that she wanted to see

Zanzibar. Ignoring interruptions from some silly ass who was shouting his mouth off about Ham being just the chap to show her the town, I arranged to let her know when next I would be going down there. She said that, duties permitting, she would like to go with me and so it was left like that.

Unfortunately we did not meet for quite a long time. I was always flying and at no time did our Naval duties bring us together. Apart from routine air testing, I was carrying out a number of special flights in a programme of tropical research on various aircraft, which kept me busy. Our next meeting was almost accidental. I was due to fly a Defiant up to Nairobi; the evening before the flight the duty transport officer rang up and asked if I could take a Wren Officer with me. The Defiant was a two-seater fighter and so there was a spare seat.

The following morning, I was sitting in the cockpit of the plane running through my pre-flight drill when a staff car arrived and, to my great surprise, out stepped Second Officer Sanderson. She climbed into the cockpit behind me and off we went. After landing at Eastleigh, the R.A.F. Station at Nairobi, we parted company again. I told her, however, that if she kept in touch and had finished her business in Nairobi by the time I was ready to go back she was welcome to hitch another lift.

It so happened three days later that we were both ready to leave at the same time. I was given a fairly good 'met' forecast at Eastleigh, but by the time we reached the point of no return the weather had deteriorated. For some time I had been concerned at the way dark clouds were gathering, but reasoned that if it were anything serious the 'met' men would have had something to say before we took off. Then suddenly it hit us. The rain came down in torrents. It was as if someone was emptying a bath over us. Lightning flashed with blinding intensity and black clouds stretched up to 20,000 feet. I tried to contact Port Reitz on the radio; they could not hear me but I could hear them warning of bad weather ahead. Since my cockpit was half full of water, and visibility so bad that the aircrew was occasionally out of sight, their warning was superfluous. I had not bothered to arrange any intercom with my passenger, so she just sat there in water up to her knees hoping the pilot knew what he was doing.

The mountains of Voi lay ahead of us, and since they went up to eight thousand feet they had to be avoided at all cost, for we were at two thousand feet with no prospect of climbing any higher. All this time I had been attempting to navigate the plane as best I could, but now the air speed indicator packed up, making any serious attempt at further navigation impossible. I steered a course which I hoped would take us past the Voi Mountains and pressed on towards Mombasa. When I felt sure we must have passed the mountains, I concentrated on the next problem; the range of hills on the approach to the airfield. There was, in fact, a gap in those hills which could be flown through safely in good weather; today, any such thought was out of the question, so I decided to fly out over the Indian Ocean and then turn and come into Mombasa from the sea. I allowed what seemed a reasonable period to pass and then began the descent. The transmitter was still unserviceable, but the receiver was picking up Mombasa control tower, indeed I could recognize the voice of Dr. Pat Tyser calling me with monotonous regularity. (Incidentally, Pat is my son's second godfather.) I continued to let down through the murk until suddenly water appeared below. Feeling very relieved, I gave my passenger the thumbs up sign over the cockpit. In actual fact she did not know what I meant for she had been sitting in lonely and unhappy isolation, soaked to the skin and, though appreciating the seriousness of our position, quite oblivious of the various problems confronting her pilot.

Receiving no animated response to my gesture I turned back to the controls in time to see a boom defence flash by. I was startled out of my wits, but fortunately appreciated what had happened: instead of being out over the Indian Ocean we were in the bay of Port Reitz. We had never been over the Indian Ocean. In coming down I had, by pure chance, passed through the one and only gap in the hills covering the airfield and was now a few feet above the water of the Bay. The airfield was on a cliff which projected out into the Bay and was some two hundred feet above sea level; I had, therefore, flown past the airfield beneath the level of the runway. Pat Tyser had had the interesting experience of calling an aircraft he could not see but which he could hear flying past beneath him. I pulled up over the Port of Mombasa and found my way in over the coconut trees. I was one hour and ten minutes overdue when we landed and as I taxied the aircraft off the runway the propeller stopped: we were out of petrol. Ambulances, Fire Tenders, and a conglomeration of vehicles arrived looking rather like small ships as they cut their way through the six inches of water which covered the field. I jumped down from the cockpit and made to help my passenger but she, as if to uphold the prestige of her sex and have the final word, stepped on to the wing, slipped, and fell flat on her back in the water below. When she got to her feet more or less unaided, the relief I felt was the first inkling that I would one day ask her to marry me.

★ ★ ★

One day, flying from Nairobi to Mombasa on a high altitude consumption test, I was surprised to find that my view of the ground was obstructed by cloud. This was most unusual in this part of the world, and if I had not been day-dreaming in the cockpit I would have seen the weather closing in below. As it was, waltzing along up there at twenty thousand feet on this rather boring flight I had got lost.

My usual method of navigation was to fly towards the coast and when I hit it to decide whether I was north or south of Mombasa-this was not too difficult as the coastline was well defined and had distinctive features. Having adopted my usual procedure this time there was now no way of knowing where I was; all I could do was fly along and look for a break in the cloud. After a time I saw what appeared to be a river below me and reasoning that it must flow to the sea, followed it and eventually hit the coast. I presumed this to be the river that flowed out of Kelifi creek but soon found out that I was wrong: Mombasa did not turn up when it should have done. Puzzled, I flew on and presently reached Mombasa; I then knew that I must have been some ninety miles off course. I consulted the maps but no river was marked in the area I had flown through.

I was discussing the experience in the club in Mombasa that evening when a man came up to me and asked some questions which showed that he knew the coast very well. When he asked me if I would drop silver markings on the Cape road – which was actually a sand track – to mark where my imaginary river flowed out to sea, I thought he was – mentally speaking – a little off course himself; nevertheless I agreed to do it. The next time I had the opportunity of looking for my imaginary river I took a couple of silver bombs and dropped them on the Cape road as requested. My friend took a party up the road and on reaching my markings headed inland following the track I had seen from the air. About a month later he and his party discovered the lost city of Geddes.

Although we were many miles from the principal theatres of war there were armed merchant raiders and an occasional German or Japanese submarine in our waters. The merchant raiders operated mainly in the Indian Ocean, the submarines in the Mozambique Channel. One Sunday afternoon several of us were sunbathing on a sandbank some fifteen miles up the coast when we heard an aircraft flying around. It was about three p.m. and someone remarked that the pilot must be an awful heathen to fly at that hour in the tropics on a Sunday; it simply was not done.

That evening I was with a friend of mine called Jon Ansell in the R.A.F. officers' mess at Port Reitz drinking pink gin when the Wing Commander came in. We started pulling his leg, telling him we were glad that at long last the Air Force had pilots who would fly on Sunday afternoons. He let us go on for a bit and then said that none of his aircraft had been airborne and that, therefore, it was a Naval heathen's plane that had disrupted the peace of that Sabbath afternoon. We assured him that no Naval planes had flown, and then it dawned on us all that this was something serious: there was a convoy sitting in the harbour waiting to sail. Further investigation confirmed the fact that no R.A.F. or Naval aircraft had been airborne since noon. It was eventually established that a Japanese seaplane had flown in from a submarine which Intelligence had warned us was operating nearby. The officer of the watch of His Majesty's ships admitted that he thought the seaplane had odd markings, but that he could not believe the Japanese would be so stupid as to send in a plane at such low level! If that plane had been correctly identified it could have been shot down with a pea-shooter. There were a lot of red faces about for some time; the only fellow who had shown any acumen that afternoon was the chap who said: 'that pilot must be a dreadful heathen', for he was right.

A little later we had more trouble from another submarine, this time a German one. She came right out through the Mozambique, sinking several ships. Our people plotted her on the chart until she reached the Mombasa area when a striking force was despatched from one of our carriers to deal with her. They found her, and claimed that she had been damaged, or possibly destroyed, when they had attacked. A week later an R.A.F. Wellington on a training flight from Aden saw a submarine beached on a very lonely part of the African coast. They came down low enough to identify it as a U-boat, and although they had no depth charges or bombs, succeeded in informing the German commander that, should he attempt to destroy his ship or put to sea, the submarine would be bombed. Their bluff worked. The R.A.F., in answer to the Wellington's wireless message, sent out another aircraft (with bombs) to relieve them, and for one week, until a naval shore party arrived, the R.A.F. kept up a day and night patrol above the submarine.

The most interesting thing to come out of this submarine was a tiny helicopter. It had no engine, and no body to speak of. Its chassis was multi-tubular: rather like a modern sports-racing car, and was shaped like a kitchen chair. The pilot sat in this chair. There was a pillar behind him with a shaft which held a rotor. Forward momentum was given by a cable which was attached to the submarine on a winch. A telephone line ran down this cable giving the pilot air to sea communication. When he was ready to take off the pilot would start the rotor with a flick of his hand and the man on the winch would play him out behind the submarine like a kite until he was flying at four or five thousand feet. The submarine would then submerge, leaving a tiny dot in the sky to inform them of the presence of a convoy over the horizon or the approach of hostile ships.

We informed the Admiralty of our 'find' and asked for permission to fly it. Unfortunately, their lordships refused permission.

A few weeks later an aircraft I was flying had an hydraulic failure; I was forced to land without flaps and with only one wheel down. The aircraft was obsolete and was due to be destroyed; my 'prang' saved the breakers' gang trouble, for though my one wheel landing was quite good, the port wing stuck in the ground when the plane toppled and it cartwheeled, throwing me out. I was not too badly knocked about but accepted from a kindly native a drink of water which gave me a serious kidney disease. For some time my life was in danger, but eventually I rallied. My convalescence coincided with the end of the war and soon I was on my way home to England for demobilization. The day before I left, my friends threw a party for me; it is something I shall always remember.

Looking down on the East African coast from the seaplane in which I flew home I realized that a chapter in my life was ending. Not only was I leaving Mombasa and the Navy, I was leaving a way of life that I had enjoyed. It had been fashionable to curse the heat of the tropics, the red tape, the frustrations of service life, and curse them I had. But what of the compensations? The firm friendships, the wonderful comradeship, the esprit de corps that only routine and discipline can instill in a man, all that had been good. Good enough for me to feel that if some walk of civilian life could offer a little of the adventure and excitement of the Naval aviation life I was leaving I must seek it out; for if I was successful in my search, and such a life was open to me, I was going to enjoy the future.

CHAPTER SIX

HILL-CLIMBS AND EARLY RACES

The first few weeks of demobilization leave were very lonely. Both my parents were dead (my mother had died in the early days of the war) and all my friends – particularly Angela Sanderson – were in other parts of the world. Death duty on my parents' estates had been heavy, and there were many legal and technical complications which had to be resolved before probate could be declared. As a result I spent a lot of time talking to lawyers and insurance company officials as I worked through the maze of documents associated with the estates. My sister had been reunited with her husband who had been in Burma for four years. Then Angela came home in time for Christmas, much to my delight, but within a few weeks tragedy knocked at my door again: my sister died in childbirth, the baby survived.

Meanwhile Angela had agreed to marry me, but only on condition that I gave up flying. This was rather a blow, for I had been offered, and had accepted, a very good job with an

American aviation company. However, I cancelled my acceptance and began looking around for something else. My sister's death had further complicated probate of my parents' estates, for she was a beneficiary, and the estates' liability for death duty was increased. A desk job, in the conventional sense, did not appeal to me. Eventually my love of cars led me to look for something in the motor business. Angela had an uncle who was a friend of Bertie Henly, the chairman of Henlys Ltd, and he arranged for me to meet the big man. The interview was a success, and I landed a job in the Henly organization buying and selling motor cars at the Camberley branch. In June 1946 Angela and I were married in Holy Trinity, Brompton, and went to live near Camberley. I stayed with Henlys until my mother's, father's and sister's estates had been cleared up; then, feeling that I had learned enough about the business of buying and selling cars to fend for myself, set up on my own. By this time my son Adrian had been born.

Before the formation of my own company, and while I was still with Henlys, the first post-war hill climbs and sprints were organized. Now that I could no longer fly, I transferred my affections from the cockpit of a Seafire to the somewhat stark and exposed cockpit of a single-seater two stage blown R-Type M.G. which had been owned by Sir Malcolm Campbell. I bought this car from Leslie Hawthorn, Mike Hawthorn's father, and used it for sprints and hill-climbs. It had independent four wheel suspension and a very high revving engine. The first time I used it was at Prescott on July 28th 1946. It was at this meeting that I met John Cooper for the first time. He had built an ingenious 'special' out of two Fiat 500s, by cutting them in half and joining the two halves together with steel tubes. The engine was at the back and the car's appearance and unusual design attracted a lot of attention. Some spectators were inclined to scoff at so revolutionary a machine, but the knowledgeable knew that John's father, Charles Cooper, had been Kaye Don's mechanic and had built one of the first 'Flying Fleas'. If John had supervised the construction of this car they were sure it would be a sound engineering job. They were right of course, but no one imagined that they were looking at the early prototype of a racing car that was one day to win the World Championship.

That winter most of my spare time was spent in taking the M.G. to pieces and then putting it together again; this is the only way to learn and I was happy learning. I entered it for as many hill climbs as possible in 1947 and I enjoyed myself thoroughly. The sport was very amateur in those days and a wonderful spirit prevailed. In saying that, I am not criticizing modern motor racing, but merely commenting on the happy-go-lucky atmosphere of those early days.

One day, while competing at Shelsley Walsh, I saw the most beautiful Bugatti; it was a 2.3-litre 35B, painted red, and with all the steel work brightly polished. After much negotiation I managed to buy this splendid car with its cast wheels and twin rears. I drove it in hill-climbs and sprints through the latter part of the 1946 season, and for most of the 1947, winning the odd small trophy and, what was much more important, having a lot of fun. I enjoyed the fun and the success, but what I remember best about this Bugatti was the way it advanced my knowledge and appreciation of fine machinery. Bugatti was an engineering genius and to work on one of his cars was an education. A veterinary surgeon, Holland Birkett, was a great help to me with advice on the maintenance and preparation of the car for hill climbs and sprints. He had an encyclopaedic knowledge of Bugattis and I shall always be grateful to him for his kindness in passing on so much of his know-how.

One day I took the Bugatti to an airfield for some high speed trials. Rumour had it that circuit racing was just around the corner and I wanted to be prepared. Unfortunately all did not go well: on braking for a corner the front brakes locked on so hard that the axle was screwed through 180 degrees. One of the front wheels was a complete write-off, and though I had a spare it was not of the pukka Grand Prix type but a solid one. I towed her home and set about repairing the damage. Once again Holland Birkett came to the rescue, telling the mechanic who was helping me and myself exactly what to do.

We worked all weekend to get it ready for a meeting at Shelsley. I was so anxious to road test her when we had finished that I did not take into account the fact that we had fitted twin-rears in readiness for the hill-climbs. I arrived at the exit doing perhaps fifty miles an hour, only to find that though my front wheels passed through safely enough, the gap was too narrow to accommodate twin-rears, and I left the entire back axle assembly behind. There was nothing for it but to begin all over again. We worked all day – various odd friends lending a hand from time to time – and then right through the night; it was not until ten-thirty the next morning that she was ready for the road once again.

I was so tired that I completely forgot about the twin-rears and proceeded to execute a repeat performance of the previous day's happenings. Once again the back axle assembly and the car parted company, to the astonishment, not only of myself, but of all the well-wishers who had gathered to lend a hand and to offer encouragement. My mechanic, no doubt overcome by fatigue after working all night, became grossly insubordinate, he proffered advice of a most unseemly kind, and made ridiculous suggestions as to what I should do with the rear axle assembly. My humble acceptance of all responsibility for the contretemps placated him, and after a stiff drink we went back to work. The next day, believe it or not, we recorded the fastest Bugatti time at Shelsley in its class.

Towards the end of the 1947 season I entered both the M.G. and the Bugatti in the Brighton speed trials. This is a sprint meeting: the cars covering a timed kilometre along the front. Originally, it had been my intention to send the M.G. on the back of a lorry, and to drive the Bugatti down myself. At the last moment the mechanic who was going to drive the lorry became ill and I was forced to improvise a means of getting both cars to Brighton. Using a makeshift tow-bar, I attached the Bugatti to the lorry, in the back of which the M.G. rested. Angela was to follow me in an Armstrong-Siddeley Hurricane drop-head coupe which we had just bought. At first all went well. I drove the lorry quite slowly, and very carefully, for I was mindful of my valuable cargo.

Suddenly, going down the hill into Guildford I saw the splendid honeycomb radiator of a Bugatti in the outside rear view mirror. Presuming it was a competitor bound for Brighton I moved over and waved him on. He did not overtake me immediately but hung back as if not sure of himself. Wondering what he was up to I glanced round and saw that it was a 2.3-litre 35B painted the same colour as my own. 'He's obviously looking at mine and comparing it with his own' I thought and motored on. Suddenly the Bugatti began to accelerate and drew level with me. I turned to look at the driver only to discover that the driving seat was empty. The awful truth dawned on me – it was my own car, gathering speed fast, and heading off the road towards two women who were standing with their backs to us. Fortunately I reacted quickly. I banged the gear lever into third, simultaneously accelerating the lorry and applying right lock, so that the bumper of the lorry struck the side of the tail of the Bugatti causing it to veer left, and miss the two nattering women. It continued across in front of me, mounted the pavement, and hit a tall concrete electric lamp standard which snapped into two, the upper half falling to the ground with a fearful crash.

We were now in the middle of a residential area; doors opened, faces appeared at windows, and a general hubbub broke out among the people who had rushed to the scene of the accident. At first everyone was mystified as to where the driver had gone. One man actually lay down on his stomach to make sure no one was under the car. Speaking quietly, I tried to explain what had happened and in so doing received some pretty queer looks. No police came, and after a time all the adult spectators left, leaving an odd assortment of children who kept poking at things .and asking ridiculous questions. Angela – who had been frantically hooting from behind the lorry – coaxed these kids far enough away from the Bugatti for me to take stock of the damage.

The front axle and springs were broken, but fortunately the radiator was all right. The car was certainly repairable but at considerable cost, and it was not insured against this unusual type of accident.

After a time we got hold of a breakdown truck and had the Bugatti carted away, but still no police turned up. Angela was worried about the broken lamp standard, for wires were poking out all over the place inviting children to play with them. I was all for pressing on to Brighton, arguing that we could deal with the problem of the lamp standard on the way back, and that if we left a notice saying 'Danger' that would suffice. She would not hear of this, and insisted that I get in touch with the Electricity Board. While we were arguing, I noticed that a man – who had watched the entire proceedings without ever offering to help – was taking a keen interest in what we were saying. He was leaning on the front wall of his garden apparently taking notes. I walked over to him and asked if he could tell me where the Electricity Board's offices were. To my surprise he answered: 'I should be able to, I'm the manager'. After sorting everything out we went on to Brighton where the M.G. recorded second fastest time in its class.

* * *

With the approach of the 1948 season, and the promised return of circuit racing, I began to look around for a suitable car. The only racing cars available were pre-war, and all the good ones were in the hands of people who had no intention of surrendering them.

One day a friend of mine, George Abecassis, phoned me to say he had just bought a Grand Prix Maserati, after locating it in the engineering workshops of the Cape Town Railway Department. I was amazed, for I had heard of this car when stationed at Mombasa and had made a few tentative enquiries without getting anywhere. It had been specially made for Villoresi and had gone out to the Union to race in a Grand Prix just before the war. George had had great difficulty in importing the car and, having succeeded, was very pleased with himself. He drove it in the Jersey Road Race, finishing second to Bob Gerard in his faithful E.R.A. The mechanic he took down with him was Alf Francis who was attending his first road race. Alf was later Stirling Moss's mechanic and later still prepared Rob Walker's cars. George agreed to sell the car to me but only on condition that he drove it in the race. I went over to Jersey where there was some talk of my being nominated as second driver. In fact I appeared on the programme as second driver, but George was too cunning actually to let me drive in the race. His pit stop to refuel was very quick, and though I waited hopefully to see whether he wanted me to take over, no sooner were ten gallons of fuel in the tank and the oil checked than he was away without giving me so much as a glance. He was quite right of course: he was well up in second position and I had never as yet driven in a road race. We took the car back to George's garage at Walton where he eventually sold it to me with no conditions attached.

I had just sold the M.G. and now decided to sell the Bugatti as well and really get down to this business of circuit racing. However, before finally parting with the Bugatti I decided to have one more fling, and took it to a meeting at Prescott. Five times we tried to get to the top of the hill and five times we hit different things. To begin with we knocked down the palings at the first corner. At the next attempt we took the bumper off an ambulance which was parked near the second corner. Third time up we left the road and all but hit a couple in the Bugatti members' enclosure. Fourth time up we hit a tree, denting the tail. Fifth and last time we made a splendid climb, arriving at the top going great guns but, unfortunately, without brakes. The car flew straight over the hedge, turned a complete somersault, landed on all four wheels, and stopped. I was unhurt, though shaken; the car was rather bent. While I was standing there contemplating how much it was going to cost to restore the car to its former immaculate condition, a small man, carrying a brown suitcase, approached me. 'Why do you always change the sixth plug?' he asked. I thought this rather an unusual remark to address to someone who has just somersaulted over a hedge, but recovered sufficiently to explain that number six plug had a tendency to become wet, so we changed it before a run just to make sure we would not lose a cylinder half way up the hill. He nodded, and then asked: 'Are you sure there is nothing wrong with the piston ring or piston?' 'Nothing at all', I said, 'we've had the engine down and it appears to be perfect. These engines do run hot, and softer plugs such as one uses for ordinary road work eliminate the trouble'. He was silent for a moment then asked: 'Would you sell this car?' Now it was my turn to be silent. I looked at the dent in the tail and wondered how the back axle had taken it all: I wondered whether the steering was as badly damaged as it looked as if it might be; I thought of what I had just paid for the Maserati and I said: 'Yes'.

'How much?' he asked. I mentioned a figure. He nodded his agreement and then opened the suitcase he was carrying; it was full of five pound notes. Solemnly he counted them. 'I'd better let you have the suitcase', he said, 'you'll not get this lot in your pockets', and with that he handed it over.

In the paddock I was met by an anxious Angela. 'Are you all right?' she asked, 'everyone says there has been an accident'.

'I'm fine', I said, 'just fine'.

'Where's the car?' She looked worried.

'Oh the car! Oh it's in here', I tapped the suitcase. She took me by the arm.

'Come along dear, I'll take you home', and she led me to the car park.

'Poor old Ham', said a bystander, 'he must have taken quite a knock'.

My first road race was the British Empire Trophy on the Douglas circuit in the Isle of Man. I practised very hard for this event, doing many laps round the perimeter of an airfield where the C.O. was a personal friend. The Maserati was going very well and, to my amusement, went faster during practice on the Douglas circuit than a new one-and-a-half-litre Alta which George Abecassis had acquired soon after selling me the Maserati. Tony Rolt – with whom I was to win at Le Mans in 1953 – was driving in this race and he gave me much good advice. My driving had apparently alarmed him, and I remember him saying: 'The object is to get round quickly, not to kill yourself'. He was a fine driver, who had won this race pre-war while still in his teens, driving the ex-'Bira' E.R.A. *Remus*. During the last practice before the race I discovered how wise his counsel had been, for I spun on the back leg of the circuit, clouted a bank, and nearly wrecked the car. It was only after working all through the night in a local garage – during which George Abecassis and his friend John Heath demonstrated how a six-foot crowbar and a twenty pound hammer could straighten the bent steering of a racing car – that the Maserati was ready for the race.

We got away to a good start and settled down lapping in about sixth or seventh place. I remember passing Wilkie Wilkinson who was driving an E type E.R.A. and then, coming down the hill into Onchan village, I left my braking far too late and went into a series of left and right hand slides, scattering straw bales in all directions and finishing up by entering a bank at high speed. That was the end of my first road race. I was quite unhurt, and spent the rest of the afternoon sitting on a straw bale outside a pub drinking glass after glass of the quite excellent beer they brewed.

★ ★ ★

My next race and, incidentally, one of the most enjoyable of my career, was at Zandvoort in Holland. It was an invitation race, the only participants being members of the British Racing Drivers' Club who had been invited by the Mayor of Zandvoort to open the new circuit. This circuit had an interesting history: it was built by the Dutch during the war under German supervision. The Mayor of the time had convinced the German commander that there was a danger of the sea coming in, and that the construction of artificial sand-dunes was necessary for the protection of the town. The German commander had been successfully hoodwinked, and as a result the Mayor was able to keep most of his male population working on this sandbank, thus preventing their deportation to Germany. The new circuit, of 2.7 miles, made use of certain roads that had been built to supply the men working on the sand dunes, and it was a very fine one.

Our party received a royal welcome. The Mayor and Mayoress were there with children, garlands of flowers, flags, and a brass band which played with hearty enthusiasm. It was my first taste of the way in which racing motorists are feted on the Continent; it contrasted vividly with 'the man's a madman' attitude I had encountered at home.

There was no limit to engine capacity, and though most of the cars were supercharged 1.5-litres, there were others of greater capacity such as Tony Rolt's 3.8-litre Alfa-Romeo; Kenneth Bear's 3.3-litre Bugatti and Ken Hutchinson's 2.9-litre Alfa-Romeo.

The Dutch were wonderful hosts and entertained us in grand style. Just before the race half a dozen of us visited the Bols gin factory and received such hospitality that my subsequent placing in the first heat was not due only to the performance of the Maserati. I finished third, easily qualifying for the final. Indeed, when we all shot away at the start of the final I was not unaware of where I had spent the morning. One newspaper reporter wrote: 'Duncan Hamilton driving in only his second race on the old 6 cylinder Maserati (which Abecassis drove at Jersey, remember?) exhibited style, coolness and a knowledge of how to do it which resulted in fourth place in the final.' What an unsolicited testimonial to Bols gin!

The race was a very exciting one, Prince Bira and Tony Rolt passing and repassing one another for the forty laps of the final. In the end Bira won by one tenth of a second at 73.25 mph after 108 miles of racing. Reg Parnell, in a 1.5-litre Maserati was third, and I followed on, fourth.

I learnt two lessons in this race: firstly, that one must so learn a circuit that one's gear changes occur at precisely the same places every time round. In this way it is possible to drive without constant reference to the rev-counter, or indeed without a rev-counter at all, as I had to do from the second lap onwards. I had practised the routine so thoroughly that I was able to drive without ever over-revving the engine. The second lesson was that without proper information from your pit you cannot know your exact position in a race. What brought this home was an incident that occurred on the last lap of the final. I came round the corner near the pits to see a Maserati – which had spun off – waiting to rejoin the race. I slowed down and waved him on, only to discover afterwards that the driver was Reg Parnell who was lying third. Had I passed him – as indeed he was waiting for me to do – I would have finished third. At the time I did not know what my position was for I was not receiving any pit signals. In a race of any length it is quite impossible to know your exact position (unless you happen to be leading) for after a time cars start lapping one another, others call in at the pits and then rejoin the race, and everything gets a little involved. If you are driving really fast you do not have time to notice all the things the spectators may be aware of.

After the race came the prize-giving, and then back to the hotel for a bath and some more Bols gin. Tony Rolt and I decided we might as well have an evening out, so we borrowed Gordon Watson's jeep and drove off in search of a restaurant. We found one, parked the jeep, and went inside. Once the proprietor discovered that we had been driving in the race that afternoon nothing was too good for us. We ate a stupendous meal and sampled just about every drink he had in the place.

After a time Tony pointed out two policemen who appeared to be taking an interest in our jeep. Presently they transferred their attentions to us – having evidently decided that one of us must be the owner. It is possible that, viewed through a partly steamed up window, we appeared somewhat the worse for wear. It is also possible that when we stood up and toasted their health through the window that they did not think it funny. It is certain that when I fell down after drinking their health (to the great amusement of Rolt) they were not amused. Tony thought, therefore, that it would be imprudent to go out and get into the jeep. Some subterfuge was necessary. While we were plotting our escape Tony saw, in a glass jar, the most enormous eel. A happy thought came to him: why not buy it and put it in Freddie Dixon's bed while he was asleep? I was so overcome by this brilliant suggestion that the policemen were temporarily forgotten, while we wrangled with the poor proprietor, who did not want to sell his eel. Eventually he gave in, reluctantly rolled it up in a newspaper and handed it over. It was so slippery, that I had to wrap a handkerchief round the paper before I could carry it.

We said goodnight to everyone, and sauntered outside. Our plan was to wander down the street past the jeep pretending it was nothing to do with us, then, when the policemen relaxed, run to the jeep, jump in, and make off. Our plan was only partly successful, for one of them was very quick off the mark. He actually succeeded in getting his hands on me. There was only one thing I could do, and I did it, losing the eel in the process. That was the last we saw of them. We bore them no malice; and though they failed to land the big fish they were after we hoped the eel was some compensation for their trouble. Tony put the final mark on a splendid evening when he drove the jeep up the steps into the foyer of our hotel and parked it there.

Shortly after we returned from Holland, the Duke of Richmond and Gordon opened his new motor racing circuit at Goodwood near Chichester. I entered the Maserati for the Easter handicap and had the pleasure of finishing fifth after leading for some time in the early stages. For a long time a photograph of the Maserati and myself leading an assortment of E.R.A.s and other Maseratis was featured on all Goodwood circuit propaganda, posters and programmes.

In those days the compulsory wearing of crash helmets was unknown; neither did anyone wear clothing which might protect him from fire. People often drove in short sleeved Aertex shirts, thin trousers and cloth helmets; I remember seeing Peter Walker driving bareheaded and without goggles. Later on we all appreciated how foolish we had been, but not before one or two had suffered the consequences of the general folly. One day, George Abecassis – who had taken his Alta to Switzerland for the Swiss Grand Prix – phoned from Berne to say that he was unwell, and that he might not be able to drive in the Grand Prix. He asked me whether I would take his place if he was still unfit on race day.

A few days previously I had met a friend who had told me he had just bought a small aeroplane – an ex-service Proctor Mark 5. When I found that no airline could sell me a seat that would enable me to arrive in time for the race I contacted my friend and asked him if he would like to fly to Berne and watch the Swiss Grand Prix. He was agreeable, and the following morning we took off from Blackbushe and headed for the Continent. I piloted the plane and we reached Basel-Muhlhausen without any trouble. We cleared customs, refuelled, and then flew on to Berne where we found George Abecassis in good health and full of apologies. As it happened I was too late to practise anyway, and since Achille Varzi had been killed that day it is doubtful whether the Swiss officials would have let me race without first practising.

I watched the race, and it was a very good one. Jean-Pierre Wimille won in an Alfa-Romeo. Unfortunately there was a fatal crash at the beginning of the race when a Maserati left the road and its driver, Kautz, was killed.

George Abecassis failed to finish. A telegraph pole got in his way and removed the back of the Alta and one of its wheels.

The next day we left Berne and attempted to fly home. The weather was poor, but we made Basel-Muhlhausen without too much trouble. But, while we were clearing customs a storm broke over the airfield and made it impossible for us to leave. For three miserable days we waited for an improvement in the weather, but no improvement came; it rained continuously, and cloud base was very low.

On the fourth morning the rain stopped, and the Polish pilot of a Swiss-owned Rapide, which was equipped with radio-aids, decided he would take off. He suggested to me that I follow him over the mountains; he was bound for Paris, and once we were over France I could set course for England. I did not like the idea very much, for if we lost the Rapide in cloud we would be in very serious trouble. My friend, and another Englishman – to whom we had given a lift in Berne – were in favour of taking a chance, and so I agreed to follow the other aircraft. The inevitable happened, of course, and we lost sight of the Rapide soon after taking off. Visibility was nil, and I had no idea where we were for the Rapide had taken an unusual course on leaving Basel-Muhlhausen – presumably to fly through a gap in the mountains – and in so doing had taken me miles off the course I would have flown had I been able to see. I dared not descend through cloud since we were obviously over mountainous terrain. A church spire flew past my port wing, greatly upsetting the chap we had given a lift to. He began to rush about the aircraft, and I was compelled – with the aid of a fire extinguisher – to make him lie down. A moment later I saw – through a gap in the cloud – some flat land. I put the plane down at once and attempted a landing. We bounced and bounced and bounced. The undercarriage broke, the port wing came off, and eventually we stopped. There was a long silence while everyone considered what had just occurred from their own point of view. Only I appeared to appreciate how lucky we were. My friend was upset because his aeroplane was broken, and the passenger was upset because the fire extinguisher was broken – the fact that it had broken on his head may have prejudiced his point of view.

It was snowing quite heavily, and since there was nothing to suggest that anyone would know that we were there I thought it best to go and look for help before the weather got worse. The cabin of the Proctor was intact and gave us reasonable protection – it kept out the snow and sheltered us from the wind – nevertheless, we could not live there for long without food and drink, and our clothing was anything but adequate for sub-zero temperatures. We were in fact on the top of the Belfort Gap, though we did not know it at the time. The passenger had a particularly heavy overcoat, and since I was going in search of help I suggested he lend it to me. He was most uncooperative, however, and not only refused to part with his coat but suggested that he did not care whether I froze to death or not.

I left my companions in the plane and set off down the hillside. After a time I came upon a house. Its sole occupant was a witch-like creature surrounded by dogs and cats; she could not understand me nor I her. She insisted on giving me an umbrella, and I found, during the course of the three hours that passed before I met another person, that it did give me some protection from the freezing wind. The man I met was a Monsieur Rine. He was a splendid fellow. He arranged a rescue party, fixed us up with hotel accommodation, and subsequently paid my air fare to Britain. Later when I attempted to pay him back he would not hear of it. He was, apparently, glad we had won the war, and this was his way of saying thank you.

Angela, who had been waiting to hear from me, first knew of my adventure when she read an account of my crash in the evening paper. The report went on to say that the plane had sunk in a swamp. Angela could not reconcile the top of a mountain with a swamp, so wisely waited until I returned home before attempting to find out what had actually happened. She presumed I was all right because the press were more interested in the plane than its occupants, a sure sign that the occupants must be safe and well.

★ ★ ★

During the winter of 1948, my good friend Philip Fotheringham-Parker suggested that we go into partnership for the following season's racing, and enter the Maserati in as many events as possible. We had a fine season's sport together, beginning with the Easter meeting at Goodwood in which I finished second in the handicap.

Shortly after this Goodwood meeting we took the Maserati over to Jersey for the famous road race. With George Abecassis driving, the car had finished second the previous year and I was hopeful that we would do well again. Philip drove for the first half of the race, handing over to me when he brought the car in for refuelling. I lapped quite fast but picked up a stone which punctured the radiator and eventually caused the engine to seize solid when the car was doing about one hundred and thirty miles per hour. The Maserati spun round five or six times and then shot off the road into the car park of a garage. I jumped out unhurt but shaken, resolving that I would take note of my instrument readings in future, It was quite obvious what had happened for there was steam everywhere. Had I been watching the water temperature the accident could have been avoided. A dear old lady gave me a cup of tea and a doughnut, and boiled water for the Maserati; after filling it up I actually managed to start it down a slope and drive back to the pits. Although we patched it up and I drove on for a couple of laps the damage had been done, and I had to retire with a very sick engine. Distorted pistons were the principal trouble and getting the engine repaired was a very expensive business.

I remember well a later race on another island, not so much for itself, as for the evening we had afterwards. Tony Rolt, Peter Walker and myself breezed into our hotel to be welcomed by a sour faced manager whose manner (ever since we had arrived) had made it clear that he had no intention of doing any of us a favour. His attitude had been caught by the rest of the staff and we were fed up with the treatment and service we had tolerated. When the manager asked us, rather pointedly, when we would be leaving, the answer was 'As soon as possible'. We had endured a good deal during the last few days and were thoroughly browned off. The last straw – for Peter Walker at any rate – was when at dinner we waited for fully half an hour without being served after giving our order. Peter got up and stormed out, to return some two minutes later wearing an overcoat and carrying a suitcase; he announced that he was leaving the so and so hotel and that he had never experienced such treatment in his life. In the middle of his harangue a very important looking head waiter marched up and curtly told him that hotel guests were not allowed to wear overcoats in the dining room neither were they allowed to leave luggage there. Peter took off his coat, handed it to the head waiter, and told him that if he wanted the case put in the hall he could put it there himself. To cries of 'bravo', he then walked to our table and sat down. A hushed silence followed: no one spoke; no one moved. The head waiter – his chin twitching up and down as if he were about to cry – stood holding the coat beside the suitcase, too baffled to retaliate. Peter had put up with too much to care whether the man was upset or not; if the fellow's feelings were hurt, well, that made two of them.

Seeing that his behaviour had not had any effect on Peter, the head waiter summoned a boy and the coat and suitcase were removed. No sooner had this been done than a large blowsy woman entered carrying yet another suitcase but to our surprise the head waiter made no attempt to stop her; he smiled a greeting and bowed her in. She walked briskly to a stage in a corner of the room where she was joined by a very small frail looking man who also bowed politely and offered her a chair. She sat down, and opening the suitcase, revealed a large accordion. The little man moved forward to lift the accordion out of the case just as she attempted a similar feat with the result that his head collided rather vigorously with her amply proportioned bosom. He bounced off and they soon sorted themselves out, but not before their little contretemps had quite taken our minds off everything else.

The little man sat down at the piano and played a few mournful chords while the lady put on her accordion. It was not easy for her. Indeed, anyone viewing her in silhouette could have been forgiven for thinking she was getting a roll-on over her head. She played, standing up, with an abandon it was fascinating to watch, for her accordion and her bosom did not move as one: it was difficult to watch her act without continually blinking.

For a while she entertained, but soon my stomach began to rumble and I was reminded of the deplorable service we were enduring. I signalled to Tony Rolt to follow me outside. From my bedroom window I had noticed earlier a yard full of ducks; why not let them make a contribution to the evening. We collected a suitcase from my room and then went outside and found the sleeping ducks. We got about fifteen of them into the suitcase and returned to the hotel. Surprisingly enough they did not make too much noise. We walked into the dining room, put the suitcase down near our table and resumed our seats. The head waiter rushed over, 'I have told you gentlemen suitcases are not allowed in the dining-room. Really this is exasperating!'. With that he snatched up the suitcase and made to leave the room. Unfortunately for him I had undone the catches, so as soon as he lifted the case the lid opened and fifteen terrified ducks tumbled out on to the floor. They scattered in all directions, making a fearful row and startling the other diners out of their wits.

The lady with the accordion was just as startled as the guests, but true to the best traditions of her profession she proceeded to play a galloping sort of tune which fitted the circumstances perfectly. There were ducks everywhere, quacking like mad as they took evasive action all over the room. Waiters and guests ran here and there as they tried to catch them, while those guests and ducks who tried to leave by the door were prevented by the people who were trying to get in to see what was happening. Still the good lady and her companion played on: it was bedlam. I looked at Tony and he at me, both of us aware that things were now out of hand. We left surreptitiously through the kitchens, found a restaurant in the town, and after a quiet meal returned to the hotel. There were police in the foyer and we feared the worst but, as it happened, they were looking only for a statue of Queen Victoria which had left its plinth in the main square. It was found eventually in a racing driver's bed wearing lipstick, rouge and mascara. How it got there no one could imagine.

After the police had gone a few friends gathered in my bedroom for a night-cap. Some ragging started, and in trying to stop someone throwing my bed clothes out of the window I slipped and fell head first against the wall. This wall turned out to be a flimsy affair of beaver board; my head went straight through it and stuck on the other side. For a moment I was in darkness, then a switch clicked and a light came on. I saw that my head was wedged in the wall between two single beds containing two elderly ladies. 'Oh my goodness!' said the one on the left, 'what are you doing?'.

'I slipped,' I said rather weakly.

'Well go away at once, you're a very rude boy.'

'I'm stuck.'

'Oh dear! 'exclaimed the one on my right, 'what must we do?'

Before I could answer someone took hold of my legs and gave a fearful tug. My head nearly came off and I yelled out. The old dears nearly had a couple of fits, but they could not help, because it would have been improper for them to get out of bed in their nightgowns, or so the one on my left said.

'It's all right Duncan, I'll have you out in a jiffy'. It was Tony's voice, and a moment later he knocked the wall down with the leg of a chair. Propriety was forgotten: those two old dears, fearing assault was imminent, shot out of bed and into the corridor just as the wall gave way and I fell into the room. Fortunately they were prevailed upon to return and to accept our sincere apologies and a noggin. Finally, after telling us we were very naughty boys, they forgave us. The hotel management were not capable of such magnanimity: they did not forgive us. When we left after settling up the next morning we carried our own suitcases: the entire hotel staff was too busy getting Queen Victoria downstairs to spare us a glance, which was perhaps just as well. When I got home, complete with hang-over and car, there was wonderful news. Angela had had a daughter, Caroline.

★ ★ ★

The great thing about my partnership with Philip Fotheringham-Parker was that we both raced purely for the sport. We tried to win, of course; but our main consideration was to enjoy an afternoon's driving on the limit of the car's performance and our own ability. Philip, who was some twelve years my senior, had first raced in the twenties on motor cycles; later he graduated to cars by way of a chain-drive Frazer-Nash. He was a regular competitor at Brooklands where, incidentally, he once achieved the unenviable distinction of shooting over the top of the banking without hurting himself. During the war he raced captured Alfas and Maseratis round Addis Ababa until stopped by his C.O. who thought it was too dangerous – after all someone might have been killed!

In September, we took the Maserati over to Eire for the Wakefield Trophy, which was run on the Curragh road circuit some thirty miles from Dublin. We put the car in the old Guy transporter we used from time to time and drove to Liverpool. We resolved not to hurry but to complete a survey of all attractive pubs and hotels en route. The journey took us three days, and we were, in fact, lucky to catch the boat on the third evening. The crossing was a bad one and I was very happy to leave the booking of hotel rooms to Philip. He drove the Maserati through the streets of Dublin to the Gresham hotel and then drove the thirty miles to the Curragh where I was waiting. Apart from the fact that a crowd gathered every time he stopped he had no trouble. It was only afterwards that we realized that he had broken just about every possible road regulation: the car was not insured for road work, it had no registration number or trade plates, no mudguards and no silencer – only open exhausts. It ran perfectly in the race, gave no trouble, and finished – Philip doing all the driving on this particular occasion.

We came back from Eire and motored to Goodwood where, the following Saturday, I drove the Maserati into second place in the Autumn handicap.

A fortnight later we were due to share the car in the British Grand Prix at Silverstone and went up well in advance to practise. I was practising on the Thursday afternoon when the engine blew up. One of the hollow connecting rods had broken and come out through the side of the aluminium crankcase complete with piston, the piston actually flying out through the bonnet. Louis Giron looked at the mess and, to our great surprise, said he was prepared to try and get the car ready for the Grand Prix. Spare parts were practically unobtainable, but I remembered seeing a spare connecting rod in Ireland in a garage. After several fruitless telephone calls we located the rod, bought it for an exorbitant price, and arranged for it to be flown to London Airport where we had a car waiting. We then took the Maserati to the house of my old friend, Tim Seccombe, and started on the repairs. At first, we worked in his garage, where he had a wonderful selection of tools; but later, at his suggestion, moved the car into his drawing room where the light was better and the surroundings more comfortable. Louis was in charge of operations while Philip, Tim and myself helped. We were faced with a formidable task, for apart from the damage I have mentioned, the oil gallery, which ran along the side of the crankcase, was perforated. To Louis, however, all things were possible, so we knuckled down to it.

About seven o'clock on Friday evening the phone rang; on the other end of the line was an old friend of Tim's, Bing Grinling. Bing reminded Tim that he was invited to dinner; should he wear lounge suit or dinner jacket? Tim told him dinner jacket. When the immaculately dressed Bing arrived in the drawing-room and saw his host lying under a Maserati he was surprised, but took off his jacket and mucked in with the rest of us. He enjoyed his coffee and sandwiches as much as we did, and when he went home after breakfast had the satisfaction of knowing that he had played a part in getting the car ready for the British Grand Prix. Philip and I shared the car – changing over half way – and finished the race. Louis Giron had done a great job, and Tim Seccombe's drawing-room had made a contribution to the sport that even that indefatigable enthusiast could hardly have envisaged. So ended the 1949 season. Philip and I had had some success and a lot of fun, so there was nothing to complain about.

CHAPTER SEVEN

MASERATI AND LAGO-TALBOT

So far as I was concerned the 1950 season began with the Goodwood Easter Meeting. I won the Easter Handicap in the Maserati in appalling conditions: not only did it rain but there was a high wind as well.

After this race I decided the Maserati could do with an engine overhaul and entrusted the task, naturally, to Louis Giron. While this work was in progress Angela and I were busy moving into our long-time home, Clare Court.

The overhaul completed I took the Maserati to R.A.F. Odiham for a thorough road test. After several fast laps one of the front tyres was looking a bit worn so I told my mechanic Jack Cotterill to change the wheel. This he did. Unfortunately I omitted to tell him to check the tyre pressure on the new wheel with the result that the tyre came off when I was doing about 100 miles an hour down one of the runways. The car turned a complete somersault, throwing me out on to the grass, where I slid along for some time before coming to a stop. The car landed the right way up and – the throttle being jammed open – proceeded to race round in circles rather like a decapitated chicken. An eye witness described what happened as follows: 'Well guv, you lies there like you was dead, and all the lads is noddin' to one another an sayin' youse bought it, when all of a sudden like you sits up. Then, afor we can get to you, you stands up, staggers a bit, and then ups and after the bleedin' car like you was missing a bus. Then she turns a bit sudden like and gives you a fourpenny one. You goes arse over tip out for the count. She's just about 'ad 'er lot as well. She coughs a bit, and then packs it in, and that's the lot for both of yer.'

Fortunately all the damage was confined to the car and myself. If the Maserati had struck a dispersed aircraft, or some unlucky R.A.F. mechanic, the consequences might have been serious. I travelled home lying face downwards in the back of a pre-war Jaguar. On arrival I was carried to my room, undressed, and put to bed still face downwards. My doctor, John Embleton, diagnosed two broken ribs and bad bruising as the extent of the damage; so once again I had been lucky. He told me my back reminded him of a rather beautiful Persian carpet upon which some thoughtless person had wiped his boots.

My convalescence took rather longer than expected and I was not well enough to drive in the British Grand Prix at Silverstone in the middle of May. This was a great disappointment to me, but I tried to accept it philosophically and concentrated on getting well for the twenty-four hour race at Le Mans which was to take place towards the end of June.

I had not driven at Le Mans before, so had been only too

willing to accept an invitation from Tony Rolt to join him in driving Donald Healey's 3.4-litre six-cylinder Nash-Healey. This car was something of a hybrid and various troubles developed in practice. Donald Healey ironed them all out, however, and by race day the car was running beautifully. Its top speed was no more than about 140 mph but the engine was very rugged and reliable. Tony and I decided to apply the law of opposites and to drive fast when everyone else was easing up: at night for instance, or in the rain.

When the flag fell sixty drivers raced to their cars; fifty-nine got away leaving a poor unfortunate desperately trying to start a Delahaye with a flat battery. Raymond Sommer led the first time round and went on increasing his lead until his advantage over Louis Rosier (Talbot) was more than a minute. He was unable to keep this up, however, and after several pit stops finally retired leaving Rosier well in the lead. By the eleventh hour half the entries had been eliminated; many of them simply because they had pushed their cars too hard. At halfway (0400 hours) Rosier led by six laps, a little later by seven; but then just before five o'clock in the morning, he had a pit stop which lasted forty-four minutes, during which time he changed a rocker shaft. At five-thirty the Talbot went off again driven by Rosier's eldest son, Jean-Louis; it was now one lap behind the Talbot of Meyrat and Mairesse. Louis Rosier could not rest while his son was driving, and after only two laps called him in and took over again. He drove – save for pit stops to refuel – until the end of the race, winning by over ten miles from Meyrat and Mairesse at an average speed of 89.713 mph, a truly remarkable performance. Sydney Allard and Tom Cole were third in the 5,434 cc Allard, and Tony and I fourth. Our average speed was 87.636 mph. We had thoroughly enjoyed ourselves, and by driving sensibly, and refusing to join in the unholy dice at the beginning, we were well placed at the finish of this endurance test which thirty-one cars failed to endure. Our only regret was that had we made other arrangements over one of our pit stops we might have snatched third place; we were only two and a half miles behind the Allard at the finish.

Both our wives had been in the pits at Le Mans and their presence had undoubtedly helped to make our visit such a happy one.

Our next race was the Jersey International in July. Philip and I drove the Maserati. The race was won by Peter Whitehead in a Ferrari. The Maserati did not run well and trouble with the brakes caused me to spin at the Le Marquands corner, to the great alarm of Charles Mortimer who was just behind me in Buster Baring's Alta. For a short time we motored side by side; I was pointing in the direction we had come from and was taking the corner a shade faster backwards than he was forwards!

My twenty-month-old son Adrian was already very interested in cars. Like his father before him he loved to sit behind a steering wheel and to fiddle with any of the controls he could reach. We always made sure that there was no ignition key in the car and that the hand brake was on. One day he escaped out of his nursery and found his way into the driving seat of a Vauxhall in the garage. The ignition key was in the car and the hand brake was off; the car had been left in gear. As usual, he played with the controls, only this time the controls were 'live', for when he turned the ignition key and saw a red light he decided to leave it on. He pulled out the choke – which was coupled to the

Above: My first car.

Centre: A Boston at Hatston in the Orkneys. This was the very aircraft in which the American Admiral was 'christened'.

Left: September 1940 – the dashing young Fleet Air Arm officer. It was a long, hard war.

Left: Angela and I off duty in Mombasa.

Below: One of the compensations – 'MB340', my personal Seafire.

Above: A minor misjudgement – off-line in my first real race during the British Empire Trophy driving a Maserati 6CM entered by George Abecassis. I was still learning.

Below: The 6CM was a pretty little car. Here I'm at my first Continental motor race, ducking inside Ken Hutchinson's classical P3 Alfa-Romeo, with the ERAs of Leslie Brooke, Fred Ashmore and David Hampshire in pursuit – all pre-war cars.

Left: The Maserati, myself, Angela, Joan Gerard, Philip Fotheringham-Parker and our mechanic Jack Cotteril at St Helier, Jersey, where I was quite looking the part in the pits.

Right: Hang the expense – the Maserati after my involuntary somersault at R.A.F. Odiham.

Left: What the well-dressed racing driver wore 1949-style, during the British G.P. Hard crash helmets are not yet compulsory.

Above: With teammate two-year-old Adrian.

Below: Familiar conditions for a Naval chap! In the Silverstone final it rained…
The International Trophy was abandoned after six laps in these conditions when
I was second. None of us took the result very seriously but, unlike so many of my
rivals, I always quite liked racing in the wet.

Left: One had to show the Talbot who was master – this is full lock with my left hand having moved through nearly 360-degrees.

Right: The H.W.M. tyre problem at Silverstone…

Below: 16 May 1953, Ulster Trophy, Dundrod – Whoops! A slight miscalculation in the H.W.M. I had won my heat from Stirling Moss's Connaught and then finished sixth in the final.

Above left: 13/14 June 1953 – Le Mans. Here is our broken windscreen and my broken nose after I hit a bird at 150 mph on the Mulsanne Straight.

Above right: Lofty England's hand on my shoulder as I leap athletically into action, Tony having just come up the steps onto the pit counter.

Below: 'Smile, please' – we really were delighted with the win. Tony Rolt's wife, Lois, is partly hidden here behind Angela.

throttle – and then the self starter. The engine fired and the car moved forward. It demolished the wooden back of the garage and careered on to the main road where it collided with a passing tractor. The tractor driver was very shocked. The suddenness of the assault and his subsequent encounter with the Vauxhall's driver proved almost too much for him at the end of a hard day.

I had great fun filling in the insurance company's accident form. Age of driver: twenty months. Previous experience: Nil. Has he a current driving licence: No. Was he driving with your permission: No. And so on. Adrian was unhurt and quite unimpressed by the accident. The only thing that upset him was the attitude of the tractor driver when he tried to compare the driving positions of the two vehicles.

The August meeting at Silverstone is one I like to remember; for it was in the *Daily Express* production car race of that year that I won the three-litre class for Donald Healey in one of his works entered 'Silverstone' Healeys, beating the great Raymond Sommer in the process. Donald had asked me if I would drive a works car when we had met at Silverstone early in August, and I had accepted. I was more than surprised, therefore, when the famous Italian ace Nuvolari turned up during practice claiming that he had been engaged to drive the Healey. I was asked to stand down and let him drive, but I refused on the grounds that I had been engaged officially to drive the car and would only stand down if Donald Healey asked me to. Donald was crossing the Atlantic at the time so the promoters cabled him requesting that the position be clarified. His answer confirmed my appointment as works driver. He went on to say that he had previously discussed the possibility of Nuvolari having one of his works cars but that the great man had not communicated with him since their conversation and so he had presumed he was not interested. It was all very embarrassing for me, for obviously the crowd wanted to see the renowned Italian and my stubborn refusal to give up the car denied them this pleasure. Fortunately, Jaguars offered him one of their XK120s which had just come out, and in so doing lifted a great load off my mind. Nuvolari practised in the Jaguar and said he was delighted with it; he fell ill, however, and was unable to drive on race day; so my row petered out like a damp squib.

My principal opponents in the three-litre class were the Aston Martins of Sommer, Reg Parnell and George Abecassis. Sommer's best practice time was 81.24 mph, while Reg Parnell and myself had both clocked 80.61 mph. Sommer had come over from France to drive the B.R.M. in the Formula 1 race; this was the race in which it failed to leave the starting line, much to the disgust of the crowd, it rained heavily during the second heat for the Formula 1 race (it was actually in this heat that the B.R.M. failed) so that the track was wet and slippery when we took up our positions for the Le Mans type start. Charles Mortimer was standing next to me, nervously watching the starter, while his wife and other friends were in fits of laughter at the prospect of seeing him racing to his car. Why, I do not know, for he made a splendid start and was away before me; mind you, I am not exactly built for the Le Mans type start! Notwithstanding being behind Charles, my start was a good one, and after I had passed him (he was also driving a Healey) I settled down to tackling the Astons. I was soon past Eric Thompson and then sped after Reg Parnell, finally getting by on the inside at Stowe corner round about half distance.

The XK120s of Peter Walker and Tony Rolt were leading the race from Sydney Allard (in one of his own cars) while Raymond Sommer lay fourth and myself fifth. The track was still wet, and Maggots corner was smothered in oil where Peter Whitehead's XK had 'blown up' earlier. The Healey was handling splendidly and I went faster and faster until eventually, towards the end of the race, I managed to get by Sommer coming out of Stowe corner. I was so thrilled at my success that I very nearly overdid it at the corner past the grandstand: in my exuberance I arrived there backwards, and was lucky to be able to spin the car the right way and to continue without losing my place. I finished winner of the three-litre class from Sommer and Parnell, and fourth overall to the Jaguars of Walker and Rolt and the Allard of Sydney Allard. The Healey was giving away a full litre to the Jaguars, and much more to the Allard. It was a great day, not for myself only, but for Geoffrey and Donald Healey whose moderately priced sports car had beaten the works team of expensive Aston Martins.

When I crossed over to Eire, some two weeks later, for the Wakefield Trophy, I was still flushed with my success at Silverstone, and fairly hurled the Maserati round the Curragh circuit. This was a period when I drove with very great confidence and never considered the possibility of having an accident. There are times in every racing driver's life when he feels like this; it is a dangerous time: too much confidence can be a killer. The risks a good driver takes must be calculated risks; he must know his own limitations as a driver and understand the limitations of his car. If he does not his life may still be gay – in the old sense – but it will probably be short.

The Wakefield Trophy was a one hundred mile handicap

race. The scratch man was Joe Kelly, driving his Formula 1, 1.5-litre, two-stage supercharged Alta, and it was generally supposed that he would win: not only did he have the fastest car in the race but, being a local man, he knew the circuit better than anyone else. It was not to be however; for though he worked his way through the field and into the lead, he made the fatal mistake of easing up a little on the penultimate lap, enabling me to close the gap between our two cars. When we came round to start our last lap there was only a second between us. He tried to correct his mistake, but I managed to put in a very fast final lap and, passing him on the back stretch, ran out a winner by three seconds. This victory brought to a conclusion a very happy season's racing. There had been successes and failures and, therefore, the opportunity to learn, an opportunity I had tried hard to take.

★ ★ ★

Early in 1951 Tony Lago made it possible for me to drive one of his wonderful 4.5-litre Lago-Talbots. I had admired these cars ever since they had first come over to this country to race in the British Grand Prix of 1950. They really merited the description 'fabulous'. When you sat in the car the first thing of which you were conscious was the size of the rear wheels: you sat so low that they were level with your ears. The ground clearance of the car was only four and a half inches and this, together with the fact that there were no mudguards or anything else to stop you from seeing the road below, gave an impression of great speed, even when motoring gently – insofar as you could motor gently in a Lago-Talbot. When on the controls, your feet actually pointed up-hill, and the prop-shaft, which was offset, ran about level with your hip. At the back of the gearbox there was a train of gears which moved the prop-shaft over to the side of the car and brought it down along inside the chassis to the back axle which, of course, had to have an offset differential. Everything about the car was big and impressive: the engine, the bonnet, the wheels and tyres, the brake drums; but what really 'sent' the enthusiast was the glorious bellow of the exhaust. I remember an Irish priest, who had stood in respectful silence as if listening to an organ voluntary, remarking after I had switched off. 'Merciful saints! I don't believe it'.

The engine ran on methylated alcohol, and was lubricated by that wonderful old-fashioned oil, Castrol R, which gave it a real sort of Bisto smell. Of all the cars I have driven this one holds my special affection.

When the car arrived in England, shortly before the Goodwood Easter Meeting of 1951, I was so excited at the prospect of driving it that I could neither sleep nor eat. Louis Giron came from France specially to run his eye over it, and passed the car as ready to race. My mechanics had been infected by my enthusiasm and all of them wanted to go down to Goodwood to see the car perform. I agreed to close my Byfleet garage at lunch time, and arranged to meet them down at Goodwood, where we had to present the car for scrutineering. The racing numbers had already been painted on the car; all they had to do was load it into the old Guy transporter and take it to the paddock at Goodwood.

I went home to Wokingham for lunch and then drove down to Goodwood, overtaking the transporter near Midhurst; I was surprised how well it was nipping along. The Duke of Richmond – who owns the land on which the circuit is laid out – was there when I arrived; he told me how much he was looking forward to seeing the Talbot in action.

By the time the transporter arrived quite a crowd had gathered near my allotted paddock number. The Guy backed carefully into the space reserved for it, and my senior mechanic got out. He was very proud, and unlocked and opened the door with a commendable display of showmanship. The crowd craned forward; then a gasp went up – there was no car in the transporter. Someone had dropped a clanger. I looked at the Duke and he looked at me, then suddenly we both laughed; there was nothing else we could do. The crowd joined in till the paddock rang with laughter; the only people unable to see the joke were my red-faced mechanics. When I told them to get back to Byfleet as quickly as possible, and not to dare to return without the Talbot, they were really glad to go. To their credit they wasted no time and had the Talbot down and ready for the first practice session.

The car went well in practice, but one or two faults developed on race day, and it was not capable of its best performance. I did have one successful race in this meeting, and that was in the E.R.A. *Remus,* which I had bought from Peter Bell a few weeks previously. Angela and I went up to stay with Peter and his wife Mary in their home in Rosset, North Wales. Peter had entered *Remus* in a local sprint meeting and the idea was that I should drive *Remus* in the sprint and if I liked him, buy him. *Remus* went very fast indeed, and Peter and I did a deal. I have a nostalgic memory of this meeting which has nothing to do with *Remus:* it was here that I met for the first time that lovable fellow Peter Collins. It was, I believe, his first competition appearance; he drove a Cooper 500 and finished second.

To revert to the Goodwood meeting: I drove *Remus* into third place in the Formula 1 Richmond Trophy race behind Bira in a 4.5-litre O.S.C.A. and Shawe-Taylor in his 'B' type E.R.A. It was no runaway victory for the hybrid O.S.C.A. – which was then the latest model – for as Bira went through the chicane my twenty-three-year-old car was coming round the corner off the straight.

I did not drive *Remus* in many races for I still had the Maserati as well as the Talbot. Philip Fotheringham-Parker drove him several times and Tim Seccombe had at least one drive at Boreham. The E.R.A. cannot be compared to a modern Grand Prix car, for with its solid beam axle the cornering technique was so very different. On a corner, the back-end broke away very quickly; so you just let it go, keeping the power on all the time. The E.R.A. was built for this cornering technique and I loved driving it; in fact, I have always liked sliding the corners; but on the more modern cars, with their advanced suspension designs, this technique only wasted time, particularly on slow corners.

Remus had belonged originally to Prince Bira who had raced the car for a couple of seasons and then sold it to Tony Rolt. Tony had won the British Empire Trophy at Donington Park in 1939 in *Remus* when still in his teens. The car required light handling, and Freddie Dixon had stiffened the chassis for Tony, but it still remained a tricky car to handle. Poor St. John Horsfall was killed in this car, and John Bolster carried the mark of its filler cap on his back, a memento he collected when he turned it over. Philip and I did not race the car very often and eventually I sold it to a man in Liverpool who never entered it for a race.

Remus turned up some years later in the hands of one Bill Moss: they were a successful partnership, winning many club races. Moss then sold him to the Hon. Patrick Lindsay of Christie's auction fame who went on winning with him for many years.

Another car I bought at the beginning of this season was in every way different from the two I have just mentioned: this was an XK120 Jaguar 'LXF 73I'. This car began its competition life by finishing third in the one hour production car race at the *Daily Express* International Trophy Meeting at Silverstone in May. The race was won by the then youthful Stirling Moss – also in an XK120 – at 84.5 mph. Charlie Dodson the ex-motorcycle TT winner was second in another XK120 and I was third. The first two cars were works entries, specially prepared for the race; my car was, at this time, virtually standard, so I was very pleased at the result.

The big race of the day was the International Trophy, and this event had attracted a splendid field. Fangio, Farina, Sanesi, Bonetto, were in Alfa-Romeo 158s, Reg Parnell had a 4.5-litre 'Thin Wall Special' Ferrari, Bira the 4.5-litre O.S.C.A., Louis Rosier and John Claes, Lago-Talbots like myself, de Graffenried a 4CLT Maserati, Manzon and Trintignant, 1500 Simca-Gordini's. There were other 4CLT Maseratis and numerous E.R.A.s including *Remus,* driven on this particular occasion by Philip Fotheringham-Parker.

There were to be two heats and a final; the Talbot ran badly in the first heat forcing me to make a pit stop to try and rectify misfiring. I carried on, most of the time on four cylinders, and qualified for the final. My heat was won by Fangio at 91.88 mph from Reg Parnell.

While heat two was in progress, my pit staff, under instruction from Louis Giron, dropped the petrol content of the fuel I was using to make it more volatile. This, with a change of plugs, completely cured the misfiring. Meanwhile, heat two had been won by Farina from Sanesi, both in 158 Alfas; Bira was third in his 4.5 O.S.C.A. Fotheringham-Parker drove *Remus* in this heat and qualified for the final. The winner's speed was 93.35 mph.

The final was run in a tropical downpour and I do not think I can do better than quote the following from an eye-witness report: 'As the cars assembled for the 35 lap (103 miles) final the clouds rolled across the landscape – and came a splutter of rain. Rapidly the shower became a downpour, and then the heavens really opened and a cloudburst exploded over the circuit, with lightning ripping to earth not far away. Indeed, the announcer's microphone at Becketts corner was struck, fortunately when he was not using it.

'The start was the most shattering spectacle I ever remember. The field toured off the grid led by Bonetto, but the rest was a blur of spray, smoke and steam. The cars were almost completely hidden from sight in the spume, while spray shot from the wheels higher than the grandstand roof. No driver could see more than his own bonnet. The hail lay on the track, so that on corners brakes merely locked the wheels and the cars went straight on, and if there was another car or a marker tub in the way, the driver could not even see it. Cars went off on to the grass, they spun round, they travelled forwards, backwards and sideways. The enormous power of the Alfa-Romeos was a millstone round the drivers' necks. Bonetto led lap one, then out of the wall of water shot Parnell, lapping unbelievably at over 60mph where others were groping through at 45mph, and he rushed past in a smother of spray to thunders of applause. Another roar of cheering – next through the rods of rain shot Duncan Hamilton's Talbot: two Englishmen in the lead – rest nowhere.'

That was how the race appeared to a spectator; as a competitor I am in complete agreement with his description of the weather. I made a good start: the Talbot being a heavy car handled well in the wet. On the inside going round Stowe, I passed Fangio – who was finding the Alfa-Romeo a handful – then slipped past Bonetto. Just after passing the grandstand I took Sanesi and with three Alfas behind felt I must be somewhere near the front. Visibility was practically nil and my cockpit was half-full of water. There was a car in front of me but it was some time before I recognized the tail as that of Reg Parnell's 'Thin Wall Special' Ferrari. A lake began to form at Abbey corner, and another water patch at Stowe sent me off the road behind the straw bales in front of the grandstand. I motored along the grass, spotted a gap in the straw bales and shot back on to the track without losing my place. When Reg was going into Abbey I was some hundred and fifty yards behind him so had time to brake very hard when I saw him spin on the lake. He went round and round several times, but kept his engine running (in typical Reg fashion) and shot off down the course as soon as he stopped gyrating; it was a splendid piece of driving. I took notice of where he had entered the lake and taking to the grass missed the deepest part which must have been four to six inches deep.

The chequered flag appeared and we all came into the pits. Louis Giron was full of congratulations insisting that I had finished second. I would hear nothing of it and told my boys to change the tyres and top up the petrol tank. They demurred, saying the race was over. This seemed so unlikely to me that I bet Louis Giron the prize money that as soon as the rain stopped the race would continue. As a result of this rash statement Louis collected second place prize money, for the stewards had decided to award the prizes to the leaders at the time the race ended. I had been placed second in front of Fangio and Graham Whitehead who, it was eventually decided, had tied for third place. This taught me a lesson: any rash wagers I lay nowadays are for very modest stakes. I could not believe a 35 lap race could be stopped after only six laps and the prizes awarded on the basis of cars' positions when the chequered flag went out. Still that is what the stewards decided and it is difficult to see what else they could have done. One thing is certain – Reg deserved his win; his driving in impossible conditions had been wonderful.

★ ★ ★

Donald Healey had once again invited Tony Rolt and me to drive his works entered car at Le Mans and we had accepted the invitation. Following discussions we had had earlier in the year Donald had decided to build a saloon for the race. There were several reasons behind this decision. In the first place a saloon would offer less wind resistance than an open car and this was important: the type of engine we were using was somewhat restricted in the amount of power it could develop, being basically a touring engine. The capacity was increased from 3.4 litres to 3.8 litres which put up the output a bit, but the power available was no match for the twin-cam Jaguar and Ferrari engines. On the other hand, the unit was robust and very reliable.

The car – as in the previous year – was fitted with overdrive. This overdrive was operated by a kick-down on the accelerator pedal and worked perfectly; it had a lock to prevent it jumping into the next gear. The car was very pleasant to drive, and we quickly noticed the complete absence of fatigue which protection from the buffeting of the wind gave us. There is no doubt about it, an open car is more tiring to drive than a closed car. The same thing applies to aeroplanes. Fresh air rushing past you causes mental and physical tiredness; I know of no better way of becoming thoroughly tired out than to do a day's sailing. Our only worry was the possibility of a windscreen wiper failure so we took the precaution of having an extra one fitted to the top of the windscreen. Another thing that eased our lot in an endurance test such as Le Mans was being able to carry little luxuries in our saloon. Tony filled the passenger seat with every kind of sweet available, while I, sticking to fruit, had apples, oranges and so on all over the place.

The week before Le Mans I took my XK120 down to Oporto for the Portuguese Grand Prix. Tim Seccombe went with me, and it was our intention to motor up to Le Mans after the race, unless the XK was u/s., in which case we would fly to Paris and then go down to Le Mans by car. Two other XKs were competing, one driven by Tommy Wisdom and the other by George Wicken. Unfortunately, on race day we all suffered mechanical failure of one kind or another and were compelled to retire. After a couple of days' work on my car it was fit to be driven to Le Mans; however, since Le Mans was some eight hundred miles away I felt it might be more prudent for me to fly to Paris rather than break down in the Pyrenees or some other remote spot. Tommy Wisdom, whose car had also been repaired, was of like mind, so we arranged for Tim Seccombe to take our Jaguars to Le Mans along with our mechanics who could share the driving.

Count Antonio Heredia very kindly drove Tommy and myself down to Lisbon and put us up for the night in his beautiful home. First thing next morning we went round to the airport to book our air passages to Paris. There, to our dismay, we learnt that an International Police conference was taking place in Lisbon and all plane seats had been commandeered. There was also a small strike at the airport which complicated things further. The British Consulate could not help; the French Consulate Office sold us two tickets which it subsequently turned out were valueless and none of Tommy's newspaper contacts were able to suggest anything. Apart from everything else, we were four hundred miles south of Oporto.

After an unsuccessful day we went back to Tony Heredia's house. Dinner over, Tommy and I visited a nightclub to drown our sorrows, but while our heads were still above water we met a charming air hostess who, on hearing our troubles, offered her help. We were not too optimistic even when she told us to meet her at five o'clock in the morning, but we turned up, carrying our grips, and accepted the tickets she gave us. When we presented them at the window of the ticket office at the airport it was in a spirit of 'what harm can it do'. It did no harm, for although we were not on the passenger list we were allowed to board a plane for Paris. Right up until the moment we were airborne I was sure something would go wrong, but all went well, and we eventually got to Le Mans with half an hour to spare before the night practice session. This was cutting things a bit fine, for the following day was scrutineering day when it is obligatory for all drivers to be present. Tim Seccombe rolled up the next day full of what a pleasant and uneventful journey his party had had. He was quite hurt when we told him where he could go.

The early hours of the race were dominated by the duel between the XK120C of Stirling Moss and the Talbot of J.F Gonzalez. Moss finally won this battle, raising the lap record to 105.233 mph in the process. At quarter-distance Stirling and co-driver Jack Fairman were established in the lead, followed by Peter Walker and Peter Whitehead in another XK120C. The Talbots of Rosier/Fangio and Gonzalez/ Marimon lay third and fourth but others were already ailing. Louis Chiron, who was sharing a Ferrari with Pierre Louis Dreyfus (driving under the nom de plume of Helde), was disqualified for taking on fuel out on the circuit. This disqualification had a farcical side to it. What happened was this: Louis had been so preoccupied dicing with Eddie Hall's Ferrari that he omitted to refuel after the minimum 25 lap period and went on until he ran dry. Cars were allowed to take on fuel only in the pit area so that was the end of his race. However, some minutes after the loudspeakers had announced the reason for his enforced stop he drove into the pits. His mechanics refuelled the car as if nothing had happened and Pierre Louis Dreyfus took over. The subterfuge did not work; Charles Faroux appeared on the scene and poor Louis Chiron broke down under cross-examination and confessed the truth: he had refuelled out on the circuit. The Ferrari was called in and disqualified.

In the early hours of the morning the Moss/Fairman Jaguar retired; then the two Talbots came in. The Rosier/Fangio car with a split oil tank, the Gonzalez/ Marimon car with a blown cylinder-head gasket. At half time the Walker/Whitehead Jaguar had an eight lap lead over the Walters/Fitch Cunningham. The Ferrari of Hall and Navone was third, the Aston Martin of Macklin/Thompson fourth, the Nash-Healey of Rolt/Hamilton fifth. We were driving to our plan and the car never missed a beat. By breakfast time the number of retirements had reached record proportions. The Hall/Navone Ferrari refused to start after a fuel stop because the battery was flat; push starting not being allowed, it was out of the race. The big Cunningham lost a lot of time after spinning off, never got back in the running and eventually finished eighteenth. The Jaguar ran out an easy winner, having covered 2243.887 miles at an average speed of 93.495 mph. The 4.5-litre Talbot of Meyrat and Mairesse was second, seventy-seven miles behind the Jaguar. Lance Macklin and Eric Thompson drove their 2.6-litre Aston Martin into third place, while Tony and I finished sixth behind the Talbot of Pierre Levegh and Rene Marchand, and the Aston Martin of my old friends George Abecassis and Brian Shawe-Taylor. There was a tragi-comic incident on the very last lap: Jean-Louis Rosier overturned his baby Renault and failed to finish. He escaped bodily injury, but his feelings suffered terribly under the lash of his father's tongue.

There was a lot of talk that evening about the merits of closed and open cars; Tony and I came out strongly in favour of the saloon. Our argument that the drivers of closed cars finished the race much fresher than the drivers of open cars must have had some substance to it: long after our fellow drivers had gone to bed to sleep off the effects of twenty-four hours of racing Tony and I were still celebrating.

★ ★ ★

During the month following Le Mans I drove in three Grands Prix: the British at Silverstone, the Dutch at Zandvoort, the German at the Nurburgring.

The British G.P was won by Gonzalez in a 4.5-litre Ferrari from Fangio's 1.5-litre S/C 158 Alfa-Romeo and Villoresi in another Ferrari. I had a spectacular spin at Stowe corner and cut my arm on a marker barrel. It bled quite badly, and since the Talbot's oil pressure was dropping I decided to call at my pit to take on oil and have my arm bandaged. In the pit there was oil in abundance but no first aid equipment, so I drank two glasses of beer and rejoined the race, eventually finishing a sore but philosophical twelfth.

When I went over to Holland my arm was still bothering me but I soon forgot about it when the Talbot's brakes all but packed up soon after the beginning of the G.P. I drove for most of the race without brakes, and the last half on five cylinders. Louis Rosier won from Philippe Etancelin, both of them driving Lago-Talbots. Stirling Moss was third in an H.W.M. in front of Fischer's Ferrari; I was fifth.

I drove to the Nurburgring with Louis Giron in my XK120. We booked in at the circuit and were told where accommodation had been arranged for us. We were wearing flying jackets, and the lady of the house where we were to be billeted took us for R.A.F. officers. She had no love for the R.A.F. – having lost most of her relatives during the war – and greeted me by taking a swipe at my head with a broom. Fortunately she missed, but as soon as she had regained her balance she tried again. I did not know enough German to reason with her so had to run for it. She pursued me all the way down the path to the gate where Louis was getting our cases out of the XK. He quickly put them back, we both leapt into the car and drove off at speed. We knew enough German to appreciate that the R.A.F. and our flying jackets were responsible. Accordingly, we hid them, and some time later tried again. We stopped the car just past her gate; Louis – having won when we tossed to decide who was to approach her the second time – was in the driving seat. I got out and looked up the path to the front door of this inhospitable place. There were flowers in the garden and such an atmosphere of tranquility that it seemed impossible that the door could suddenly open and a she-devil appear. Nevertheless I ensured that Louis had first gear engaged and the engine running before making my second overture. I knocked on the door, and this time a smiling, friendly face appeared. Before she could recognize me I blurted out who and what I was and was invited into the house. It was not until after my second drink that a plaintive blip on the throttle of the XK120 reminded me that the loyal Louis was still at his post with cramp in his left leg and fear in his heart. I called him in, and after a time we were all the best of friends. Indeed she long corresponded and we always exchanged Christmas cards.

The Talbot was not as yet fully reliable. It would run splendidly in practice and then, just when you thought everything was fine, some trouble would develop. The Nurburgring was no exception: the gearbox casing split during the last practice session. This, I was sure, had put us out of the race, but my mechanics refused to be daunted, and after working all night had the car ready in time to take its position on the starting grid.

My car was the only British entry so alone I had to endure a very embarrassing experience before the start of the race. As usual, all car positions were determined by their practice times, and in order to build up atmosphere for the start of the race the announcer called each car driver to the grid individually. As each car was pushed out from the paddock the national anthem of the country concerned was played. When it came to my turn instead of playing 'God Save the King', the band played 'Rule Britannia'. Louis Chiron, who was in the next car, indicated to me that this was no accident. I agreed with him, so forbade my mechanics to wheel the car out. Various officials were gesticulating vigorously but I took no notice. The band played 'Rule Britannia' again; still I refused to move. They played it a third time, but I held my ground. There was a long pause; then, a rather mournful version of 'God Save the King' echoed round the Nurburgring and, to the cheers of the French contingent of drivers and mechanics, the green Talbot was wheeled to the line.

After this minor triumph it would be nice to record that the car ran faultlessly and won. Alas! It was not to be. Despite the Herculean effort of my mechanics in repairing the gearbox in time, and my stubborn refusal to go to the line until the appropriate honours had been done, I had to retire at half distance. Lack of oil pressure was the cause. The race was won by Ascari's big Ferrari from the 158 Alfa-Romeo of Fangio; Gonzalez's Ferrari was third.

Although I had been busy racing the Talbot I had not forgotten my other cars and had, in fact, spent quite a lot of time on my XK120. It was now completely stripped for racing. Special light seats had been fitted; air scoops were added to assist brake cooling; the wheels were lightened, and much work had been done on the engine; it was now a very fast car.

When I took the XK to Boreham in August I felt we had something up our sleeves and so it turned out. We won the W Lyons Trophy race for Jaguar XK120s with something to spare and then went on and won the unlimited sports car race from an entry studded with Frazer Nashes, Connaughts, Tony Rolt in an Aston Martin DB2, a 2.6-litre Alfa-Romeo, Jack Fairman in Rob Walker's 3-litre Delahaye, Sydney Allard in an Allard-Cadillac. Although I knew my XK was probably the fastest car in the race, what gave me great pleasure was the fact that I won on a wet track in pouring rain. This was a time when critics were saying that Jaguars were no good in the wet, that their great power could not be used because their road holding was suspect. Having always said that that was nonsense, I was pleased to back up my opinion with a practical demonstration.

In September I went over to Eire to defend the Wakefield Trophy. I was driving one of two works H.W.M.s, Stirling Moss had the other. Stirling was in great form and won the race at 81.21 mph. I lapped consistently at around 81 mph but could not overtake Stirling; I eased up a little towards the end and finished a comfortable second. My overall average speed – despite easing up – was 79.45 mph, over one mile per hour faster than the previous year in the Maserati. Philip Fotheringham-Parker drove my XK120 in this race and drove it very well, lapping at around 75 mph. He had a splendid duel with the Dublin driver Cecil Vard – of Monte Carlo Rally fame – who was also in an XK120. After passing and repassing one another several times they both eventually retired. Vard, without brakes; Philip, with an overheated engine.

CHAPTER EIGHT

I JOIN JAGUARS

In 1952 I had a very full season's racing. I drove regularly for H.W.M., competing in most of the European Grands Prix. This was the year promoters favoured Formula 2 cars for their International meetings, for the withdrawal of Alfa-Romeo from Grand Prix racing had robbed Formula 1 of its attraction. I drove the Lago-Talbot whenever I could – mostly in Formule Libre races. So far as sports car races were concerned, I drove in the Jaguar team at Le Mans, and bought the first C-Type Jaguar sold to a private owner and raced it both at home and abroad.

It was not always the big meetings that gave me the best sport, some of the lesser ones were great fun. There was a Formule Libre race at Snetterton in May when Tony Rolt and I had a grand dice on a very wet track. He was in his 1.5-litre two-stage blown E.R.A.-engined Delage, I was in the Talbot. The circuit was very treacherous, and I achieved a spectacular slide at the Esses right at the beginning of the race. I was fighting wheel spin all the way round and could never use the car's power. Tony's predicament was similar, but he drove very cleverly and avoided trouble until right at the end when he opened up too much down the final straight and snaked all the way to the finish with me right behind him.

When I went to the Nurburgring, towards the end of May, to drive an H.W.M. in the Formula 2 race which had taken the place of the Grand Prix, the memory of my previous visit was very much in my mind. This time, however, instead of being the lone British entry waiting for the band to play the national anthem, I found myself, along with Stirling Moss and Ken Wharton, occupying the front row of the starting grid. It was the first time in post-war racing that three green cars had been so placed. Ken was in a Frazer Nash, Stirling in an H.W.M. like myself. The race was won by Rudi Fischer in a Ferrari which went surprisingly fast for a two-litre; there were many people who were astounded by its speed down the straight. Stirling Moss was second – after leading in the early stages – and Ken Wharton nosed me out of third place in his Frazer Nash. Both Stirling and I suffered minor misfortunes which amused everyone but ourselves. Stirling's fire extinguisher went off accidentally in his cockpit and soaked him; while my seat collapsed, forcing me to drive sitting on the oil tank, a position not recommended for the Nurburgring.

I flew from Germany to the Isle of Man for the British Empire Trophy and there in the pits saw for the first time my new C-Type Jaguar. Tim Seccombe had collected the car from the works, driven it to Liverpool and then shipped it to the circuit.

The car went fabulously well in practice and, despite a wet track, broke the sports car record for the circuit by seven seconds. I was very hopeful of winning the Trophy, but it was not to be: a combination of a full tank and Kavanagh's Bridge taken at speed proved too much for the tail brackets supporting the back-axle, and after waltzing crazily for two hundred yards I was out of the race after completing only five laps. There were many retirements and the race was won on handicap by a Lester M.G. driven by Pat Griffith.

After the car had been repaired I decided to drive it home on the road; Tim Seccombe came along for the ride. When the boat arrived at Liverpool a downpour was in progress and the prospect of driving an open sports racing car across England was not attractive. Still we had no real alternative so made the best of a bad job and headed out of the town. Visibility was so poor that when I stopped at some lights on the outskirts of a northern town I did not notice that a car which skidded to a halt behind me was a police car. I saw four doors open and four men in shirt sleeves jump out and make towards the C-Type. At that moment the lights changed and I departed, leaving the four men behind. According to Tim Seccombe they ran back to their car and made as if to follow us; he could not be sure because the acceleration of the C-Type did not allow detailed observation of following vehicles. We motored into the centre of the town and found ourselves in a square; visibility was so bad that we could not read the signposts, and I did a couple of circuits while Tim tried to sort out the various alternative routes. Suddenly he shouted: 'I've got it. You'll have to go round again'.

I accelerated round the square and came up behind a police car which was ringing its bell and sliding on the wet road; they were obviously chasing someone or answering a call. I turned out of the square, down the road Tim indicated and we motored home. It later transpired that this police car was the car that had stopped behind us at the lights. They had followed us into the town and had apparently arrived behind us in the square at the precise moment Tim had found the right road for home. The C-Type's acceleration had taken us round the square so quickly that we had arrived behind the car that was following us; naturally we both presumed they were following someone else, or answering a call, and never connected their bell-ringing with ourselves. The start of the trouble, we learned later, was my failure to see a built-up area sign in the rain; they had pursued us unsuccessfully for some time but had never got near enough for us to hear their bell. Why they were all in their shirt sleeves I do not know; if they had been wearing uniform I would have recognized them at the lights when they left their car. This was only part of our trouble: we had also been timed at 102 mph between two points in the built-up area. The summonses were not delivered for some time so I will come back to the incident later.

A week later I was in Northern Ireland for the Ulster Trophy as an official member of the Jaguar team. We discovered in practice that due to the special surface of the road our tyres would last only seven laps – a distance of fifty miles. One of my tyres shed a tread at about 110 mph and I was lucky to be able to walk away from the car afterwards. The race went badly for our team; all the cars retiring with mechanical trouble. This race was run on a Thursday, and on the following Saturday the Italian G.P at Monza was due to take place. Prince Bira, who had flown to Ulster in his own plane, had promised to give Fangio a lift to Monza after the race but, due to some misunderstanding, left without him.

Poor Fangio, unable to get a seat in any civil plane, drove

from Ulster to Monza in some forty-eight hours and arrived one hour before the start of the race. He had had no sleep for two days and nights and was too late to practise; nevertheless, the Italians allowed him to race; putting him on the back row of the starting grid. As the flag dropped Bonetto, Ascari and Farina shot off closely followed by Gonzales and Villoresi. I made a good start in the H.W.M. and was moving briskly in the middle of the pack with Ken Wharton in a Cooper-Bristol beside me. As we came out of the tricky Lesmo curve on the far side of the circuit something suddenly fell out of the sky in front of Ken and myself. I instinctively avoided it, as did Ken, and in so doing left the track; ran up the bank at the side at about 80 mph, spun round and stopped. Italian police ran forward and push started me but not before I saw that the object Ken and I had avoided was Fangio. His car had somersaulted and he had been catapulted out into the middle of the screaming pack. He was a very lucky man to survive this accident, though his injuries kept him out of racing for some time. Bearing trouble put me out of the race which was won by Ascari from Farina and Simon all driving 2-litre Ferraris.

★ ★ ★

The 1952 Le Mans will always be remembered for the epic drive of Pierre Levegh in a Lago-Talbot, who drove for twenty-three hours, and then broke down while holding a commanding lead. His stubborn refusal to hand over to his co-driver proved to be his undoing: utterly exhausted, he changed into first instead of third gear, an error which caused the crankshaft to break and put him out of the race. This allowed the Mercedes-Benz of Lang and Riess to win.

All the Jaguars were out of the race within three hours by reason of overheating. A new sloping nose was the cause of the trouble. The cooling system, which had served so well the year before, had to be redesigned to fit under the lower body. The new system was tested at Lindley on the Motor Industry Research Association's circuit but, unfortunately, speeds of only 120mph were possible there. When we pushed the cars up to 160mph on the Mulsanne straight overheating started. We had evidence of this in practice, and team manager Lofty England was worried; however, there was no time to alter the body work before the race so we all pressed on and hoped for the best. Tony Rolt and I lasted longer than our team-mates Stirling Moss, Peter Walker, Peter Whitehead and Ian Stewart. To keep the car going until we had completed enough laps to allow us to take on water, I used to tuck myself in behind one of the little DB Panhard Monopoles, switch off the engine, and let the Panhard's slipstream pull me down the Mulsanne straight at 100 mph. As a result of this ploy I managed to complete the necessary number of laps and we were allowed to replenish our water supply. Unfortunately the damage had been done, and as the water was put in steam came out of the exhaust pipe; sadly we pushed the car away.

The Mercedes were not impressive that year; they did not have the speed on the straight that we had been led to believe they would have, and it was a tragedy that Levegh's pride made him go on for too long. If he had allowed his co-driver, Rene Marchand, to drive for only one hour I believe they would have won easily. The Mercedes-Benz of Helfrich-Neidermayer was second; the Nash-Healey of Leslie Johnson and Tommy Wisdom (our old car) third. A good performance was put up by the fourth car, a

Cunningham, driven by Briggs Cunningham and Bill Spear. Briggs drove for twenty-one of the twenty-four hours.

Although everything had gone wrong there was a wonderful spirit in the Jaguar team; a spirit that proclaimed: 'We will be back next year'.

My last memory of this Le Mans is of the Germans waiting for their national anthem to be played and the French stubbornly refusing to play it. They gave them the trophies and prize money but not *'Deutschland Uber Alles'*. It was the first time in the history of the race that the winners had been denied this honour. When I passed in front of the spectators who stood below a plaque erected on the stands in memory of Robert Benoist, the great pre-war champion, who was executed by the Germans in 1944, I could understand why.

From Le Mans I drove down to Oporto for the Grand Prix; my C-Type had already been shipped there from England. When I went back to the hotel after the first practice session it was to find a telegram from Angela informing me that five summonses awaited my return home, one for dangerous driving. I was more puzzled than worried, for I could not think what these summonses could refer to. In fact, they referred to incidents in the C-Type in a northern town, though at this time I did not remember any incidents.

Mechanical trouble put me out of the race which was won by the up-and-coming young Italian driver Castellotti.

On my way down to Oporto I had been accompanied by a friend, Jerry Grey. Near Vittoria we had stopped to enquire after the occupants of a Morris Minor with G.B. plate which had hit a tree. We learnt that the driver, a Naval Commander, was in hospital with minor injuries, but that his wife had been killed. I went along to see the man, hoping there was something I might do to help. As it happened he did not know his wife was dead and the doctors asked me to break the news to him. This was a distressing task, made all the more difficult by the way the stricken man reacted to the news. On my way back to the U.K. I stopped at San Sebastian, and learned from a Spanish newspaper that a Naval Commander and his wife had been killed in a Morris Minor near Vittoria. I knew the Commander had had only minor injuries so rang up the British Consul. He was very charming, and told me this was the Spanish way of being tactful: the Commander had committed suicide by jumping out of his hospital bedroom window shortly after I had left him. This news on top of five summonses left me feeling very depressed.

On returning to England I took my traffic problem to that fine counsel, Ralph Gibson, who was able to explain to the Magistrates how I had inadvertently and unknowingly exceeded the speed limit. The dangerous driving charge was dismissed, and in the end a forty-shilling fine was imposed for jumping the traffic lights. I have always been grateful to Ralph Gibson for the way he handled this affair.

Shortly after this court case I had an unusual experience while driving an H.W.M. in the British Grand Prix at Silverstone. The car was running well in the middle of the pack at 120-130 mph when suddenly I felt something plucking at my cheeks. It was as if I was driving through very light rain. While I was wondering what might be causing this sensation my front off-side tyre burst, and I was lucky to be able to keep the car on the road. The plucking was caused by tiny bits of rubber breaking away from the tread. The next time I experienced this sensation I braked hard, for I recognized the symptoms. The tyre, unable to withstand the strain put upon it, threw a tread and then broke up. I mention these two incidents to show how a racing driver profits by his experience. The third time it happened I slowed down gradually, braked gently, and stopped the car before the tyre burst.

For the Nine Hours race at Goodwood in August I was once again in the Jaguar team. Again we were dogged with troubles and when it seemed certain that the car driven by Stirling Moss and Peter Walker was going to win it spent thirty-six minutes in the pits having a new axle location arm fitted. They eventually finished fifth. Tony Rolt and I were put out by a broken half-shaft when lying a comfortable first after six and a half hours' racing. The remaining car crashed. The race was won by Peter Collins and Pat Griffith in a DB3 Aston Martin.

There were many other races I have not mentioned: at Winfield, in Scotland, where Stirling Moss, George Abecassis and myself finished in that order in H.W.M.s in a Formula 2 event. Then Snetterton, where I won in an H.W.M. at the circuit's first meeting, and so on – one cannot mention every race.

CHAPTER NINE

WE WIN
LE MANS

My greatest personal ambition was achieved in 1953: to be in the winning partnership at Le Mans. I felt I was driving faster than ever before, and though success eluded me in the early meetings at Goodwood and Silverstone, I knew I was driving well.

My first success came in the Ulster Trophy race at Dundrod. The event was run in two heats followed by a final. I won the first heat, driving a works H.W.M. from Stirling Moss in a Connaught. Stirling had some trouble early in the race and was forced to make a short pit stop; this enabled me to establish a commanding lead, and though he drove splendidly and reduced the distance between us, he had no real chance of catching me. Just after Stirling went into the pits, Jock Lawrence, in a Cooper-Bristol, passed me; we both enjoyed some fine motor racing for a few laps until I repassed him and eventually drew away. The second heat was won by Mike Hawthorn in a Ferrari. I could only finish sixth in the final, which was won by Mike from Ken Wharton in a Cooper-Bristol, Bobby Baird in another Ferrari, and Peter Whitehead in a Cooper-Alta. Louis Chiron – O.S.C.A. was fifth. My H.W.M. could not match the speed of the cars in front but went very well. My method of negotiating the hairpin attracted some attention: I would slide the car round the corner and let the bank stop the slide, then belt on up to Quarry. It was an effective method and, as it happened, no damage to the car resulted.

The C-Type Jaguars which Stirling Moss, Peter Walker, Ian Stewart, Peter Whitehead, Tony Rolt and myself were going to drive at Le Mans were similar to the 'Boilers' of the previous year in general construction – though the sloping nose had gone – but with two important modifications: disc brakes and Weber carburettors. These Dunlop discs gave us a great advantage over our principal adversaries, and we knew that they would last the twenty-four hours of racing without having to be nursed. The drivers of other cars with a chance of winning the race outright (i.e. other than the Index of Performance) had the serious problems of 'fade' and wear to contend with and, as always, were forced to overwork their gearboxes and transmissions to conserve their brake linings if called upon to lap as fast as possible. When all cars depend on drum brakes the problem is a common one; in 1953 we Jaguar drivers no longer shared the common problem.

The other modification, the substitution of three Weber twin-choke carburettors, had greatly increased the torque of the engine in the lower ranges and, consequently, the pick-up when coming out of the slower corners.

The Jaguar team consisted of three cars numbered 17, 18 and 19. Tony Rolt and I had No.18. There was a reserve car which, for some reason, had also been numbered 18. This duplication of numbers led to terrible trouble during the last practice session.

From the beginning the cars went wonderfully well; No. 18 quite a bit faster than the others. On Thursday evening I set up an unofficial record for the course, lapping at 110 mph, a full second faster than Ascari in the 4.5-litre Ferrari. Stirling Moss was very impressed with the performance of our car and asked to be allowed to drive it. We told Mr. Lyons (as he then was) that we did not really want anyone else to drive our car: this was no reflection on Stirling's skill, but merely a feeling we had that there was no point in his driving the car. If he was unlucky enough to have some trouble and the car could not be repaired in time we would be out of the race. In short, we wanted to carry full driver responsibility ourselves. Mr. Lyons was both sympathetic and understanding and suggested that Stirling try the reserve car with a lower axle ratio. Now, unknown to him, the regulations with regard to practice sessions had been changed since the previous year, and practice cars were not allowed. The pit staff knew this of course, but in the general confusion the practice car, with its No. 18 marking, came out and did some warming-up laps in the hands of Norman Dewis, Jaguar's chief tester. The Ferrari pit protested; their protest was upheld by the promoters, and Tony and I were told we were disqualified. Mr. Lyons asked for a special enquiry into this alleged breach of the regulations, pointing out that the reserve driver had driven the reserve car which, although marked No. 18, was not in fact our car. They granted his request and said they would hear his protest the following morning – the morning of race day.

Tony and I were bitterly disappointed. We knew how ruthlessly the regulations were enforced at Le Mans, and did not believe we had a chance in a thousand of being allowed to race. Accordingly, we decided to drown our sorrows in the usual way. Our wives gave us up as a bad job and moved in together, telling us we could share the same sorrow, the same bedroom and, on the morrow, the same hangover. They need not have bothered: Tony and I never saw our bedroom.

After a night of steady imbibing we drifted eventually into Gruber's restaurant for a cup of coffee. We were sitting there feeling ill, miserable and dejected, when a Mark VII Jaguar drew up outside and William Lyons got out. He hurried over to us with the news that he had paid a 25,000 Fr. fine and we were back in the race. I looked at my watch; it was 10 a.m.; in six hours' time the starter's flag would fall. Neither of us had had any sleep, and twenty-four hours of racing lay ahead. We ordered more black coffee and enquired if there was a Turkish bath in the town. There was not. We went back to our chateau and had hot baths; we drank more black coffee; we listened to our wives, and by two o'clock in the afternoon we felt dreadful. I knew I could not race feeling as I did; there was only one thing and that was a little of the hair of the dog. I ordered a double brandy; immediately I felt better. Tony tried the same medicine with equally happy results; by four o'clock we both felt fine. We had not had very much, just a medicinal pick-me-up.

It was a lovely day. A dust haze – set up by thousands of cars rolling over the sandy soil into the car parks – hung above the circuit as if reluctant to leave the scene of so much excitement. Sixty cars were lined up on one side of the track; sixty drivers opposite them. The flag was raised. A moment of silence followed, and then the patter of running feet as the flag fell. Sixty engines burst into life and, for half a minute, the air rang with the snarl from departing exhaust pipes. Twenty-four hours of racing had begun. An excited hubbub broke out as the crowd commented on what they had just seen, and speculated on what they would see when the field came round for the first time – who would be leading? I sipped my brandy and waited.

When they swung into the straight from White House, Sidney Allard was leading, closely followed by Villoresi's Ferrari and Stirling Moss. Tony lay seventh just behind Tom Cole's Ferrari and just in front of Mike Hawthorn's Ferrari. Satisfied that all was well I settled down to await my turn. Sidney Allard was soon out, his brakes having packed up, and when on the fourth lap Stirling passed Villoresi the order was: Moss Jaguar, Villoresi Ferrari, Cole Ferrari and Rolt Jaguar. Tony was driving magnificently, and presently managed a lap at 111 mph, a new lap record. The three Alfa-Romeos which had been well back at the beginning were now in fifth, sixth and seventh places but were not in any way threatening the leaders. Shortly after five o'clock Stirling came in with fuel-feed trouble and Villoresi took over the lead, though not for long: Tony, seeing Stirling was in the pits, passed Villoresi, and once more a Jaguar was out in front. Tony was lapping at a steady 107 mph and no one could do anything about it. Stirling got going again, only to have to make a second pit stop, which dropped him to twenty-first place. The pace quickened, and Tony, Villoresi and then Sanesi, in the 3-litre Alfa-Romeo, took it in turns to break the lap record. At 7.10 p.m. Tony came in to refuel and handed the car over to me. Before handing over to Ascari, Villoresi finally left the lap record at 112.76 mph. When going down the Mulsanne straight at some 150 mph a bird hit my windscreen, breaking half of it away, so that I was forced to lean to the left in order to obtain protection.

Ascari took over from Villoresi and pressed me very hard; he had a bigger and more powerful engine; I had better brakes. At the end of the Mulsanne straight we Jaguar drivers could bring the cars' speed down from 150 to 30 mph in less than three hundred yards.

So the race went on through the night. Ferrari snatched the lead for a short time when we refuelled but we soon had it back again. The Alfa-Romeo of Kling and Riess was the only other car on the same lap as the Villoresi/Ascari Ferrari and ourselves. Then, after eleven hours of hard driving, both Alfa-Romeos were out of the race with back-axle trouble. The Carini/Sanesi car had been lying fourth two laps behind its team-mate. These retirements left the Walters/Fitch Cunningham in third place ahead of Peter Whitehead and Ian Stewart who in turn were followed by Stirling Moss and Peter Walker whose car had moved up sixteen places since their second enforced pit stop. We now began to draw away from the Ferrari, and at half distance (twelve hours) had covered 152 laps to their 150. First light coincided with the arrival of the usual mist and our disc brakes really paid dividends: I was never in danger of overshooting at Mulsanne whereas poor Ascari was obliged to brake early just to make sure. When I brought the car in around 5.30 a.m. the mist lifted, and Tony set off as fast as ever in excellent visibility. I ate a very good breakfast, and greatly enjoyed my coffee and cognac; I felt so well and so excited at the prospect of winning that I could hardly wait for Tony to come in again. About 6.30 a.m. the lap chart keepers announced that Tom Cole's Ferrari was missing; it later transpired that he had crashed at White House corner and had been killed; the news saddened us all for he was very popular.

There was great excitement when Tony came in at 8.30

a.m., for Ascari brought the Ferrari in at the same time
(Ascari and Villoresi had been driving for different periods
to Tony and myself so that Tony had actually driven against
both of them). Although we had a lead of two laps the
presence of the principal protagonists in the pits at the same
time added to the heightening tension, and in my desire to
get away before Villoresi I shot out of the pit and only just
missed one of the small French cars as it passed by; it was a
very near thing.

When Villoresi accelerated out after me it was obvious to
all in the pits that his clutch was slipping badly and that the
Ferrari had shot its bolt. He never challenged me again and
soon lost second place to Stirling Moss and then third place
to the Cunningham. Villoresi actually kept this beautiful red
car going for two hours before it finally stopped out on the
circuit. The Cunningham continued to lap very consistently
and remained a danger to us if we made a mistake or had
mechanical trouble. Neither of these contingencies
occurred and we eventually ran out winners by 29.1 miles
from Stirling Moss and Peter Walker at an average speed of
105.85 mph; the first time the magic figure of 100 mph had
been exceeded. By two o'clock we had covered 278 laps,
one more than the winners of the previous year, and by
three thirty the scoreboard had run out of numbers. When
the flag was dropped to signal the end of twenty-four
hours' racing it coincided with my arrival on the line. It was
the end of a perfect day's racing and I had achieved my
dearest sporting ambition. Tony's driving had been
wonderful; the way in which he had taken the lead when
Stirling was delayed, and had stayed in front of Villoresi
when the latter's car still had perfect brakes and transmission
was masterly. He may have had disc brakes, but he was

giving away a litre to the Ferrari which had been beautifully driven by a very fine driver.

Both Tony and I will always remember our dice with those two great Italians Villoresi and Ascari. In their refusal to give up while their car would still run they showed courage and determination of the highest order.

The Index of Performance winner was the Panhard of the Chancel brothers. The Panhard of Bonnet and Moynet was an unlucky second: it ran out of fuel on the last lap and had to be pushed to the finish; but for this error it would have won.

We received a wonderful ovation from the crowd and found that we were now back in favour with our wives: there was no further mention of our night out. Angela and Lois Rolt had been in the pits all through the twenty-four hours, cooking, washing-up and generally looking after everyone, as indeed had my old friend Tim Seccombe. William Lyons, Mort Morris-Goodall, Bill Heynes and Lofty England must have seen twenty-three and a half hours' racing at least; no one goes to bed at Le Mans while their car or cars are still in the race. On the other hand most of them sleep the night before. In the case of Tony and myself, neither of us had had any sleep for forty-eight hours. It is amazing what good cognac and the will to achieve an ambition can accomplish! Needless to say we celebrated that evening and it was the early hours of Monday morning before either Tony or myself got to bed. We were very tired and happy men.

After the official prize-giving, which took place in Le Mans on the Monday afternoon, our very happy party split up. Tony and Lois Rolt returned to England with Mr. Lyons and the remainder of the Jaguar party, while Angela, Len

Hayden (Jaguar's mechanic) and myself headed for Oporto and the Portuguese Grand Prix. We had a lovely drive down in a Mark V Jaguar drophead coupe and passed the first night in St. Jean de Luz. The next day saw us through Spain and up into the mountains where we spent the night at Guada in Portugal. This is an interesting town which has splendid views of the Spanish plains. It is well worth while getting up early to watch the sun rise: the dawn contrast of light and shadow is quite wonderful.

We arrived in Oporto on the Thursday afternoon and went straight to the Infanta Sagres, a luxury hotel, where we had booked accommodation. My C-Type had arrived by sea and Len Hayden lost no time in getting the car ready to race. This car was not as fast as the Le Mans cars, having only two SU carburettors as against three twin-choke Webers, but it was a very fast car all the same. It had been modified by myself to the extent that the pistons were of special French manufacture and very much lighter than those fitted as standard; the valves were sodium filled; the cylinder head modified, and the fly wheel lightened. Munger Haynes of Jaguar, who had designed the engine, told me that my modifications would lead to disaster, a view which has not been borne out in practice; in fact the car was still running perfectly when this was first written, owned by Captain Jack Howey of Romney, Hythe & Dymchurch railway fame.

I made the fastest time in practice and, as I told representatives of the Portuguese press who interviewed me at the hotel, was hopeful of winning. My principal rivals were Taruffi in a Lancia, Oliveira, Pinto and Castellotti all in Ferraris, and Tony Gaze in an Aston Martin.

My practice laps had been done with only some eight to ten gallons of fuel in the tank; in the race I was carrying forty. I expected, therefore, that the Ferraris, with their bigger engines, would give me a lot of trouble in the early stages, but that as soon as my tank began to empty I would be able to quicken up. My only regret was that the car did not have disc brakes.

Angela and Katie Gaze were in the pits acting as timekeepers for Tony Gaze and myself while an old friend, Giles Holdroyd, was voluntary acting unpaid pit manager to the Hamilton equipe.

The circuit was interesting: it began along the sea front, up the main boulevard into the back of the town, then down a winding section which was a mixture of tramlines and pave, and back to the sea front. It was a drivers' circuit.

Before the G.P there was a race for motorcycles which was to be started by the President. All the motorcyclists lined up in readiness for his signal only to discover that the President could not be found. After a time they were compelled to switch off to prevent damage to their engines which were overheating. Just about the time the last motor was cut the President turned up. The riders could not restart their bikes because the engines were too hot so the President went away to give them time to cool down. After a while the order to start up again was given and the riders got ready for the drop of the flag; but once again the President was missing; so they all switched off. No sooner had they done this than the President appeared carrying a flag. The marshal told the riders to start up again, to find that half of them could not do this because of the same trouble as before, so the President went away again. By this time the British contingent, which had been trying to conceal its mirth, was in a state of collapse; the fact that the Portuguese appeared unaware of the humour of the situation only made matters worse. I am happy to say that eventually the President and the motorcyclists resolved their problem and the race was started.

I did not make a good start to the G.P. but even so led into the first corner. Going up the boulevard I could feel the difference my full tank was making compared with my practice laps and was not too surprised when a 4.1-litre Ferrari passed me. I was alongside him at the next corner but could not get by due to the odd line he took. By the end of the lap I knew that he was no driver of calibre and that he was in fact hard put to stay on the road at all. Three times I drew alongside him only to have to fall back because of his erratic conducting. Going into the fast right hander on the approach to the sea front I took the corner inside him; our cars touched, and in taking the necessary avoiding action I lost control and left the course on the outside of the corner. As I headed for an electric pylon at some 125 mph I remembered advice Ascari had given me when we had been talking while on the massaging tables at Le Mans: 'Duncan, if you are going to have a shunt have a neat shunt head-on'.

Instead of brushing the pylon I twitched the wheel and rammed it head-on so that the front of the chassis and the engine were between me and all that steel. The pylon was cut in half; the car cartwheeled, throwing me out right across the track and into a tree, where I hung for a moment, fourteen feet up, before falling on to the side of the road. I was still conscious and an instinctive sense of self-preservation made me pull my legs off the road just as a red car whipped by and took the boot off my left foot. A crowd gathered round me and two men tried to sit me up. I resisted them for I knew my ribs were broken, and was afraid my lungs might be punctured. They seemed to understand and contented themselves by putting something under my head. The next thing was the arrival of an English-speaking Portuguese who gathered from the grunts I gave to his questions that I badly needed an ambulance, I am a little hazy as to what happened after this; I know that an ambulance came and took me – not to the British Hospital – but to a hospital in the dock area of the town, but I have no recollection of details.

The next thing of which I was consciously aware was looking up at my nude reflection in the chromium-plated light above an operating table. The light was not working, for the simple reason that I had knocked down one of the pylons which helped to carry the current to the hospital. I could see that my chest had been ripped open and that my face was a mess. An enormous man with a shaved head stood eyeing me as he contentedly puffed at a cigar. I was about to dismiss him as an interested bystander when I saw to my horror that he was wearing a butcher's apron and carried what looked like a carving knife in his left hand. He advanced closer and began poking and prodding – as one would poke and prod a dog which had been hurt. Every time I groaned he nodded with satisfaction; I now saw that a nun stood beside me and that another one stood near the doctor. Desperately I tried to tell them that I needed water, but they could not understand. Fortunately, a small boy who spoke English turned up and I was able to make him understand what I wanted. After consultation with the nuns he told me that the water was contaminated and could not be drunk, but that they could offer me port. So port it was.

Meanwhile the doctor had got to the stage where he thought he might do a little sewing and was playing with the loose skin and flesh round my chest. Fortified with port I could just about stand the pain, but not the thought of the ash on his cigar – which was fully two inches long – falling into my open chest. As it happened he was a tidy man, and before such a catastrophe could occur he tapped the ash into a metal bowl one of the nuns was holding in case I felt sick.

He made quite a good job of stitching me up including some tricky work on my torn mouth, gum, and broken jaw. I was told afterwards that he was sorry he could not give me an anaesthetic, but the anaesthetists had the afternoon off to watch a motor race.

After the doctor had finished with me I was put in a small dark room and left alone. The atmosphere was stifling, for in true Continental fashion all the windows were closed. I was very relieved when Angela turned up with Giles Holdroyd, for they soon saw to it that I was transferred to the British Hospital in another part of the town. The rumour had got around that I was dead, and Angela and Giles had been frantically visiting every hospital in Oporto in search of the truth.

I was very well looked after in the British Hospital; the Matron, a Miss Nolan, being particularly kind. I had nine broken ribs, a broken jaw, a fractured collarbone and several other superficial injuries. At any rate that was what the hospital X-rays and examinations revealed; however, when I had a final check-up in England – on my return home – it was discovered that I had also fractured my neck. But for the fact that my injuries had compelled me to lie still and allow my neck to mend, I would have died.

Tony Gaze, who had crashed on the same lap as myself, was also in the British Hospital for a few days. He had been the victim of another inexperienced driver.

I was in hospital the best part of a month, and though Miss

Nolan and all the hospital staff were very good to me, I was pleased when I was discharged. Angela and I had quite a job getting back to England: none of the airlines would fly me because I had suffered internal bleeding; and no ship wanted me as a passenger because of the risk of my dying on the high seas. Eventually we came home in a cargo boat which had accommodation for three passengers: Angela, myself and a very battered C-Type Jaguar.

★ ★ ★

Shortly after my return from Portugal I drove an H.W.M. in a Formula 2 race at the Crystal Palace. My ribs were still strapped up, and my drive was a painful one. I was up with the leaders in the early stages but eased up when I realized really determined driving was impossible. The race was won by Tony Rolt in a Connaught from Roy Salvadori, who was similarly mounted, and Les Leston in a Cooper-Jag. Tony drove in his usual impeccable way and won easily, after leading from the start. The following Saturday saw Ascari win the British G.P. at Silverstone in a 2-litre Ferrari. I drove the H.W.M. again but without success. My happiest memory of this meeting is the lap of honour Tony and I were asked to do in the Le Mans-winning C-Type.

Earlier in the year Peter Whitehead had asked me if I would share his C-Type in the twelve-hour Pescara G.P. in Italy. The prospect of a visit to the Adriatic Coast had appealed to me so I had said yes. Accordingly, on August 10th, we crossed the Channel and pointed the nose of my Mark V drop head coupe Jaguar in the direction of Milan, where we proposed spending the first night. At the last moment David Yorke joined us and the three of us shared the driving. We wasted very little time; stopping only for meals, and for a short while on the St. Gothard Pass to take in the wonderful scenery. Fourteen hours after leaving Calais we rolled into Milan. I remember sitting in the foyer of the Arcade near the Opera House sipping a drink and listening to the wonderful singing next door; it seemed an appropriate ending to a good day's motoring.

The following day we motored to Pescara, stopping only for an excellent spaghetti lunch. After booking-in at the rather rough hotel where the promoters had provided accommodation we went off in search of Arthur Birks, Peter's mechanic, who, accompanied by an assistant, had driven down a lorry containing the C-Type some days previously. We found them, and listened to a harrowing tale of adventure and difficulty, the most interesting part of which was their descent of the St. Gothard without brakes. Both they and the C-Type had come through it all without harm, though not without difficulty.

We drove round the course the next morning and saw that it was an interesting one. It began down a straight which ran parallel to the sea front and then went into the middle of the town. A sharpish right hander followed and the circuit went up into a village, and then on up into the hills and away round until it came down to the sea front again. The circuit measured some 15.8 miles.

The weather was insufferably hot and we were glad that the first practice session was to be in the relative cool of the evening. The race itself was to begin at noon and end at midnight. We soon found that due to the great heat (temperatures were around the 100-degree Fahrenheit mark) the road gave off a haze that made it difficult for one to see as far ahead as was necessary on the straight where we were reaching 160 mph. It was also difficult to know when to cut off for the corner at the end of the straight. At speed all the houses were pink blurs and there were no suitable landmarks. I resolved the problem by cutting off at a large advertisement which proclaimed the virtues of an Italian contraceptive. Visibility was so bad that if you could see the corner at the end of the straight before you braked you had left it too late. Another disconcerting thing was the way people walked about on the road apparently oblivious of the fact that racing cars were practising on them at very high speeds.

On race day, we learnt, to our surprise, that the promoters had given us the pole position for the Le Mans-type start. This was because both Peter and I had been victorious at Le Mans. Our principal opponents were Hawthorn and Maglioli and the Marzotto brothers, both pairs in 4.1-litre Ferraris. After a mild dispute as to who should drive first, Peter and I tossed for it. He won and said I should drive. I was rather disappointed at this, for I was so affected by the heat that I had intended to sit in the sea while Peter drove for the first two hours or so. However, it was not to be, and after an early lunch of iced melon I ambled to the start.

There was a holiday atmosphere in the air. All the shops were closed and the entire population for miles around had gathered to watch the race. In the various villages the elders put their chairs on the pavements and, tilting them back against the wall, lounged at their ease not caring about the dangers they exposed themselves to. Their heirs occupied places of greater safety: upstairs windows, trees, the tops of buildings – watching and waiting – as if ready to drop down and claim their inheritance if their seniors succumbed.

There was a mix-up over the start. First of all Paolo Marzotto told me that a flag would be dropped on the right, then that it would be dropped on the left, then that a siren would be used, and then – following a lengthy loudspeaker announcement – that a hooter would be sounded. I did not know whether I was coming or going but on hearing a rumble of ball bearings, which I took to be the hooter starting up, decided to go, and raced across the road to the car. A subsequent photograph on the cover of '*Autosport*' showed Mike Hawthorn leading the cars away from the start; the caption might have remarked, but did not, that Hamilton was not in the picture as he had already left.

Now, before the race, Arthur Birks had relined the front brakes but, due to a misunderstanding, had told me merely that he had adjusted them; consequently, when I braked for the first corner the combination of new unbedded linings and 45 gallons of fuel in the tank saw to it that I could not get round. I lost it and spun off into a sand-pit at the side of the road. My front wheels and bonnet rested right on the apex of the corner, and as I looked back whence I had come I could see sixty sports cars bearing down on me at about 140 mph. I let the revs go sky-high and let in the clutch with a bang; the wheels spun, gripped, and I shot out and away before the howling pack reached me. As I accelerated past the station I was only too well aware of what a narrow squeak I had had. When I came round on my second lap I saw that three Ferraris had crashed into the wall behind the sand-pit in which I had been sitting. Had my rear wheels not gripped all three of those cars would have hit me.

I held a good lead until about halfway round the second lap when Mike Hawthorn ran close behind me and slipstreamed me all the way down the coast road and on to the straight approaching Pescara. He passed me just outside a small village on the outskirts of the town and as we entered the village led by perhaps thirty yards. The width between our cars was no more than twenty feet and our speed about 160 mph. Suddenly I saw that an old lady was crossing the road. At the speed at which we were travelling I do not suppose she was in my sight for more than a couple of seconds, yet my eyes recorded the fact that she was an old woman, dressed in black, with a black shawl over her shoulders, and carrying a shopping basket. Mike passed right behind, I right in front of her. How we both missed her I will never know. A quick look in my mirror revealed that she just kept walking as if oblivious of what had occurred.

Going into the corner at the end of the straight – the one at which I had spun off – Mike made a mistake; I passed him and shot away determined to open up as big a gap as possible before he could recover. As I approached a 100 mph corner just outside a village I saw what appeared to be signs of a nasty crash: a pall of thick smoke was billowing across the road and flames rose high into the air. I braked very hard and came down to about 40-50 mph; an incredible sight confronted me: an Italian stood stoking a bonfire in a garden which ran adjacent to the course. Before I could get over my surprise I was in the middle of what resembled a London fog; I was not in it for long, but here was an unnecessary hazard which could easily have killed a man. It is not surprising that road racing is no longer allowed in Italy!

After a time I handed over to Peter. I was quite exhausted: the heat and the unpredictable behaviour of the locals made road racing a tiring occupation. I changed into bathing trunks, put on a paper hat and went and sat in the sea which, as I have already explained, ran along the side of part of the course. It is the only time I have watched a Grand Prix sitting up to my neck in water.

When Peter had finished his stint I took over again. We were now lying fourth, but with some of the fastest cars retiring, had every hope of finishing second or third if not first. I had another surprise in store, this time high up in the uppermost part of the circuit: going round a corner at a point where the road is very narrow I was confronted by a cow, which a policeman was pulling vigorously by the tail. I missed the policeman, but touched the cow; she took off over the hedge, followed by the policeman, who had not slackened his grip in time. This shunt led to our eventual retirement, for shortly after taking over from me for the second time Peter came in complaining that he could not steer the car. Examination revealed that the cross member on the chassis had sheared through so we were out of the race. It was a great pity, for we were lying third after eight hours of racing. The eventual winners were Mike Hawthorn and Maglioli in a Ferrari.

Peter and I left Pescara the following morning and drove back to Calais. We took things easily, for we were both driving in the Jaguar team at Goodwood in the Nine Hours Race on the coming Saturday. I was also driving a works H.W.M. at Zandvoort in the Dutch G.P. on the Sunday, and my itinerary read something like this. Thursday, practice at Goodwood; Friday morning, fly to Holland, practise and qualify for the Grand Prix; Friday night, return to England by boat; land at Harwich, where a driver and car would be waiting to take me to Goodwood (the idea of returning by boat was to ensure that I got back irrespective of weather conditions); Saturday, Nine Hours Race at Goodwood; Sunday, fly to Holland and drive in Dutch G.P. Practice times at Goodwood on the Thursday showed that the Jaguars were quite a bit faster than the Aston Martins, and

Lofty England looked very happy at the end of the session.

I flew over to Holland the next morning and was out practising before lunch. John Heath told me that the car had just had a new engine fitted and that I had better take things quietly for a few laps. I did three running-in laps and then began to open up a little. On my fourth lap I was doing about 125 mph going down the straight, when Ascari, who was driving a Ferrari, drew alongside and pointed down at my engine. I did not know what he meant but looked down and saw sparks and flames shooting up between my legs. I lifted my foot off the throttle only to find that it stayed open, while the flames and sparks became positively personal in the way in which they attacked me. I switched off the engine and braked hard, simultaneously steering on to the side of the track while other practising cars whizzed by at 130 mph. Before the car came to a halt the flames between my legs had become so potentially dangerous that it was a case of stand up or spend the rest of my life as a counter-tenor.

I stood on the seat, and then jumped out on to the sand-dunes. The car went on at about 30 mph fortunately without hitting anyone, until it too came to rest in the sand. What had actually happened was that the mechanic who had fitted the new engine had inserted the tommy bars to line up the engine bearers and had then gone off to lunch. On his return he had omitted to insert the engine bearer bolts and knock out the tommy bars, with the result that I went off with an engine supported only by tommy bars. They had worked loose and part of the sump had dropped on to the road, hence the flames and sparks. Fortunately the car was not damaged, and after another engine change it was ready to race in the Grand Prix, though I did in fact qualify in another car.

The Nine Hour Race was a tragedy so far as our Jaguar

team was concerned, for with only one hour to go the cars of Stirling Moss and Peter Walker, and Tony Rolt and myself led the first Aston Martin of Reg Parnell and Eric Thompson by two laps. Then at 1.18 p.m. with only fifty-two minutes to go, the Moss/Walker car retired; two minutes later Tony and I did the same thing. The trouble was lubrication failure caused by the incessant surging of oil on the corners.

Goodwood, with its succession of right hand corners, sees to it that the oil in a wet-sump engine is continually surging to the left-hand side of the sump; should the oil level drop, due to consumption during the race, bearing failure can result. This trouble does not arise in a dry-sump engine. The next year the new D-Type Jaguar had a dry-sump engine.

In the early stages of the race Stirling and Tony had swapped the lead several times; when Peter Walker and I took over we did the same thing; we were not racing – as some people imagined – but merely having good sport and driving well within the safe 'rev limit' of our engines. We could in fact have gone a good deal faster but had no need to. Our team-mates, Peter Whitehead and Ian Stewart, had brake trouble, which prevented their being up with us; even so they finished third, but could not challenge the Astons of Reg Parnell and Eric Thompson, and Peter Collins and Griffiths when we fell out. So Aston Martin won for the second year running, and Jaguar, after leading for eight hours and eight minutes of a nine-hour race, had to be content with third place, and the knowledge that wet-sump engines can be vulnerable in certain circumstances.

The next afternoon I drove in the Dutch G.P. The Ferraris of Ascari, Farina and Villoresi ran away with it and finished in that order. Only Mike Hawthorn was able to live with them and he finished fourth in a Cooper-Bristol. I finished seventh. The engine stayed in the car this time but the brakes left something to be desired. All in all it had been quite a fortnight.

The last meeting of the season was at Goodwood and the first race (the Madgwick Cup for Formula 2 cars) turned out to be the shortest of my career. I was driving R. J. Chase's Cooper-Bristol, and with people like Stirling Moss, Tony Rolt, Roy Salvadori, Ken Wharton and Bob Gerard in front of me knew that I had to make a good start to have any chance of finishing among the leaders. The flag fell; I let in the clutch, and with a bang the left-side rear stub shaft snapped and the wheel rolled slowly up the track after the departing cars leaving me sitting on the line.

Mike Hawthorn stole most of the thunder at this meeting winning the two Formule Libre events in Tony Vandervell's Ferrari 'Thin Wall Special'. In the first, for the Woodcote Cup, he beat Fangio who was driving a B.R.M. and established a new lap record in the process. In the second, for the Goodwood Trophy, he again beat a B.R.M. driven this time by Ken Wharton, and raised the lap record to 94.53 mph.

In the handicap race for sports cars my C-Type went splendidly and recorded the fastest lap at 81.82 mph which was not bad for a car that had been a total wreck after the Portuguese G.P. It was at this meeting that I was first introduced to that charming young man, King Feisal of Iraq. He was very interested in motor racing, and also in fast cars. We were, presently, to become very good friends, but more of that later on.

And so the actual racing season ended. Tony and I received several awards for our success at Le Mans: The E.R.A. Trophy, the Sir Malcolm Campbell Memorial Trophy, *The Motor* Twenty-four Hundred Trophy.

The Motor Twenty-four Hundred Trophy had been in existence for many years waiting for someone to average 100 mph for the full twenty-four hours; it was an award in perpetuity. With the Trophy we also received replica clocks; mine is one of my most treasured possessions.

There is a little story connected with the clock. When Eric Adlington of *The Motor* called on the clock-makers (Charles Frodsham, clock-makers to the Kings of England) to give them details of the names to be engraved on the clocks, the white-haired engraver laughed. 'Duncan Hamilton, how can he still be alive?' When Eric asked him what he meant he told him that he had served under me in Africa: he was Warrant Officer French, my old Senior W/O.

★ ★ ★

After the hurly burly of a season's racing it was nice to settle down in Wokingham and quietly take stock of things. I noticed how my family was growing up, how the puppy of yesterday was now a dog, how the autumn tints and hues reminded me that spring had passed. Had there been no blossom this year? I began to wonder if the life I led was the right life for me. Was it sensible to risk one's all and perhaps the future of one's family to satisfy a competition urge to go faster and faster? When my mother-in-law asked me why I did it was I as unconvinced by my answers as she was? Sometimes I felt so. After all, I had shared the winning car at Le Mans and achieved my racing ambition. Why go on and risk a repetition of my crash in the Portuguese G.P.? There was no answer I could give to those who questioned the wisdom of what I did, for our incompatibility of spirit prevented understanding; while those who understood had no reason to ask any questions. Anyway, as I soon found out, danger is not confined to the race track; misfortune can befall you anywhere.

On the evening of the 21st December 1953 my manager, Ken Atkins, and myself were returning to my works in Byfleet from a business trip to Essex. It was a dark wintry night and I was driving very carefully when suddenly on rounding a corner on the Esher side of Cobham I saw four sets of headlights coming towards me. I got well over to the left but the outside vehicle – a stolen lorry as it happened – struck us and my car, a Mark VII Jaguar, spun round three times, knocked down a bus stop, broke open, and threw both Ken and myself out onto the road. It then went on and demolished a police box. I received a bang on the head and must have passed out for a few seconds for when I came to I was sitting on the spare wheel with Ken lying over my knees. He was unconscious, I suspected, badly injured; for he was making the most awful noises. The police and an ambulance soon arrived and we were taken to Kingston Hospital. I was discharged the following day but Ken was there for several days with head injuries. The lorry was found abandoned with its payload – Christmas trees; the thieves were never apprehended.

The foreign press was misinformed as usual and reported that I had been killed. Apparently a news agency broadcast this inaccurate report; it was picked up by other agencies, and I was duly written off. Indeed I could claim, as once Mark Twain said: 'the reports of my death have been greatly exaggerated.'

Angela received many letters of condolence and we had quite a job convincing people that I was alive and kicking. One letter from Holland came from a priest we knew there who, in fact, was one of six brothers – five of whom were priests. The sixth was to become my racing mechanic. The priest finished his letter by saying: 'After all he is now in a better place'. I acknowledged his condolences myself ending with the words: 'Looking forward to seeing you soon'. He loved the joke and both he and his brothers told the story for years afterwards. So ended 1953.

CHAPTER TEN

LE MANS IN
THE RAIN

E arly in 1954 I persuaded Jaguars to sell me a works
C-Type which had been built specially for the Pan-
American road race. Jaguars had withdrawn from the race
and the car had remained at the works. It had in fact gone
to Le Mans, as the spare car, in 1953, and was the car over
which there had been a rumpus, but it had never raced. Of
heavier gauge aluminium – to withstand the buffeting it
would have received in South America – than the other
works cars, it was otherwise substantially the same as the
car Tony and I had driven to victory. With its three Weber
carburettors and disc brakes it both went and stopped
better than my old C-Type. This latter car had now gone
to Jack Howey who was remodelling it and retained it for
a long time.

Towards the end of February I flew, with Tony Rolt, James
Tilling and Philip Fotheringham-Parker, to Klosters in

Switzerland, ostensibly to get fit for the new racing season. Our hotel was the Wyneck and its proprietress, Frau Guler, was a splendid hostess.

I found skiing a hazardous sport and was not surprised to learn that Swiss doctors know as much about broken limbs as any medical men anywhere. I soon discovered that, as in motor racing, it is the ability to negotiate corners at speed that separates the men from the boys. My speed in a dead straight line was – I am told – impressive; but my cornering technique left everything to be desired – I was incapable of turning at speed. This failing caused me to have two major shunts and, far from getting me fit for the motor racing season, my new sport nearly sent me home on a stretcher.

My first shunt came at the end of a long descent when my inability to turn made me somersault into a pit. I landed on my head and was knocked out. It was a good thing members of my party missed me, for I was still unconscious when found. I took things easily for a day or two, but then rash confidence and enthusiasm sent me up the slopes again. I tried to come down slowly but found that it required more skill than I possessed. The harder I tried to control my progress the more erratic my course, and the faster my speed became. Eventually I was in a sort of snowy no-man's land going faster and faster to nowhere in particular. Then, with a dreadful suddenness, two figures appeared ahead, and as they drew nearer I saw that a man was instructing a girl in some of the finer arts of, I suppose, skiing. All my shouting was in vain, and though I missed the girl, I bounced off the man, causing him sufficient injury to put him in hospital for a month. I was unhurt but, naturally, very upset. I had done all I could to attract their attention, and had been shouting a warning at the top of my voice for a good two hundred yards before I hit the fellow, but all to no avail – neither of them had heard me. It is wonderful how two people can so concentrate their minds as to be oblivious of the world around them.

To finish off this holiday, one of the engines of the twin-engined plane that flew us home failed, and the pilot made London Airport only with difficulty. As I drove home, observing the antics of my fellow motorists, I mused that you cannot run away from fate. Shakespeare wrote: 'Even in the temple of a King keeps death his court'. The operative word is 'even'. If the fates are on your side motor racing is no more dangerous than anything else.

★ ★ ★

A little over a week after my return from Switzerland a remarkable Dutchman joined my business: Fredricus Gorelius Boelens. Fred was the only unordained brother of the Dutch priest who had written to me after my accident just before Christmas, and he was a remarkably fine mechanic. He absorbed technical details as a blotter absorbs ink and in no time he knew just about everything there was to know about a C-Type. When we went up to Oulton Park in April for the first race of the season I knew that my car could not have been better prepared. The race was for the British Empire Trophy, transferred from its usual venue in the Isle of Man. There were three heats and a final. The heats were scratch races for the different capacity classes while the final was on handicap. My heat was an interesting one for Ecurie Ecosse had entered the three Le Mans cars of the previous year; they were driven by Tony Rolt, Ninian Sanderson and Jimmy Stewart. After some very enjoyable dicing I won by half a length from Ninian with Tony third. The final was won on handicap by Alan Brown in a Cooper-Bristol from Roy Salvadori's two-litre Maserati and Peter Gammon's 1,500 Lotus-MG. I was fourth; but had the satisfaction of being the fastest car off the scratch mark, unfortunately, there was no scratch prize.

The following Saturday I went to Goodwood and collected a couple of second places in the two races for which I had entered the C-Type; Jimmy Stewart, in another C-Type, was the man who pipped me both times. I drove also a 2-litre H.W.M. in the Lavant Cup. The race was won by Reg Parnell in a Ferrari. The only thing I remember about the race was the experience of driving the under-steering H.W.M. after the over-steering Jaguar.

The previous October, a Jaguar prototype competition model had been timed over a measured mile of the Jabbeke road in Belgium at 178.383 mph. Those of us who drove for the works knew that this was the new D-Type, and we all hoped the car would race at Le Mans in June. Tony and I went up to the factory after the Goodwood meeting so that the design department could sit us in a 'mock-up' and take the necessary measurements. Jaguars are always wonderfully good at this sort of thing and do their best to see that their drivers are comfortable. We learned also that we would have a chance to test the new car in the near future.

I had entered the C-Type for the Coupe de Paris at Montlhery, and decided to drive the car to the meeting, race it, and then drive home again. Accompanied by Fred, I drove to Newhaven, shipped the car to Dieppe and then drove on to Paris. It was a lovely day and we made very good time. Our trip was quite uneventful and the car ran perfectly. I have always believed that sports racing cars should be driven to the track whenever possible. If they cannot be driven on the road it is a reflection on their design. Apart from fitting softer plugs my C-Type was in racing trim. All Fred had to do before the race was fit hard plugs, check water and oil levels, ensure tyre pressures were correct and that the car was carrying the right quantity of fuel. The only spares we carried were the sort of spares any keen motorist would take with him on a motoring holiday.

On arriving in Paris I dropped Fred – who was staying with friends – and then drove round to Claridges Hotel in the Champs Elysees.

The first day's practising was marred by the death of Guy Mairesse. This fatal accident was caused by an idiot in a 4 CV Renault who drove at 50 mph in the middle of the track ignoring all the international flag signals the marshals gave him. Poor Mairesse came round a very fast corner at about 140 mph and saw this goon in the middle of the road and right in his line. He braked hard, and spun through a concrete barrier killing three children and himself in the process. It was a sad accident, and quite unnecessary. I was not far behind Mairesse, but seeing a pall of smoke rising and guessing that there had been an accident I was able to slow down and miss the Renault.

The C-Type handled beautifully on the banking, and I recorded the fastest practice time which gave me pole position on race day. The race was started by some important gentleman who, quite clearly, had never started a race before. When he held the flag aloft I saw that it was attached to a pole and that if I jumped the start it would probably decapitate me. Alternatively, he could not bring it down other than in front of me which meant I would have to drive over it. While I was worrying about this pole a

Gordini, which had been revving away in the middle of the pack suddenly blew up and caught fire. The officials panicked, and in the general excitement the important gentleman dropped the pole. I shot off, followed by one other car, while everyone else stayed behind. When I took the hairpin bend, some two miles from the start, and looked back down an empty straight, I guessed what had happened, so motored slowly on round to the start, while excited marshals jumped up and down gesticulating madly. They, poor souls, thought I would arrive behind the crowded starting grid at speed and that a dreadful accident would occur.

I won the actual race very easily. The C-Type quite outclassed everything present and I won as I pleased at an average speed of 93 mph. I was getting 155 mph on the straight and 135-140 mph on the banking.

The next meeting was the *Daily Express* meeting at Silverstone. The Trophy race was won by Gonzalez in a 2-litre Ferrari from Behra in a Gordini. The foreign cars had things very much their own way, and the highest placed British car was the Connaught of Tony Rolt in sixth place. Gonzalez was also successful in the sports car race, driving the monstrous 4.9-litre Ferrari. This car could really accelerate and Gonzalez ran away from everyone, winning by forty-six seconds from George Abecassis in a Jaguar-engined H.W.M. I finished sixth in the C-Type.

Lofty England had been at Silverstone looking – or so I thought – very pleased with himself, and a couple of days later I knew why. Tony and I went up to Coventry and lunched with Lofty and Munger Heynes and then repaired to Gaydon Airfield to test the new D-Type. Norman Dewis was there with the car which, with its bare metal finish and streamlined appearance, looked wonderfully functional. Both Tony and I drove the car and did our best to put it through its paces. Lofty had marked out a course so that we could sample the car's handling characteristics and, true to form, I was the first person to spin off. Brake and cockpit temperatures were taken and all our comments noted so that when the car arrived at Le Mans it would be as we wanted it. It says much for the factory that they were able to prepare their team cars and pander to the whims of their drivers all in the space of four weeks.

My next date with the C-Type was at Hedemora in Sweden, and on May 19th accompanied by Angela, Fred, the C-Type and my XK120 drophead coupe, I set sail for Oslo in the S.S. *Blenheim*. Apart from the fact that I ate too much *Smorgasbord* and became ill, the trip was uneventful. We disembarked at Oslo and drove in convoy to Hedemora where we had arranged to meet Michael Head and his wife. Michael had, until recently, been military attache in Stockholm. George Abecassis was also staying in our hotel, as was Prince Bertil of Sweden. The Prince, who is a motoring enthusiast, was in great form and entertained us to dinner. The race was won by Casimiro d'Oliveira of Portugal in a Ferrari 4.5 from George Abecassis in his H.W.M. with myself in third place. Michael Head won the race for standard production sports cars, so we all had some success as well as a lot of fun. Once again Prince Bertil played host: he gave a splendid dinner to all participants after the racing was over. Fred took the C-Type and went on ahead of us while Angela and I travelled home with Michael and his wife Joan. It had been a very enjoyable interlude.

I do not know whether the Swedish air had agreed with me, but the Saturday after my return to England I won the first race held at Aintree car circuit. The race, for sports cars, took place in pouring rain, and the C-Type ran beautifully. Jimmy Stewart's C-Type led in the early stages, but I passed him on the seventh lap, as did the then-new American driver, Carroll Shelby, who was driving a DB3S. I managed to increase my lead over Shelby and won fairly comfortably. This was one of those occasions when I felt master of the situation. The track was new, wet and very treacherous, yet I drove with tremendous confidence, and indeed almost ignored the adverse conditions. A retrospective view of this race causes me to shudder when I think of the abandon with which I went into the corners.

After its success I thought it would be a good idea if Fred were to take the head off the C-Type and give the car a thorough check-over. The next race for which it was entered was the Oporto G.P and that was a month away. Meanwhile, I was to share Peter Whitehead's new Cooper-Jaguar in the twelve-hour sports car race at Hyeres on the French Mediterranean coast and then travel up to Le Mans for the Twenty-four Hours. I flew from London Airport to Marseilles where Peter Whitehead met me in his XK120 fixed-head coupe. Although June had only just begun the heat was intense, and the interior of Peter's car was quite insufferable, so hot indeed that we had to take our shirts off. Fortunately our hotel in Hyeres was beside the sea and we were soon in the water.

The Cooper-Jaguar had independent suspension on all four wheels and I was most curious to see how its handling compared with the C and D-Type Jaguars. Arthur Birks had brought the car down to Hyeres and had lost about a stone in the process: the cabin of his transporter had been even hotter than Peter's XK. Peter drove the Cooper first and then handed it over to me. I liked the car, and after three or four laps, during which I got the feel of things, I began to drive fast.

I was coming down the backleg of the circuit towards the hairpin and had just changed down into third when I either heard a sound or just sensed that something was wrong. I braked, and to my horror, the pedal went down to the floor and stayed there without in any way retarding the car's progress. I changed into second, then first, but it was no good, I was going too fast to get round the hairpin and I could not go through the barricade because it was lined with children. There was only one thing to do. I whipped the wheel round and spun the car. Round and round it went finally stopping six feet short of, and broadside on to, the flimsy barricade and the children who stood behind it. Not one of them had moved: they had no time – only when I began to spin did they know that anything was amiss. Two very shaken gendarmes helped me push the car off the track while the delighted children gathered round. It was not every day that they could examine a racing car at such close quarters.

Knowing from past experience how helpful Jaguars can be on such occasions I phoned Lofty England, told him what had happened, and asked for the necessary spares to be flown to us. He had these spares put on an aircraft within a few hours but, unfortunately, the plane was delayed and they arrived too late for us to repair the car in time for the race. We were very disappointed after travelling so far, but tried to make the best of things by helping in Graham Whitehead's pit. Graham was driving a DB3 with Pat Griffith. As it happened they subsequently suffered more than we had done, for in avoiding a slowing car Pat hit a concrete kilometre post, the car turned over and he received severe injuries to his back. The car also was extensively damaged. We saw poor Pat in hospital, and after ensuring that he was in capable hands left for Le Mans. The race, incidentally, was won by Maurice Trintignant in a Ferrari; his co-driver was the Italian Piotti.

Prince Chula once said something to the effect that if one allowed 'ifs' in motor racing one might just as well stop it. He was perfectly right. Nevertheless, the motor racing public, like the followers of other sports, loves its 'ifs' and 'buts' and will continue to do so as long as races are run. Bearing this in mind it is fair comment to say that the 1954 Le Mans race was a race of 'ifs' and 'buts'.

If Tony and I had not lost some ten minutes through fuel filter trouble we might well have won easily. But, as against this, the winning Ferrari was in the pits for seven and a half minutes in the vital closing stages of the race when the engine refused to start after a stop to refuel and change drivers. Tony and I also lost time when a Talbot motored across Tony's bows on the approach to White House corner; Tony was forced to take to the sand at the roadside and the nearside front wing was buckled. He was more or less compelled to stop at the pits to check whether any serious damage had been done and in so doing lost much precious time. 'But', the Ferrari supporter will say, 'the Ferraris were more handicapped by the wet conditions than the Jaguars; they could not use the great power of their 4.9-litre engines to the full'. 'Ah', replies the Jaguar man, 'if the race average of the first hour had been maintained the Ferrari would have run out of brakes; as it was, Gonzalez was virtually without brakes at the end, and was probably grateful he had a wet track to help keep his drums cool'. And so the argument will go on. No conclusion can be reached; but many opinions will be proffered. In the end it is probably best to say that the works Ferrari driven by Gonzalez/Trintignant won by 87 seconds from the Rolt/Hamilton Jaguar and leave it at that. The Jaguar supporter – refusing to leave it at that – will point out that our car was in the pits for 27 minutes against the Ferrari's 25 minutes; to which the Ferrari supporter will undoubtedly reply that 7 minutes of the Ferrari's time was taken in trying to start the car after its last pit stop, and but for that it would have won comfortably. Of course, there is an answer to that one, and a counter answer to that answer, and so we could go on indefinitely. I have no intention of doing so however; I intend merely to describe the race as I saw and experienced it.

The D-Types went fabulously well in practice and were faster in terms of maximum speed than the 4.9-litre Ferraris, though the latter naturally had better acceleration. We were getting over 170 mph on the Mulsanne straight and found that what had previously been a fast curve now became a corner. The car handled beautifully and the disc brakes were superb. The Jaguar team consisted of Stirling Moss and Peter Walker, Peter Whitehead and Ken Wharton, Tony and myself. Ferrari had: Gonzalez/Trintignant, Maglioli/Marzotto and Rosier/Manzon.

As usual, Tony began the race and, after a good start, came round in fifth place behind the three Ferraris and Stirling Moss at the end of the first lap. Gonzalez broke the lap record on his second lap going round in 4 minutes 22.4 seconds, 115.023 mph. A few laps later he improved on this fractionally, but now Stirling got in amongst the Ferrari's and put in a lap at 115.728 mph and took the lead for a short time. At the end of the first hour the leaders' average speed was 111.678 mph, at the end of the second 112.640 mph, higher than the previous record lap. Gonzalez was now back in the lead with Marzotto second and Stirling third, while Tony had passed Rosier to take fourth place; Peter Whitehead lay sixth. All these cars were on the same lap.

Shortly after this Jaguar's trouble began. First of all Stirling came in complaining of misfiring. The plugs were changed and he went off again. Then Tony came in with the same complaint, only he emphasized that the misfiring was occurring at high revs, and was at its worst on the Mulsanne straight. New plugs were put in but they did not effect a cure for one lap later he was back again. Len Hayden checked the ignition and carburation but could not find anything amiss. Lofty England told him to change the plugs again (just in case) although no one believed that that was the answer. After another two laps Tony was in again to say that the misfiring was as bad as ever; he suggested to Lofty that I drive the car to see whether I could spot the cause. Both knew that, racing my own Jaguars, I had naturally acquired some knowledge of this engine. As soon as the misfiring started I was sure fuel starvation was the answer and came in to the pit and told them so. Len Hayden took out the fuel bowl, cleaned it, and removed the filter, and we had no more fuel feed problems for the rest of the race. Unfortunately, we had lost some ten minutes, ten minutes we were not able to make up. Both our team-mates were in with the same trouble. No one ever found out how the filters became blocked – maybe they were too good!

The rain really came down soon after this, and there were times when my cockpit seemed half full of water. I suffered cramp in my left leg and was very wet and cold. How I envied the drivers of the closed cars.

And so Tony and I went on through the night. By midnight we were fourth; by four a.m. we were second; our old policy of driving as fast as possible in the dark had once again proved to be right. Occasionally the rain slackened off, but at no time was the road other than very wet, and spray was always a problem. Both our teammates had now gone. The Moss/Walker car rather dramatically, Stirling suddenly finding he had no brakes at the end of the Mulsanne straight. He came down through the gears and took to the escape road. It was a harrowing experience for him, and a terrifying one for the two gendarmes who were enjoying a quiet smoke in the middle of that road. The Peter Whitehead/Ken Wharton car had gearbox trouble, the lever eventually sticking in top gear. They motored on, but the strain of pulling the car away from the slow corners on such a high ratio proved too much for the engine, and cylinder head trouble ended their effort. After the race was over it was discovered that the gearbox fault could have been fixed in ten minutes had it been known.

Just after six a.m. Trintignant took over from Gonzalez with a 500 seconds lead over our car. By eight a.m. I had reduced this to a lap and 109 seconds and had sometimes taken as much as twenty seconds a lap off him. I handed over to Tony who continued to whittle down the lead – in deplorable weather – until he was on the same lap as the Ferrari. At 9.25 a.m. Gonzalez took over again and drove very fast, but Tony continued to gain a steady two seconds a lap. Then, at 10.15 a.m., came near-tragedy for us, a Talbot drove across Tony's bows, forcing him to take to the sand at the roadside. The car was damaged and Tony came into the pit. When he set off again we were a lap and thirty-three seconds behind the Ferrari.

I took over again just before eleven a.m. and found that the car was handling differently as a result of the bang it had taken. The Ferrari refuelled at noon and Trintignant took over once more. I gained on him at first, but then the rain stopped and, as the track dried out, so he speeded up and I could only take the odd seconds a lap off him. I handed over to Tony at one-thirty p.m. The sky was now showing blue and it looked as if the rain clouds had at last departed. I gladly accepted a glass of cognac, little guessing that another drive lay ahead of me.

Tony was in terrific form gaining as much as ten seconds a lap. Then suddenly it began to rain again. Trintignant brought the Ferrari into the pit. Oil and fuel went in followed by Gonzalez.

Then he jumped out and the bonnet was opened, then he jumped in, then he jumped out again – the car would not start. The minutes ticked by. The Ferrari pit became more and more panicky; the Jaguar more and more excited. I was standing beside Mr. William Lyons (as he then was) watching the performance; at least five Italians were working on the car although the regulations clearly stated that only two mechanics could service the car at any one time. I drew his attention to this and asked him if he thought we should protest. Without turning his head he said quietly: 'If we win this race Duncan it will be the British way – outright, not as the result of a protest'. No sooner had he said this than Tony attempted to come into the pit. He was waving his goggles indicating that he wanted a vizor. This was almost too much for us and we waved him on for all we were worth.

He saw both our signals and the Ferrari, and realizing what had happened, shot off again. Eventually, after seven minutes the Ferrari started and Gonzalez was back in the race. One minute thirty-seven seconds later Tony came by, the crowd, still on its feet, urging him on. At this moment I really thought we would win again: it seemed reasonable to suppose the Ferrari was sick and would not be able to motor as before. My theory was soon dispelled, for Gonzalez came round going very fast in a car that sounded horribly healthy. By three p.m. the Ferrari had increased its lead to one minute fifty-five seconds, and though Tony was holding on wonderfully well it was obvious to everyone that he could not see properly through goggles. He had already signalled his need of a vizor when he had tried to come into the pit and it was clear that unless he was given one he could not hope to catch Gonzalez in the present conditions.

When he had taken over from me the rain had stopped and – as I have already mentioned – it looked as if the worst of the weather was over; however, as is often the case on the Sarthe Plains, the rain had reappeared from nowhere. The track was now awash and every car hurled spray up behind it. How Tony managed to lap as fast as he did wearing goggles I do not know. It was decided to bring him in and give him a vizor.

Then someone questioned whether he could be handed a vizor while sitting in the car. The Le Mans regulations have never been easy to interpret and no one knew for certain what the position was. Clearly we could not risk disqualification at this late hour, so it was agreed that Tony be called in and I take over in his place. By dealing with the situation in this way we not only avoided the risk of disqualification, but saved the precious seconds Tony would have taken in jumping out of the car, clipping on a vizor, jumping back in, starting up, and getting away. As it was, he came in, switched off and jumped out. No sooner was he out of the car than I was in and away. He was surprised and disappointed, for he wanted to finish what he had started, but, being a team-man, took it in good part, and understood the reasons for his pit manager's decision.

A change of clothing and a few cognacs had made a new man of me and I went after Gonzalez for all I was worth. I managed a lap at 117 mph and by three-thirty p.m. I was a bare ninety seconds behind him. How I tried. I was clocked at 173 mph on the Mulsanne straight when the storm was at its worst and in achieving this speed frightened myself to death. The gearing of our D-Type was such that we could pull 5,600 rpm in top gear on the straight. This corresponded to something just over 170 mph. I saw suddenly that the rev-counter was reading 5,900 and realized that I was getting wheel spin at 170 mph in top gear. I eased my foot immediately for wheel-spin can take charge when you cannot control it. On my next lap three cars left the track, all victims of sudden and unexpected wheel-spin.

Gonzalez was impossibly good. He handled that big Ferrari superbly and I could not catch him. With fifteen minutes to go the rain stopped and, as the track dried out, he increased his lead to a final 87 seconds. I tried desperately hard right to the end, though from three-thirty p.m. onwards I made sure of finishing and took no unnecessary risks. In the half hour before that I had driven with a total disregard for the consequences and might have killed myself a dozen times. I still get butterflies in my stomach just thinking about it.

My blood was up and I simply ignored the wet track and drove as I would have done in the dry. The funny thing was that the car was always controllable and I had no real incident until I was almost on the finishing line – then the Bristol team nearly wrote me off. They were finishing 7th, 8th and 9th and knew they had won the team prize. In their elation they forgot presumably that others were still racing, for they formed up in line abreast right across the track so as to be able to cross the line together. I came up at about 150 mph and just passed between two of them.

Collectively they were throwing up so much spray that I was upon them before I knew it. I was lucky to miss them; they were lucky I did.

And so a great race ended. Gonzalez and Trintignant deserved their win, for the big and heavy V12 Ferrari was a very considerable handful in the wet. Another big car was third: the 5-litre Cunningham of Spear and Johnston which finished 157 miles behind the winner. The privately entered Jaguar C-Type of Laurent and Swaters was fourth, and Briggs Cunningham's own car, which he shared with Bennett, fifth.

CHAPTER ELEVEN

BAD LUCK AT RHEIMS

After the Le Mans celebrations were over, Angela and I set off for Oporto in my XK120 drop-head coupe, which she had brought over from England. We had a lovely run down and, save for a period when we were nearly choked by red road dust in Spain, enjoyed some fine open car touring.

Lancia, who had withdrawn from Le Mans shortly before the race, had entered three 3.3-litre cars to be driven by Ascari, Villoresi and Castellotti. It was obvious as soon as we started to practise that they were faster than any other cars entered. Indeed, with the exception of Peter Whitehead's Cooper-Jaguar, George Abecassis's H.W.M.-Jaguar and my C-Type, none of the other cars there could keep them in sight.

On race day the Lancias ran true to their practice form and streaked away from the rest of the field. Clutch trouble put me out on the twenty-fourth lap; George Abecassis had already gone on the eighteenth, so it was left to Peter Whitehead to hang on to fourth place behind the three

Lancias. He was lapped twice, but kept pegging away, and when Ascari's steering broke, seven laps from the end, he found himself in third place and there he stayed to take the flag behind Villoresi and Castellotti. Ascari was leading when misfortune befell him; only his wonderful skill saved his life. I saw the whole incident and marvelled at the way he managed to stop the car from going into the sea at tremendous speed.

The following morning Angela and I were retracing our route of a few days previously, and, wasting very little time, drove the 1,200 odd miles to Rheims where I was due to attend medical examination before practice for the Twelve-Hour Sports Car race. We arrived with half an hour to spare, which was evidence of pretty good timing. For this race I was teamed, as usual, with Tony Rolt, and we were driving the same D-Type Jaguar 'OKV 1', in which we had chased Gonzalez and Trintignant two weeks previously at Le Mans. The other members of our team were Moss/Walker and Whitehead/Wharton.

Everyone hoped this race would be in the nature of a return match between Ferrari and Jaguar, coming as it did so soon after Le Mans. But it was not to be. Enzo Ferrari found himself in a spot. The French Grand Prix followed the Twelve-Hour Race, and if he had entered a full team of sports cars his drivers would have been tired out before the G.P. began. He decided, therefore, to enter one four-cylinder 3-litre car and nominated Maglioli and Manzon to drive it. This sole entry had to take on three D-Types, two Cunninghams, Levegh's Talbot and Jean Behra in a disc-braked 3-litre Gordini. Several privately entered Ferraris were running, of which the most dangerous was a 4.5-litre driven by Masten Gregory and Biondetti.

The Twelve-Hours begins at midnight with a Le Mans-type start. The pit area was brilliantly lit, and the spectator could enjoy all the tenseness and excitement peculiar to this type of start.

A Cunningham was first away but at the end of the lap Stirling Moss was well in the lead. By the third lap he was already lapping the 750 cc cars, and by the sixth led Maglioli by fifteen seconds. Tony Rolt was third and Jean Behra fourth – the race was really on. Behra was trying desperately to close the gap between Tony and himself and succeeded to such good effect that he ran into the back of our car. Both cars had to come into the pits, the Gordini to stay, but Tony, after having the rear light repaired, was off again without losing too much time. A cursory inspection had suggested that the damage was confined to the tail of the car though we knew, only too well, that the axle might be affected.

Just after dawn Stirling's prop-shaft broke and his misfortune left Tony and me in the lead. The works Ferrari had gone out around the time we had been shunted and the only serious oppositions we now had to contend with came from other Jaguars. We were exceeding 170 mph on the straight and were averaging twelve miles per gallon. All this on the same axle ratio as for Le Mans: 2.9 to 1. At half-time we led by forty-nine seconds from our team-mates Whitehead and Wharton who in turn were fifty-five seconds ahead of the Walters-Fitch Cunningham. Soon the Cunningham began a series of pit stops and the C-Type Jaguar of Laurent and Swaters took third place. And so we went on until thirty minutes from the end when suddenly my back axle ran dry. I got the car to the pits where it was found that there was a hole as big as a half-crown in the axle casing. There was no time to do anything save plug it and this we did with chewing gum, etc. Oil went in, smoke and smell came out, and I pressed on for one more lap. Most of the teeth had left the crown wheel and I could feel the odd three or four catching as they went round. I free-wheeled down the straight at a steady 50 mph where I had previously been doing over 170 mph and somehow got the car to the finishing line. To my great chagrin our team-mates passed me and went on to win. I had to wait just short of the line and then do one more lap to count as a finisher. This was because the last lap had to be completed within a certain time. I managed it, crossing the finishing line with a dead engine and a crown wheel minus all its teeth. The Laurent/Swaters C-Type was third, making it 1, 2, 3, for Jaguar.

Angela and I returned to England, but not for long; for as soon as the British G.P. at Silverstone – in which I did not achieve any success – was over I flew down to Lisbon with Mike Hawthorn for the Portuguese G.P. We arrived in the middle of a heat wave, and were more than glad that our hotel – Harry Rugoni's Aviz – had splendid air conditioning.

The heat made practising a murderous pursuit and I could only manage five laps before coming in. The pedals became so hot that they blistered my feet, and Fred had to cut slots in the side of the C-Type before I could consider racing the car. Fred and the C-Type had been in Portugal since the Oporto race, and not only had he overhauled the car, but he had had it repainted and reupholstered as well. It looked wonderful and went splendidly but clearly could not hold the new 3-litre Ferraris of Gonzalez and Hawthorn. As soon as the five minute signal went before the race, I got out of my car and Fred poured a bucket of water over me. A gesture that was as much enjoyed by the crowd as appreciated by me. I made a very good start and led Gonzalez down the hill on the first lap. I hung on to the lead for three laps and then, trying to stop Gonzalez passing me coming into a corner, left my braking too late and had to take the escape road along with him. Mike Hawthorn, who was coming up behind, laughed so much he spun and only just got away in front of us after we had turned round. Unfortunately both Gonzalez and I hit a policeman on our way down the escape road; happily he survived his accident. In the end Gonzalez won the race by fourteen seconds from Mike, with Masten Gregory in a 4.5-litre Ferrari third. I finished fifth.

The car that Masten was driving was eventually sold to an American who crashed while demonstrating it to a friend of mine, Louis E. Wade; poor Louis was killed. My friendship with Louis was a strange one, for we never actually met. One day I received a letter from Bay City, Texas, in which the writer – who was of course Louis – asked me where I got the driving gloves I wore when racing. I told him and, as a matter of courtesy, sent him a pair. My gesture started a correspondence that went on until his death three years later. He used to ring up every Christmas morning: 'This is Louis B. Wade, calling just to wish you and your family a Happy Christmas'. He was a family man himself and left a wife and three children when he died. I shipped several cars to the States on his behalf, among them a Bugatti and a Bristol. He was one of the nicest people I have ever known; I can say that even though we never met in person.

After the race, Mike and I went back to the hotel with Harry. A tremendous party followed. The Holdroyds had come down from Oporto, Peter Whitehead had recovered from his heat stroke and Harry's friends were legion. Mike and I became separated from the main party around midnight. We then looked for, and found, a local night club where we joined in the fun. At four o'clock the club closed and we were more or less compelled to return to the hotel. Mike was on the first floor; I was on the third. Neither of us felt like going to sleep so we decided that we would change our bedroom furniture around. Using knotted sheets I lowered all my furniture down to Mike's room; he, in return, helped me pull all his up to mine. A poor drunk on the second floor who chanced to look out of his window as dawn was breaking was convinced he had the D.T.s when a large armchair went by.

When Harry called on us both some hours later he just could not work it out. If it had not been for the fellow on the second floor blabbing about poltergeists he might never have guessed the truth.

After lunch with Harry at the airport, where I attracted unwanted attention by sitting on a chair which collapsed under me, we flew back to London Airport. Mike and I hit it off with the two air hostesses, and arranged to take them up to town for supper and a show; alas, when we stepped out of the aircraft on arrival at London Airport, we found Mike's mother and Angela waiting for us.

* * *

By August 12th I was back on the Continent again, this time for the International Sports Car meeting at Zandvoort. This meeting was in place of the Dutch G.P. which was not held that year. I travelled over to Holland with Angela and George Abecassis, and after a night in the Hague, went up to the circuit to practise. Fred had taken the C-Type over a few days previously in order to have plenty of time to prepare it for the race. He was very keen that I should win in front of his countrymen. I was fastest in practice by some two seconds, in 1 minute 56.2 seconds, but both Fred and I were worried by an inexplicable drop in oil pressure. We changed the filters but could not find any metal in the discarded ones.

After the final practice it looked as if George Abecassis and I were faster than anyone else, and over dinner that night we agreed to take things easily and not to blow up our engines racing one another. Despite this pact I am not sure that either of us really trusted the other, and Angela says the sight of the two of us sitting side by side on the front row of the grid casting surreptitious glances at one another was very funny indeed. The flag fell; I departed, George stayed – in letting in the clutch he had sheared the driveshaft. At the end of my first lap I could not see a car behind me, by the fourth I was lapping the tail-enders. This circuit was made for the C-Type, so much so that it was difficult to believe that I.R.S. or a de Dion back axle would have allowed me to lap any faster. Then on my fifth lap a bearing went and my race was over. I was lucky enough to hear it go and so was able to stop before any more serious damage was done. The fact that I never used ear plugs – except at Le Mans – enabled me to hear the clatter despite wind and exhaust noise. I was very disappointed, as indeed was George Abecassis. We had a beer together and watched the rest of the race which was won by Sir James Scott-Douglas in an Ecurie Ecosse C-Type. Naturally our pact was never mentioned.

I returned to England leaving Fred and the car in Holland. Since my next race was to be the La Baule G.P. we had decided that Fred would strip the engine, fit new bearings, and then run the engine in by driving the car down to La Baule where I would meet him. George Abecassis was not driving at La

Baule but thought he would go down and watch the race, so George, Katie Gaze, Johnny Marshall and myself drove to La Baule from Cherbourg in George's Studebaker. We nearly had a bad accident on the way down when an enormous truck, pulling an even larger trailer, drove straight out of a side turning and crossed the main road at two miles per hour. Johnny clamped on the anchors and we somehow just missed the back of the trailer. It was a very near thing, and at one time I was sure we must hit the truck, or its trailer, for it was so long it went on and on and on – like a train at a railway crossing.

When we eventually got to La Baule I found Fred waiting with the car. He had driven down from Holland and told me the engine was now nicely run in. He had really put the engine together and it ran like an electric motor. The race was a handicap affair, and it was obvious that I could not give the small cars the start they had over me. Not that this was surprising: very few handicap races give the big cars an even break. I made fastest time in practice but was bothered by a rear tyre which kept catching fire! Tony Gaze who had been following me in his H.W.M.-Jaguar told me it was quite a frightening sight from behind. The cause was a couple of very sharp corners and the fine torque of the Jaguar engine.

On race day I led from the start, breaking the lap record several times. My rear near-side tyre kept catching fire just as it had done in practice, and eventually it burst. The car snaked terribly and I was lucky to stay on the road. By the time I reached the pits the hub was red hot and Fred had great difficulty in changing the wheel. While he struggled I had a couple of stiff cognacs, and then – to the cheers of the crowd – washed them down with a tankard of champagne. As soon as the new wheel was on, I jumped in the car, started the motor, engaged first gear, let in the clutch and shot off the jack which Fred had not yet had time to lower. The wheels were spinning like mad before they touched the ground. The scream of the tyres brought people to their feet, the smell of the rubber temporarily emptied my pit. I finally established a lap record which stands to this day, won the scratch part of the race, and finished fourth in the handicap. Tony Gaze was sixth. The race was won by the DB-Panhard of Cornet.

On our way back to Cherbourg another Frenchman drove out in front of us. This time on a bicycle. The bicycle vanished under the car, its rider over the roof. I was sure we had killed him, but he got up and let fly such a broadside of verbal abuse that it was obvious he had come through the ordeal better than we had. A crowd quickly gathered – we were in the middle of a village – and soon they loudly. chorused their disapproval along with the indignant cyclist. George made the fatal mistake of trying to buy him off. The man trebled George's offer; George argued. The villagers lay bicycles around the car; the police arrived. They were polite but firm: it was a case for the insurance company. After two hours of form filling and questions we were allowed to go. We were late for our plane at Cherbourg but managed to get on another one. All the delays had made us thirsty and a jolly party arrived at Her Majesty's Customs. George, who had fallen asleep in the plane, can claim the enviable distinction of passing through Customs without waking up. No one asked him if he had anything to declare; if they had they would not have got an answer.

★ ★ ★

I began September in Eire at the Curragh practising for the Wakefield Trophy; I ended the month at Seaview on the Isle of Wight in plaster. The race for the Trophy was won by Peter Whitehead in his Cooper-Jaguar; I was second. I was leading the scratch part of the race (in the Wakefield Trophy) by thirteen seconds at one time, but was forced to slow when the car began snaking. After it was all over we found that the holding nut on the end of the half-shaft had burst, and the hub, complete with wheel, was held on by the C-Type's disc, which was rotating in its caliper. In fact the knock-on nut was fully floating. With the wheel in this dangerous condition I had been doing around 140 mph on the straight. There was a fatal accident when a local driver, Joe Quinn, left the road. Two soldier marshals, a spectator and Quinn were all killed. This fatal accident led to the abandonment of future races at the Curragh. I was lucky not to be involved in an accident at the same spot; for shortly after Quinn's crash I was coming down the straight flat-out when two stretcher bearers suddenly walked across the road in front of me. Fortunately, they either saw or heard me, for at the last moment they dropped the stretcher and I passed over it without touching either of them. Needless to say the stretcher was empty.

The following weekend I was driving in the Ulster TT, this time in a works D-Type with Tony Rolt. Unfortunately gearbox trouble put us out of the race after three hours. This visit of the Jaguar works team to Ulster was beset with vicissitudes. First of all, someone dropped a crate on William Lyons's Mark VII Jaguar. This modified the car to such an extent that no one could even get into it, let alone drive it. In the general excitement this incident created, some light-fingered gentleman whipped all the team's chronometers.

Then, after practising for hours trying out a new soft tyre Dunlop had produced specially for this circuit, getting the pressures right and so on, we found that they had all been stacked together, necessitating a pressure check before anyone knew which were the front and which were the back wheels. Morris-Goodall, our assistant team manager, had a busy time placating the team when, to add to our troubles, all the cars broke down during the race. This was not a weekend to remember.

After a splendid party at our hotel in Belfast where we recaptured our good spirits, and someone dressed up as a fireman and ran about the hotel getting people out of bed, I returned to England. I only just caught the plane at Nutts Corner, and would not have done so had I not given the taxi driver five pounds and taken the wheel myself. In the plane I sat next to Harry Ferguson, who entertained me with an account of how he had first conceived the idea of his tractors. I remember his pointing down at two tractors ploughing a field and saying: 'See the labour they have saved'.

I joined my family at Seaview in the Isle of Wight and looked forward to a few quiet days of playing with my children. The Rolts were down there and, on the second afternoon of my holiday, I hired a boat and put to sea with my son Adrian aged six, my daughter Caroline aged four, Angela Rolt aged seven, her sister Susie aged three, their brother Stuart aged five, their mother Lois and last but not least Nannie Rolt (I do not mean Tony). After some time out at sea I turned the boat round and headed for the shore.

I was not familiar with local tidal conditions and did not appreciate that it was going out. Anyway the boat ran on to some rocks and we lost the outboard motor. The front of the boat was up in the air; the stern was low in the water. It was obvious that as the tide went out the angle would become steeper, and that eventually the boat would topple over. I jumped into the water and swam around and under the boat to see if there was any way I could launch it; the women did their best to keep the frightened children from rocking it. Eventually I stood on a rock adjacent to the one upon which we were marooned and, using all my strength, just managed to float the boat again. The effort cost me dear, however; for I strained my back and was in plaster for nearly a month. The whole thing was a nasty experience: if that boat had overturned, most, if not all, of those children would have been drowned. Our plight had been seen by people on shore but I doubt a boat could reach us in time.

Owing to my injury, I missed the September Goodwood meeting; it was the first time I had missed a meeting since racing had started there. I went down with Angela and we watched it all, but I did not enjoy it, for I am a bad spectator.

My plaster was due to come off on October 6th, but I had to postpone my release for a day when King Feisal's A.D.C. phoned to say that His Majesty required me to dine with him the following day. Kings do not invite you: they command your presence. I lunched with the King at Claridges and, over coffee, when he had dismissed his entourage, we had a long and serious talk. As always, he spoke about his people with great feeling and touching concern.

The day after this enjoyable luncheon the plaster came off, and the day after that I drove the C-Type to Paris in order to practise for the Coupe du Salon at Montlhéry. The Coupe du Salon takes place every year during the French motor show; it is a good meeting with an end of season atmosphere. My first date in Paris was to a luncheon given in honour of Lord Louis Mountbatten, who was then at

SHAPE. The invitation came through an old friend, Hervé Coatalen. After lunch was over I was standing talking to Lord Louis when an A.D.C. came up and reminded him that he had an appointment at SHAPE for which he was already late. Since my C-Type, stripped for racing, was waiting outside I offered to take him there post haste. He was willing, but some old Admiral pointed out that the official car with motorcycle outriders was waiting, and that this was probably a more suitable type of transport. To my great chagrin Lord Louis felt obliged to decline my offer and went off with his outriders. When his procession was in full swing I passed them in the C-Type. I waited till I was level with his car, and then opened up in second gear, just to let him see how much quicker it would have been my way.

When I got back to Claridges in Paris, after practising at Montlhéry, there was a telegram waiting for me. It read: 'Best of luck at Montlhéry tomorrow'. It was signed: Feisal R.

The Coupe du Salon was won by Jean Behra in a straight-eight 3-litre Gordini from Masten Gregory in a 4.5-litre Ferrari; I was third. I slid on some wet tar early in the race and clouted the bank at the side of the track. My front shock absorbers were damaged and thereafter driving on the banking was a nerve-racking business; in the circumstances I was pleased with my third place. I attended to the shock absorbers and the following morning, leaving Claridges at five a.m., averaged 73 mph for the journey to Dieppe.

★ ★ ★

Ken Atkins always said that the great thing about the end of the motor racing season was that it gave me a chance to look in on my motor business. Being passionately fond of motor cars, anyone visiting my showrooms would find Jaguar, Bentley, Rolls-Royce, Mercedes and cars of similar quality in my stock.

I had for some time been negotiating with Jaguars the purchase of the D-Type 'OKV 1'. An entirely new version was to appear in 1955. I sold the C-Type to Dan Margulies. I was very sorry to sell it but I needed something faster.

I went up to the factory in February, collected the D-Type, and drove it back to Byfleet. There had been a heavy fall of snow, yet it was possible to drive the car quietly and without incident thanks to its tractability. With 250bhp on tap, and a scale weight of less than one ton, one could hardly use high revs. Many sports-racing cars would be undriveable under such conditions. No one ever had to take a Jaguar to a race on a transporter. Lofty England always said that if you cannot drive a car on the road it will never be reliable in a race. I completely agreed.

A day or two after I had collected the D-Type, John Bolster came down to Byfleet and road tested the car. John had long been one of the best appraisers of a car's virtues in Britain; the report of his impression of the car appeared in *Autosport,* and I was most impressed by the accuracy of his valuation of its strong points.

CHAPTER TWELVE

LE SPORT IN MOROCCO

Just before Christmas Fred Boelens had left me when his working permit expired. He could have applied for an extension, and he wanted to; but the pull of home was strong and in the end he decided to return to Holland and the family motor business. I was very sorry to see him go, for he was a truly splendid racing mechanic as well as a charming person. He later married, had a family and ran the Rover agency for the Hague. Whenever I was in Holland I always made a point of looking him up for we remained very good friends. His successor was a young man of twenty-one, Robin Freeman. Robin had received a good training and was very keen to get into the sport.

The day after John Bolster had road tested the D–Type, Robin and I got down to preparing the car for the first race of the season, so far as we were concerned. It was to be the G.P. of Agadir, the town subsequently destroyed in the Moroccan earthquake. Agadir was a small but flourishing port four hundred miles south of Casablanca. I had received an invitation to compete in this race, and also in the G.P. of Dakar, from the local automobile clubs who had Government backing. At first I felt I must decline the invitation for, although it was possible to get the car to Casablanca, via Antwerp, there did not appear to be any way of getting it back: no shipping company could offer me cargo space. In the end, after consultation with Graham Whitehead – who had also received an invitation and was in the same predicament as myself – I decided to go, and to worry about getting the car home afterwards. Graham was of like mind so we had our cars shipped together. His car was an Aston Martin DB3S; a car he was to race for several seasons, and in which he and his half-brother Peter were to drive into second place in the 1958 Le Mans Twenty-Four Hours. Our cars were accompanied by Robin Freeman, Bob Humphreys (a trade friend of mine) and Arthur Birks. We stripped the cars of everything which we thought might attract the attention of the local Arabs, and hoped that our equipe would prevent the taking of steering wheels, gear sticks and instruments.

Some days after our party left Antwerp, Graham and I flew to Casablanca by way of Paris and Bordeaux. We had judged things nicely, and arrived the day the cars were disembarked. A representative of the Automobile Clubs met us at the airport and, after welcoming us, explained that due to the trouble with rebels a night curfew was in operation. He escorted us to the customs and, in order to get us through as quickly as possible, asked some of the stock questions on behalf of a busy official. I committed an awful faux pas, when asked if I had anything to declare, by saying: 'Oh! Only a few guns, bombs and so on.' My joke misfired and the customs men called the police. I had to apologize to everyone before they would let us through.

There were no proper service garages in Casablanca, only motor businesses, and it was not until I ran into an old acquaintance, Guy Berthomier, that we were able to find somewhere where we could work on the cars. Guy had at one time raced a C-Type, and we had met at meetings such as Oporto, where, in fact, he had had a crash which had put him out of serious racing. He owned one of the motor businesses but with an important difference – it had a decent workshop.

Both Graham and I took the cars out for a practice round the town, and whereas he was satisfied with his I was not satisfied with mine – I appeared to be getting clutch slip. We had a spare clutch with us so I thought it would be safer to put it in the car. To change the clutch on a D-Type is no easy task for you have to begin by taking the engine out of the car; nevertheless Robin, Bob and I managed it in a day.

The hotel in which Graham and I were staying was a fabulous place with the very latest luxury equipment fitted everywhere. For example all doors and windows were opened electrically, and the bedroom telephone was a box into which you spoke, and which then appeared to answer you, rather like a personal genie. I was always getting involved with this box for I never knew when the wretched thing was working. One afternoon I was lying on my bed resting after a very good lunch when suddenly two chambermaids rushed in and changed the bed linen. I wondered what was going on until I discovered that the telephone was 'live'. It had, apparently, picked up a rather raucous naval song I had been singing. The Arab at the other end had a smattering of English which enabled him to misunderstand the song and to believe the fine tenor tone to be the rantings of an angry Englishman.

Then there was the time I ordered breakfast for Graham and myself. I ordered, in my best French, eggs, bacon and kidneys, for both of us. I repeated the order several time for the man at the other end seemed to be querying my order. Eventually, after rather a long time, there was a knock on the door and a small, sad-faced Arab came in, tears streaming down his cheeks. He was immaculately turned out: tight waistcoat, beige apron, sleeves with clean white frilly cuffs, black slippers. He carried a silver tray upon which rested two plates with silver plate covers. We had heard an explosion during the night and so presumed that the poor fellow had lost someone near and dear; he was a pitiful sight. He put the tray down on the table, then, smiling bravely through his tears, removed the plate covers with a flourish revealing the two largest onions I had ever seen. For a moment we stared in amazement.

'Two onions, sir,' he said in perfect English, 'you ordered two onions.'

'I thought I said rognons,' I suggested rather weakly.

'Yes, that is right, sir, onion.'

'Rognons.'

'Yes sir, onions. They are terrible things to peel.' He wiped his eyes with a handkerchief. 'These native onions of ours are very much bigger than the onions you have in England, it is the sun you know.'

'Your English is very good'. I said.

He bowed politely. 'Thank you sir. You are very kind. I have gone to much trouble to perfect my English in order to be of assistance to our English speaking guests. Sometimes when visitors attempt the French language they have trouble with the pronunciation of words and this leads to misunderstandings, even mistakes.' He bowed politely. 'I hope you gentlemen enjoy your onions, if there is anything else you require I am at your service.' With that he left the room.

'Well,' said Graham, 'I reckon he told you everything except what to do with them. In fact,' and he laughed, 'there's a man who knows his onions.' He would not stop laughing even when I threw them at him.

★ ★ ★

We drove in convoy from Casablanca to Agadir. It had been our intention to transport the cars on lorries because we thought the roads would be too bad for normally sprung cars. We had been told that to take a car on these roads was to risk losing a sump or back axle on a rock. In fact, there was little wrong with the road and the scenery was – at times – magnificent. It later transpired that these stories about the road had been circulated by a Frenchman who hoped to transport our cars, and the cars of fellow competitors, in his lorries. Just before we left Casablanca who should turn up but Dan Margulies and Graham Hill in my old C-Type. They joined us and we all set off for Agadir. Robin Freeman was driving the D-Type, Arthur Birks the DB3S, Margoulis the C-Type, while Graham Whitehead, Bob Humphreys, Graham Hill and myself were in a Mark VII Jaguar we had borrowed.

There was no traffic on the road save for the odd lorry and one long-range bus. In the first three hours we covered 180 miles and then drove into a swarm of locusts. The boys in the open cars had a terrible time. The horrible things were everywhere: they even flew up the carburettor air intakes of the sports cars, forcing our convoy to stop. Fortunately I had put my brushes in an old pair of Angela's nylons; the brushes came out and the stockings went over the air intakes and probably saved our engines. We drove on and presently found ourselves clear of the insects. One moment they were all about us; the next instant they had gone with incredible suddenness.

After some five hours' motoring we stopped at a village and refuelled the Mark VII. The sports cars had long-range tanks so did not need fuel. We went into the local cafe for rest and refreshment followed by all the local residents who could get through the door; those who could not waited outside. One particular character attracted our attention. He was a tall thin man in a black night-gown with a cloak which he held across his face so that only his eyes peeped over the top. He was quite mad, and walked in a most peculiar way, taking very high steps, rather in the manner of a heron. He attached himself to Graham and, when we went outside with our drinks, followed him closely. Graham told him to go away – or words to that effect – but it made no difference; he stood there as if awaiting an opportunity; worrying Graham, who was not sure what sort of an opportunity he was awaiting.

After half an hour or so we prepared to go on our way only to discover that Robin Freeman had lost the key of the D-Type. We looked around on the floor of the cafe and then in the cracks in the cobbles outside. The locals were fascinated, particularly our mad friend, who, after a loud cry of 'Ha', put his nose some six inches from the ground and, taking the same high steps, moved about in this highly complicated and distorted position. Like some Pied Piper, his antics attracted the attention of the many children there who formed up behind him and mimicked his contortional act. Even when Robin found the key in his pocket and we went to our cars our mad friend continued his unavailing search. We drove out of the town leaving them at it, feeling it was only a matter of time before the entire adult population joined in. The funny thing was none of them could have had the faintest idea what they were looking for.

Agadir was a lovely place not unlike Cannes, though of course much smaller. The race was to take place in the town and the circuit was a tortuous one; hilly and with many corners. We had known what to expect before leaving the U.K. and the D-Type had the lowest axle ratio (4.09) that I have ever fitted to a C- or D-Type Jaguar. It was in fact too low, and I left black tyre marks all over the circuit. Misfortune befell me during the first practice session when my gearbox seized solid. I was on the highest part of the circuit at the time with a long drop on to rocks on my right. As luck would have it the car spun to the left and kept spinning that way all the way round a left hand corner at the top of the hill. It finally came to rest right on the edge of a precipitous drop. I got out jolly quickly for I knew that Graham was behind me and that he would not be able to see over the hill. Fortunately he saw black tyre marks spinning over the brow and, knowing that I must have lost it, slowed down.

Thanks to the efforts of an old Frenchman who made a part for the gearbox on his lathe, and worked all night to do so, we got the car to the starting grid. This old man refused payment for what he had done, and when I tried to thrust some money on him made it quite plain that he had no intention of accepting any reward. His attitude was typical of what I have experienced all over France. They love to help *les voitures du sport*. This is not an attitude I have encountered in Britain. Unfortunately, his endeavours on my behalf, and those of Robin, Arthur and Bob – who had also worked all night – availed little for I had to retire after twelve laps with a recurrence of the same trouble. The box did not seize, but it began to stiffen up and, since I had no desire to repeat my spins of the previous day, or wreck the car, I retired.

The race was won by Mike Sparken in a Ferrari. Graham finished the race somewhere in the middle of the cars that were still running. There were several crashes and even more retirements. On the first lap I saw Picard go through a shop front backwards, and a little later a Ferrari, which was running alongside me, suddenly slid off the road and over a wall. The King of Morocco flew down from Casablanca to see the fun and had more than his money's worth: the day before the race a tornado hit the town and blew down the stands which had only just been erected. It did not last long and fortunately arrived after I had removed my car from the cliff's edge.

The Mark VII Jaguar we had borrowed in Casablanca was a ropey motor car, and on the way down to Agadir I had thought to myself several times that it would be a wonder if it managed the return trip in one piece. Various instruments had packed up, the steering left much to be desired, and the tyres were very bald: My prognosis was sound, for no sooner had we started our return journey to Casablanca than we were beset with every form of motoring vicissitude. We had five punctures – one of which nearly sent us down a ravine – a boiling radiator, the failure of virtually every instrument and accessory and, finally, a fire in the boot. We accepted the first three punctures philosophically. The first time we put on

Left: The XK that cut off the power. MDU 214, pictured after demolishing the electricity pylon at Oporto.

Below: 'Ok you chaps, let's race…' Ready for battle in the C-Type at Goodwood.

Below: 11 July 1953 at the Crystal Palace Trophy. The H.W.M. might not have had the power of the Ferraris or the Maseratis nor the agility of the Cooper-Bristols, but it was quite a handsome car. Here my ribs were still strapped after my minor Oporto shunt.

Above: 10 June 1954 – Jaguar's impressive Le Mans practice line-up of brand-new D-Types. See how the short-nose Jaguar's tailfin stopped short of the spare wheel hatch in the tail.

Below Left: Tony and Lofty, plotting Ferrari's downfall.

Below Right: OKV 1 has some scars to show after Tony had been carved up by a Talbot entering Arnage and slithered into the sandbanks. We lost over two minutes while the damage was checked and partly beaten out.

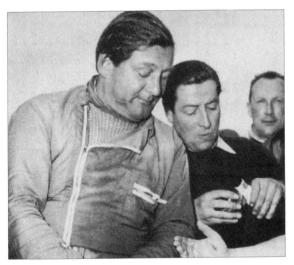

Being asked for an autograph when you've just been pipped to the post at Le Mans (in 1954) fails to lift the air of despondency. But Tony philosophically raises the Moët and, after a sip or two, we both cheer up!

Above: 'Five go on holiday together' – me, Adrian, Angela, Caroline and Joss the Springer.

Left: A drophead Coupé road car – with Peter Whitehead and the XK120. Peter's farm was at nearby Arborfield and we quite often travelled together to Continental races.

Above: I was the first private owner to acquire a D-Type Jaguar. Here we were at Agadir in 1955 leading Mike Sparken's Ferrari Monza. The whole city was subsequently tragically flattened with great loss of life in a devastating earthquake.

Below left: Oporto, 1955. George Abecassis, myself and the late Peter Whitehead.

Below right: Miami, 1956. Mike Hawthorn and myself after a good lunch.

Above: I wasn't meant to lead Paul Frere to the finish at the Rheims 12-Hours in 1956 and Lofty England fired me for it. Regardless of the furore, Ivor Bueb and I were delighted with our victory. Angela (*left*) looks a little more thoughtful…

Below: My good friend Mike Hawthorn and myself. I still have his famous peaked cap to this day.

Above: 12 April 1958 at the British Empire Trophy. There are an infinite number of ways of negotiating a corner; here I'm using full left lock around the banked right-hand hairpin at Esso Bend.

Centre: My last Le Mans – sharing with Ivor Bueb we ran second in the dry and were gaining in the wet until I rolled the car in avoiding a wandering Panhard… and woke up in a ditch.

Below: Tony Rolt and I seeing the funny side of things at Le Mans in 1953. The fun was just beginning.

Left: A moment of gravity – perhaps the bar was closed?

Below: *Cynara* – my beautiful boat.

Below: The XKC 051 – my Le Mans winner – owned by us, pictured in 1990.

the spare; the second and third times we patched the tubes. The fourth burst was a bad one and left us with only three tyres and tubes. Fortunately we had spare racing tyres and tubes of the right size but on the wrong type of wheel; Arthur and Robin somehow managed to get a racing tyre on to the Mark VII wheel and we went on. All the instruments were now useless and it was getting dark. We did not know how far we had to go for the Mark VII's speedometer had packed up and the Aston and the D-Type had the wrong axle ratios for their speedometers to mean anything. We had been warned not to travel at night on account of the terrorists who lay in wait ready to ambush any travellers.

When the fifth burst occurred it was pitch dark. We turned out all lights and Arthur and Robin set about changing a racing tyre and tube from one size of wheel to another in the dark. While they were doing this Graham and I kept watch for terrorists. Margulies and Hill were not with us on this return trip, and Bob Humphreys had gone back ahead of us with Guy Berthomier in his D.K.W. We had expected to catch them up but our punctures had prevented us from doing so. My stomach had been bothering me and I had had to stop and disappear behind a hedge from time to time all day. Feeling another attack coming on I climbed over the wall at the side of the road and wandered a few yards into the scrub land with which this part of the world abounds. While attending to my wants I was suddenly disturbed to hear the sound of heavy breathing. I remained perfectly still; my hair stood on end. I pictured a swarthy Arab, a knife in his teeth, creeping below the level of the wall waiting for the opportunity to pounce and kill. Plucking up all my courage I jumped to my feet and, shouting 'Look out chaps', ran for my life full tilt into a curious camel who had undoubtedly been attracted by the noise Arthur and Robin were making on the road, and had come over for a *shufti*.

The tyre changed, we motored on, though it was obvious from the way the car was performing that it would only be a matter of time before something else went wrong. When the engine began to seize up no one was really surprised. We stopped, and discovered – by torchlight – that the radiator hose had sprung a leak and that the radiator had run dry. We had some drinking water with us and, after repairing the hose, poured it into the radiator. We then added two bottles of Lager and the contents of a brandy flask but we still needed more liquid before we could consider going on. There was only one thing left to do and Arthur was the first to do it. Arthur is not a tall man, and it was not easy for him, particularly standing on the bumper bar in the dark. He swayed slightly and allowed a part of his body to rest, for a moment, on the red-hot header tank. The scream that rent the air was both effeminate and terrifying; I for one thought someone had cut his throat. However, like all good pioneers, he had the satisfaction of knowing that those who followed him had profited by his mistake, and were, by taking an elementary precaution, able to avoid the awful consequences of a sway forwards.

An hour or so later we came upon Bob Humphreys and Guy Berthomier. They had been held up when the D.K.W. they were following, which was being driven by a friend of Guy's, had crashed; Guy's friend had been killed. Poor Bob was particularly distressed for the accident had been a very unpleasant one. We followed them into Casablanca but before we got there a metal box in the boot of the Mark VII fell on a spare racing battery we were carrying causing a short which set fire to the contents of the boot. By the time we knew about it a good old blaze was under way, and when I lifted the bootlid flames shot high into the air. It was a wonder the petrol tanks did not go up. There are two in the Mark VII, one on each side of the boot. We threw sand – which fortunately was plentiful – on to the flames and managed to douse them, but not before the paintwork of the car had suffered. When we returned the car to its owner he was very upset. As he put it: 'Nothings in her works. You have made fires in ze boot; and ze radiator, she smells 'orrible.'

* * *

Graham and I had a very enjoyable week in Casablanca. We visited places like Fedala and Rabat, the seat of the Moroccan Government, where we purchased carpets, rugs, silverware and interesting African curios. There was a certain amount of terrorist activity in the area and the curfew was strictly enforced. We were always forgetting about the curfew and had our moments in getting back to the hotel in the early hours. One evening, after being entertained by two charming French girls in their flat, and after drinking all their booze, we found ourselves walking through the streets of Casablanca at one in the morning. I felt the sensible way to proceed was to move from doorway to doorway and keep in the shadows. Graham, on the other hand, thought it best to walk boldly down the middle of the road. His argument was that his presence would be obvious to a French patrol, from whom he had nothing to fear so far as his life was concerned, and that no one could suddenly jump on him out of a doorway. I saw point in his reasoning, but also saw that it would be easy for some terrorist to take a pot at him. My method did render me liable to surprise attack but I was not a sitting target.

Any observers must have found our progress interesting; Graham, his feet pounding the road, sending echoes down the deserted streets; I, desperately trying to keep up with him, moving noisily through the shadows as I fell over dustbins and trod on the odd cat. Eventually I gave it all up and joined him in the middle of the road. We marched briskly, and in step, whistling 'Colonel Bogey', all the way to our hotel. We neither saw nor heard a living soul. Where the French patrols were I do not know. We were inclined, the following morning, to scoff at the whole idea of terrorists until we heard that a car had been machine gunned on the outskirts of the town and that its four occupants had been killed.

Shortly after hearing of the previous night's assassinations we were having our 'elevenses' (large whiskies and soda on this particular occasion) in the main bar of our hotel when a Frenchman got into conversation with us. He told us that we must go to the Sphinx at Fedala. 'It is the most interesting place in Morocco,' he said, 'the parade is wonderful. Remember to ask to see the parade.' We thanked him for the information and after lunch set off, in a hired car, to see this fabulous place. Quite a surprise was in store for us.

Fedala is some fifteen kilometres from Casablanca; it is not a big place, and it did not take us long to find the Sphinx. All the Frenchman had said about this hotel appeared to be true. It stood in lovely grounds, in a commanding position, overlooking the sea. We parked the car and, after climbing some steps, entered the foyer. It was sumptuous. One might have been in a king's palace. Fine rugs and carpets partly covered a beautiful mosaic floor; Moorish furniture, perfectly in keeping with the atmosphere of prevailing luxury, graced this hall; fine tapestries hung from the walls. In one corner there was a bar, in another an orchestra played soft music; we were enchanted. Everywhere there were beautiful women, some with men, but the majority of them were unescorted. A charming middle-aged lady approached. 'Unless I am very much mistaken you are English gentlemen?' We nodded. 'How very nice for us, we do so like to entertain our countrymen.' The 'we' was explained by the arrival of another woman of the same age.

'What would you like to do first, Mr. er....'

'Hamilton' I said. 'This is Mr. Whitehead.'

'How do you do Mr. Whitehead. I am Miss Mary, this', she indicated her companion 'is Miss Gladys.' Miss Gladys was positively gushing.

'I believe I know who you are' she said excitedly, 'you are racing drivers.' We agreed that was so. 'Well now,' said Miss Mary, 'what would you like to do first?' I looked at Graham and wondered if he was thinking what I was thinking.

'I think we would like to have a drink,' I said.

'A very good idea, come this way.' Miss Mary led us over to the bar.

'What's going on?' Graham whispered to me as we crossed the floor. I shook my head. I did not know. Something was going on, of course, but that is not unusual in an African hotel. We ordered our drinks and took them to one of the little tables nearby. Miss Mary and Miss Gladys smiled their approval and left us to our own devices for the time being. At the table next to ours sat a very lovely looking girl drinking alone. I was wondering whether she might be English or not when she called to the barman, 'Jimmy, bring me the same again.' While the Moroccan behind the bar dealt with her request I got up and went over to her table.

'Excuse me,' I said politely, 'but are you English?' She looked up, a half amused expression on her face, 'Yes, Mr. Hamilton, I am.'

'How did you know my name?'

'I read the papers. They all carried photographs of you after the race at Agadir.'

'Won't you join us and allow us to buy you a drink?' She hesitated for a moment.

'You mean I have a choice?' I must have looked very puzzled for she threw back her head and laughed, 'Tell me who sent you here?'

'A man we met in our hotel in Casablanca.'

'What did he tell you about the Sphinx?'

'He said it was an interesting place.'

'Nothing else?'

'Nothing else.'

'You must know this is no ordinary hotel, don't tell me you haven't guessed!'

'It is, is it?' I enquired, a trifle self-consciously.

'It is.' She looked at me, and then at Graham.

How beautiful she was in her blue dress with little white polka dots scattered here and there around and across the material. The dress matched the colour of her eyes, and her auburn hair hung long about her shoulders. She was no more than twenty years old.

'Then what are you doing here?' I asked.

'I work here,' she said simply, 'does that surprise you?'

'Nothing surprises me,' I said untruthfully.

The barman brought her drink to the table along with the 'same again' for Graham and myself.

'Where do you come from?' I asked, wanting to change the subject. She mentioned a country town in England. 'Do your parents know what you are doing?'

'My parents! Good heavens, no. My father is the vicar.'

Neither Graham nor I quite knew what to say next; we never doubted but that what she had just said was true. An uncomfortable silence followed. It did not seem the moment for a Hamiltonian epigram. She was quite unabashed, however, and without any sign of embarrassment told us how she had first come to this part of the world some two years before. The life was easy; the money good. There was swimming, sailing, high living and men. 'I like men,' she said quite simply, as if to say: 'This is my chosen vocation.' By the time she had finished her story both Graham and I had downed a fair number of doubles, so many in fact that the arrival of Miss Mary with the news that the 'Parade' was about to commence was greeted with alacrity. Neither of us knew what the parade was going to be, and we had consumed sufficient alcohol not to care.

Miss Mary led us down a long corridor and, eventually, into a small room. In one corner of the room there was what appeared to be a mirror: it was in fact a one-way mirror. We could look through it into the next room; the people in the next room could only see their reflection when they looked at the same piece of glass. The room we looked into was quite large, and was, we learned, surrounded by cubicles similar to our own. Suddenly a door at the end of this room opened and in trooped some thirty girls, naked, save for their high heeled shoes. The vicar's daughter was one of them.

'Just make your choice, gentlemen,' said Miss Mary.

Graham and I looked at one another; the whole set up was

becoming a bit dodgy. We had to get out of this place, but without annoying anyone.

'What about the film show you mentioned?' I said playing for time. 'I'm very fond of the cinema, it takes you out of yourself.'

She looked very disappointed. 'Don't you want any girls? I thought you wanted girls.'

'Later, perhaps,' I suggested. 'It's very early.'

'Oh, all right, come with me.'

We followed her down more corridors till we arrived at the cinema. Miss Gladys was there, a triumphant smile on her face; I wondered how often she triumphed over her companion. Was it perhaps that her films pandered to man's illusions, that she left them with their little dreams; whereas Miss Mary's world of reality offered them fulfilment and disillusionment in the same breath, reality destroying the myths and exposing the foibles of the curious mind with the cruelty of which only truth is capable?

The film was called *The New Secretary*. We saw it through, paid our bill, and left with our illusions still intact; which is more than most people have been able to do after visiting the Sphinx at Fedala.

★ ★ ★

I awoke next morning in a cold sweat. A noise was ringing in my ears, and my head felt as if someone was attacking it with a pneumatic drill. I did not feel able to open my eyes and it was only the timely arrival of Graham that prevented the drill penetrating my skull. The noise I had heard and the sensation I had experienced were in no way connected with the drink I had consumed the previous evening; they were much closer to fact: an Arab workman had actually drilled a hole through the wall just above my head, and the dust and plaster that had fallen and rested on my face had contributed to the feeling I had on awaking that I was not well. Mind you, I was not exactly fit – as I discovered when I jumped out of bed. The workman was part of a labour force who were working on improving the amenities of the hotel and, apart from the fact that he had drilled his hole in the wrong wall, he meant no harm.

We flew down to Dakar in a Super Constellation and arrived there the same day as our cars and mechanics who had travelled down by boat. Neither of us felt very well and after an early meal we decided to turn in. The hotel was comfortable and in a good quarter of the town; nevertheless, when the native population came alive at about eleven p.m. we could hear them. The noise was dreadful: they appeared to laugh and sing all night. The local cats also contributed to the din, courting one another up and down and over every surrounding roof. I became so exasperated that I went out on to my balcony and, seizing the pots of cacti with which it abounded, bombarded these amorous stalkers of the night. The hotel management took a poor view of this and presented me with a hefty bill for flower pots the next morning.

A friend of mine, Jacques Pecquer, had offered to let Graham and me use his garage in Dakar, both as a place to keep and to prepare our cars. When we went round to see him we were surprised to find that the place was still being built. However such was the labour force available that this building, which was some 800 by 200 feet, was not only finished, but painted, twenty-four hours later.

We had to change the back-axle ratios on both cars, for

Dakar's circuit was as fast as Agadir's was slow. It consisted of two straights – one with a slight kink in it – and two rounded 50 mph corners at each end. One way was slightly uphill, the other slightly down. These two roads were separated by a narrow grass verge, so that if a car was to burst a tyre and cross the verge the possibility of a head-on collision with a car travelling on the other straight was very real.

We put a 2.75 cog in the D-Type and fitted seventeen-inch wheels. The engine pulled 6,500 rpm in top gear – round about 200 mph. In bottom gear 80 mph was available. Poor Graham found that the Aston was quite outclassed on this circuit having, as it did, a maximum of only 160 mph. On the other hand I saw that the Ferraris of Carini and Rosier, and the Maserati of Behra, were as fast as the D-Type. They did not have the top speed, but their five-speed gearboxes gave them a better getaway from the start and more acceleration out of the two corners. Their top speed was about 190-195 mph whereas the D-Type would do a genuine 200 mph.

The D-Type handled beautifully in practice; it was wonderfully stable at top speed. The only thing that concerned me was that the tyres were feathering when I braked for the corners. Although Dunlop had sent their Paris representative along to advise me there was not a lot he could suggest. No race had ever been held at these speeds in this temperature before. I decided that, no matter what happened as a result, I would come into the pit after twenty laps for a tyre check. I did, and the stop cost me a certain second place and possibly a first.

The race was started at five o'clock in the afternoon, but even so the shade temperature was ninety degrees Fahrenheit. I did not make a fast start: I could not with the axle ratio fitted. There was a strong smell of burning clutch lining and I chugged away after the fast Ferraris. The car soon got into its stride, however, and by the time we reached the end of the first straight I was up with the leaders. Carini and Behra duelled together almost to the end when Behra suddenly went out with engine trouble. Just behind them Rosier and I either drove side-by-side or slipstreamed one another all the way round. We were so close together that I could read his rev counter. He was a past-master of slip-streaming another car and it took me some eighteen laps to get away from him. Once I had got away I was able to open up a gap, and once I had opened up a gap I was loath to stop for a tyre check at twenty laps, but discipline is very necessary when you go motor racing so I came in for my check. It only took a few seconds, for my tyres were all right, but the time taken in slowing down and then accelerating away again was sufficient for him to pass me. Although I was catching him when the race ended I could not get by and had to be content with third place. The way in which the Ferrari's drum brakes remained effective surprised me. Both Carini and Rosier had to reduce speed by some 150 mph at the end of each straight and managed it without difficulty. Rosier actually put up the fastest lap on his last time round. 1 had hoped their brakes would begin to fade so that I could use the D-Type's discs to advantage. Mind you, I could brake later than they did, but lost advantage to their five-speed gearboxes on the corners. The winner's average speed was 190.783 kilometres per hour; this was the fastest sports car race ever run up to that time.

★ ★ ★

We had great difficulty in making arrangements to ship the cars to England, and in the end had to leave it to friends to do what they could to get the cars away some time. Graham and I flew back to London Airport by way of Paris wondering when we would see our cars again. The first race of the new home season was to be for the British Empire Trophy at Oulton Park. Before leaving Dakar we took the precaution of changing the axle ratios so that should the cars arrive just before this meeting we would be able to race them without having to take down the back axles.

As things turned out this was a wise precaution for they arrived at Bristol three days before the race. Robin Freeman went down to collect the D-Type and ran into all kinds of trouble. Half the car's papers had been left in Dakar and it took a whole day to sort things out with the customs.

His troubles were not yet over for he was stopped by a police car in Bristol and summonsed for, (a) not having a proper silencer; since the law does not state what a proper silencer is and the silencer fitted was the standard one the police dropped this charge: (b) The number being painted on a curved surface; after it was pointed out to them that there was no flat surface on or near the nose they dropped this one also: (c) The car not being taxed; after I had explained that the car had been in Africa for three months they took a lenient view of this last, admitted, technical offence, and after a friendly exchange of letters the whole thing was dropped.

We had very little time to prepare the car for the Trophy race and it did not handle too well. The shock absorbers had taken a fearful pounding in Africa and we did not have time to fit new ones. All in all I was pleased to finish second to Mike Sparken's Ferrari in the heat for cars of 2,700 cc upwards. The track was wet and several cars spun off. There was also an accident which might have been more serious than it was when the Jaguars of Berry and Kelly touched. Kelly's car left the road, demolished a B.B.C. commentator's box and injured three officials. Kelly and the three officials were all hospital cases; his car was completely wrecked. I was fourth in the early stages behind the Ferrari, the Aston Martin of Peter Collins and Ninian Sanderson's C-Type.

The combination of wet track and weak shock-absorbers was disconcerting on this circuit and it took me six laps to pass Ninian, and three more before I could get by Peter. The final was, of course, on handicap, and was won by Archie Scott-Brown in a Lister-Bristol from Ken McAlpine's 1.5-litre Connaught; Reg Parnell's 2.6 litre Aston Martin was third. I was seventh overall and second in my class to Dick Shattock's R.G.S. Atalanta — a glass-fibre bodied Jaguar-engined special.

Angela had travelled up to Chester with me; we stayed at the Grosvenor where — as usual — they did their best to ensure that we were comfortable. All in all we had a very pleasant weekend. Graham's Aston did not run very well and he had to be content with twelfth place in the final. Neither of our cars were capable of their best performance after Africa and the sea journey, so perhaps we should not have raced them; on the other hand we had some good sport and a pleasant weekend, which was the real object of the exercise, so really there was nothing for us to complain about.

Robin drove the car back to Byfleet and worked on it all week to get it ready for Goodwood the following weekend. This was the Easter Meeting when the racing took place on the Monday. In the sports car race for cars of over 2,000 cc, I found myself on the front line beside Mike Sparken. Both of us were watching one another rather than the starter's flag, and when he went off I followed. The Duke of

Richmond and Gordon said that it was the only time he had seen two cars in top gear before the flag fell. We were both penalized fifteen seconds; this penalty just allowed Roy Salvadori to pip Mike for first place and myself for second. Roy was driving a DB3S. Roy had a very successful day winning three races: the Lavant Cup in a Connaught; the Glover Trophy in a Maserati; and the race I have just mentioned. A thing I particularly remember about this meeting was Peter Collins's handling of the very fast supercharged 1.5-litre B.R.M. in the Formule Libre race. He was now beginning to show signs of the greatness that was to follow.

A few days later I was back on the Continent. This time in Paris to defend the Coupe de Paris. The D-Type was at its best, and after recording the fastest time in practice I was very confident. The Marquis de Portago, driving Rosier's old 4.5-litre Ferrari (the car in which Rosier had won the AN G.P. two years previously) now converted to sports car specification, and Picard in a Ferrari 750S, appeared to be the only serious opposition, particularly when Andre Pilette had trouble with the 3-litre eight-cylinder Gordini and the car was withdrawn after practice.

However, I had not reckoned on the determination of the organizers to see a French car win. They announced just before the race that Pilette would be driving a Formula 1 G.P. 2.5-litre Gordini, and that this car − which had not practised − would share the front row of the grid with Portago and myself. Portago and I protested, but it was to no avail. In the end we accepted the position, which was perhaps a mistake on our part − we should have insisted that the Gordini start on the backrow of the grid. The maximum speed of the Jaguar was equal to that of the Gordini, but the latter car, being lighter, had better acceleration. Pilette was first away at the start, but I passed him on the straight and held him on the banking; he passed me on the inside going into the hairpin, and with his lower axle and lighter weight pulled away out of the corner. I hung on, however, and hunted him right to the end. The D-Type handled beautifully and none of the other sports cars could touch it. The Gordini won at an average speed of 100.05 mph; I was second at 99.5 mph. Picard was third in his Ferrari, and Portago fourth. Poor Andre was very apologetic afterwards and insisted that we dine together that evening. I was only too happy to agree, and we had a very pleasant meal before doing the night clubs. The next day I changed the plugs in the D-Type, checked the oil and water and drove home via Dieppe and Newhaven.

I was due to drive a works Jaguar at the Silverstone International Meeting on May 7th so lent my D-Type to Michael Head to drive at Djurgard Park, Helsinki, on the 8th. He took the car over there and won the sports car race for the third time. He had previously been successful in 1952 in his XK120, and in 1954 with a C-Type.

Just before I left home for Silverstone a telegram arrived from Amedee Gordini asking me if I would drive one of the three Formula I cars he had entered for the International Trophy event. I was delighted to accept for I appreciated what an honour it was to receive such an invitation: Gordini had never asked a British driver to drive one of his cars before.

My efforts to get into the tiny Gordini amused everyone in the pit area. A local wag remarked that he had heard of a pea on a drum, but that he had never seen a drum on a pea until now. The Gordini was quite a crisp little car with a strong smell of Castrol R. The engine did not produce the power that Maserati and Ferrari could muster, but against that it was so light that the acceleration was quite good. It was outclassed on a really fast circuit, but could give a good account of itself where the corners were many. The most disconcerting thing about it was the handling at speed. It appeared to jump all over the place; if you threw it about it hopped rather than drifted.

After four laps to get the feel of things I really began to motor. I did two quite fast laps, and then, the next time round, just after I had passed under the members' bridge and was braking for the corner (speed about 120 mph) the back axle locked up and the car flew off the track. It hit an earth barricade going backwards; somersaulted a couple of times throwing me out, then fell on top of me. The cut-away part round the cockpit rested across my body. Fortunately I had landed on soft ground and was not too badly hurt; the arrival of the car on top of me changed things rather for the car rolled slightly bringing the red hot exhaust near to my face. I pushed it away with my gloved hands only to see that fuel was running out of the tank. It was a very nasty moment. Luckily for me the marshals and other helpers were soon on the scene and they rolled the car off me. I then discovered that there were two spectators on the cool side of the car. Both had received minor injuries.

I went back to the pit feeling a bit twitchy and asked Lofty England if I could go out and practise in my team car. Reluctantly he agreed and, within twenty minutes of my crash, I set up the fastest sports car time of the day. I felt I had to go straight out again just to prove to myself that I could do it. The Gordini was not repairable so it was left to team drivers Trintignant and Manzon to represent the make on the morrow. I went to hospital to have my left foot X-rayed – it had been hurt in the crash – and then to John Ansel's pub, the Jersey Arms at Middleton Stoney where Angela and I always stayed. Mike Hawthorn was also there, and despite my prang I was in good form that evening. I did not feel so good the next morning, however, and knew only too well that I had been in a crash; still I drove in the sports car race and finished fifth. A week later, while driving home from my business in Byfleet, I noticed two white lines on the road, then I saw a Vanguard with four stop lights. I was near Michael Head's house at the time so stopped and sought assistance. They looked after me for a while and then took me home; I was in bed for two weeks. My trouble was a kind of delayed concussion.

I did not waste my time while in bed but designed a caravan which I used for ages. My idea was to take it to Le Mans where accommodation during the race was very primitive. In the end my brain-child was a twenty-seven foot caravan fitted with all modern conveniences and capable of sleeping eight in comfort. Because it was over twenty-two feet in length I had to inform the police when I moved it about in this country.

Before going to Le Mans I had a very successful Whit-Monday at Goodwood winning both my heat and the final of the Johnson Trophy. I also set up what was at that time the fastest sports car lap, 86.22 mph, for the circuit. Bob Berry, in another D-Type, was second, sixteen seconds behind me; Dick Protheroe was third in a C-Type. This success proved that I had now recovered from the Silverstone accident, and that I was fit to drive at Le Mans. Indeed, I was looking forward to it, for I knew that the latest works D-Type was an even better car than its predecessor, and that had most certainly been no slouch.

CHAPTER THIRTEEN

THE KING AND I

Using my Mark VII Jaguar, Angela and I towed the caravan to Le Mans. Apart from the fact that British Railways did ninety pounds worth of damage to the caravan when loading it our journey was uneventful. We stopped in Rouen for an evening meal and, while we were eating, four young Frenchmen came over and wished me luck in the race. They told us that for the last three years they had always watched the race from a point just opposite the Jaguar pit; they intended to be there again this year and asked that we look out for them. We drove on to Le Mans, to learn on arriving there that young John Lyons had been killed in a road accident just outside Cherbourg that afternoon. This news made us very sad for he was a charming boy. We were staying with Madame Lamotte as usual and as soon as I had dropped my luggage I went round to the Paris hotel to see Lofty England. He had left for the scene of the accident, but Mrs. Heynes was there and she told me how both she and

Mrs. Lyons had had the same dream on the same night some days previously. They had dreamt that both Tony and I had been killed at Le Mans. She meant to relate their dreams to John's accident and did not appreciate that she gave me much to think about. The meal Angela and I had at the Bec Fin that night was both sad and sober.

The new D-Type had a much longer nose to improve air penetration and also new slots to help brake cooling. The comfort of the cockpit was improved: there was more elbow room and the new wrap-round screen gave good protection even on the Mulsanne straight. The cylinder head and the exhaust system were new and the engine was giving 285 bhp at 5,750 rpm. We also had a new high axle ratio: 2.53, giving 33.9 mph per 1,000 rpm in top gear. The cars handled well and all our team drivers were pleased with them. Mercedes were racing their 300 SLR sports cars. These cars were fitted with the revolutionary air brakes, and very effective they were too. During a practice session I came up behind Fangio and followed him round a couple of times hoping to learn something of his car's performance. Fangio was too canny to give much away, but nevertheless his car exceeded 170 mph down the Mulsanne straight. The first time the air brake came up I was more than surprised at the way it slowed the car. I braked hard at around 170 mph; Fangio did not touch his foot brake until after he had changed into third; in other words, the air brake slowed his car from 170 mph down to about 140 mph as quickly as the Jaguar's discs slowed it. Thus the Mercedes drivers had no need to use their drum brakes above 140 mph. Since the heat build-up and rate of wear is greatest at the higher speeds their air brake was going not only to increase the efficiency of their brakes but to extend the life of the linings as well. I reported my findings to Lofty England only to learn from him that, although their brakes might last twenty-four hours of racing, their clutches were very suspect. They were having trouble with their team cars in practice and spies had reported great concern in the Mercedes pit.

Tony made a bad start; the engine would not fire, and in the end he was the last car away but one. He was soon making up ground, however, and by the end of the first hour was quite nicely placed. The outstanding feature of the race was the duel between Fangio and Mike Hawthorn. For the first few laps Castellotti led in a Ferrari, a few feet in front of Mike who had Fangio breathing down his neck. Castellotti broke the lap record on his second lap, Fangio lowered it on the sixth, then Mike put it still lower. The crowd was wild with excitement. Fangio went faster and faster, breaking the lap record time and again, until presently he was in the lead with Mike close behind him. For two hours it went on like this and then both Fangio and Mike came in to refuel. I was standing on the counter with Angela at my side, waiting to take over from Tony, when I saw the four French boys who had spoken to us in Rouen standing on the other side of the track waving to us. We both waved back, and then, suddenly, a Mercedes was flying through the air like some great silver fish. It threshed its way through the crowd, exploded, and burst into flames. Pierre 'Levegh' was dead on the road, thrown from the somersaulting car.

A gendarme lay dead at my feet, hit by something, I know not what. A photographer and another man were also on the ground. The scene on the other side of the road was indescribable; the dead and dying were everywhere; the cries of pain, anguish and despair screamed catastrophe. I stood as if in a dream, too horrified even to think; then suddenly Tony arrived in the D–Type. I jumped down from the counter. 'Look after the girls,' I said. He nodded and went to Angela and Lois. A mechanic refuelled the car. I stepped over the gendarme, jumped into the car and was away. I do not want to comment further on this terrible accident; enough has been written already; there is nothing I can usefully add.

The race went on and developed into a duel between Mercedes and Jaguar as the Ferraris dropped out. By midnight, Tony and I were fourth behind Fangio, Mike, and Fitch in the other Mercedes. We were gaining on all of them and, in the last hour prior to the Mercedes withdrawal, we actually covered fourteen laps to the other car's thirteen laps. At one forty-five a.m. Mercedes, on orders from Germany, stopped racing, leaving Mike in the lead with ourselves second. Shortly after this Tony began to experience gearbox trouble. We lost first and second gears and, though we might have staggered on for a time, the strain on the engine of pulling a 2.53 axle on top and third gears only would have led to serious cylinder head trouble. Wisely, in my opinion, Lofty withdrew the car from the race. As a matter of interest, our third gear ratio was only 3.23, higher in fact than the 3.54 standard top gear ratio fitted to a production D–Type. Normally we would never use the 3.23 third gear under 120 mph.

The result of the race was:

1st Hawthorn/Bueb. Jaguar, distance 2594.225 miles.

2nd Collins/Frere. Aston Martin, distance 2530.862 miles.

3rd Swaters/Claes. Jaguar, distance 2487.515 miles.

Fourth, fifth and sixth places were taken by 1.5-litre Porsches; a wonderful performance by these fine little cars.

The fastest lap of the race was Mike's at 122.38; he put in this lap shortly before the accident. This was not a Le Mans I want to remember.

★ ★ ★

After Le Mans I drove, as usual, down to Portugal, for the G.P. of Oporto. And after five years of trying I eventually survived the race without personal injury or mechanical trouble. The D-Type went very well and I finished third behind the very fast 3-litre Maserati of Jean Behra and the 3-litre Ferrari of Masten Gregory. Peter Whitehead's Cooper-Jaguar was fourth.

We had left the caravan at Le Mans in readiness for a holiday in Brittany. After a quick trip home to pick up the children we went back to Le Mans, collected the caravan and took it down to Hervé Coatalen's house on the Brittany coast where we spent a very happy two months. Michael and Joan Head and their children joined us for part of the time, and I paid a short visit to Lisbon to compete in the Sports Car G.P. The car had been overhauled and repainted in Oporto, and very pretty it looked. I found, however, that it had the wrong cog in the back axle for this circuit and sent a wire to Coventry asking for another one. It duly arrived and by working all night we fitted it in time for the race. In fitting it, however, we had disturbed the brakes and they failed during the race with frightening consequences.

I made a good start and led the first time round. Then, on braking for a corner, I sensed, rather than felt, that my brakes were not quite right. Baron de Graffenried passed me in his Maserati and for three laps I followed him closely. Then, as the car's braking efficiency deteriorated, I fell back. I should have stopped and investigated the cause of the trouble, but I did not, with the result that the brakes failed completely, and though I managed to turn down an escape road, and duck under a wire which some thoughtful person had left at head height, I could not stop the car until I was in the middle of the town surrounded by trams, buses, taxis and cars. I had changed down through the gears and then switched off the engine, but the car still went a very long way before it stopped. People scattered in front of me, and a horse carrying a mounted policeman reared up on its hind legs and allowed me to pass underneath its flying hooves, one of which dented my crash helmet. We found out afterwards that a jack had pinched a copper pipe while Robin was changing the axle ratio, causing a fracture which led to hydraulic failure. All in all, quite an experience.

The race was won by Masten Gregory in a 3-litre Ferrari only two-fifths of a second in front of Baron de Graffenried's Maserati; Godia-Sales in another Ferrari was third.

I did not race again until the Grand National meeting at Silverstone in September, when I won the twenty-lap sports car race in the D-Type. Michael Head was second in another D-Type which I had recently bought. My son Adrian, who was at this time seven years old, drove an Austin pedal car in a children's race that the promoters had arranged. Unfortunately, he had a shunt early on when a female competitor cut across in front of him. He was stationary for some seconds and was never able to get up among the leaders. The race was won by eight-year-old Edward French, a nephew of Reg Bicknell.

At Goodwood, the following Saturday, I was again successful with the D-Type, and then on the Sunday went up to Snetterton for the last meeting of the season and made it three in a row. Before the race started I had debated whether or not to change the near-side rear tyre: there was not quite as much tread on it as I like to see. I decided it would be all right for the race and told Robin not to bother to change it. George Abecassis borrowed my other D-Type and finished second some three and a half seconds behind me. Just as I was about to cross the finishing line the rear tyre burst; the car spun round and crossed the line going backwards. This was the only occasion I have won a race with the nose of the car pointing in the wrong direction.

I had another spectacular spin in the Invitation Handicap. After setting up the fastest lap time of the day (87.3 mph) I overdid it a bit on the last lap and spun right off the track. I had to be content with fourth place; Colin Chapman won on handicap in his Lotus-Climax.

Because of the Le Mans tragedy there was no racing at Montlhery during the Paris Motor Show week and for me, at any rate, the season did not so much end as peter out.

The day after the Snetterton Meeting I lunched with King Feisal. He asked me to come in the D-Type, and this I did. The police were expecting me and allowed me to leave the car in Brook Street outside the main entrance of Claridges where the King always stayed. This annoyed the owner of a Bentley whom they had just moved on; he would not believe I could be calling on the King in such a car. I had understood that we were lunching at Claridges, but the King decided that we would go to the Coq D'Or so that he could give me a run in his new red Mercedes 300SL. The distance between Claridges and the Coq D'Or was about half a mile: our time for the journey was about thirty seconds. There was nowhere to park in Stratton Street so the King stopped the car in the middle of the road and got out. He must have read concern in my face for he laughed and said: 'One of my chauffeurs will park it.' With that, a Mark VII Jaguar, which had presumably taken forty-five seconds for the same journey as ourselves, drew up and one of four chauffeurs got out and drove the Mercedes away. As was usual when we visited the Coq D'Or the entire dining room staff lined up, and most of the other diners stood.

During the course of this lunch I was commanded to go for some long drives with the King, and also to arrange for an aerodrome circuit to be put at his disposal. The drives were very good fun. The first one was to Bath and back and the King drove very well and very, very fast. He constantly asked me questions and was both keen and willing to improve his driving technique. When we went to an aerodrome he would ask me to drive, to show him how to take such and such a bend, to change gear without using the clutch, how to correct an incipient skid, and so on. He was most attentive and never missed a point. He would sit unflinchingly beside me when I was cornering on the limit, a thing not many people have been able to do. He had excellent nerves and never panicked. I remember once down at Odiham aerodrome he lost it completely and we spun round and round on a very wet track. When we stopped gyrating he said: 'See Duncan, I have kept the engine running'. Then he made me take over and show him exactly what he had done wrong. The hours I spent with this charming and unassuming man have left indelible memories in my mind.

On one occasion when I was lunching with Feisal at Claridges he announced that he would like to see my home and to meet some of my friends. This was more or less a Royal Command to throw a party, and of course I obliged.

The King had a penchant for oysters, and since he did not eat meat I decided to concentrate on sea food. The date of the party was fixed by the King, and Angela and I got on with the preparations. Before we had got very far the inspector of police in charge of the bodyguard the British Government provided for the King phoned and asked for a list of the people I proposed inviting to the party. A couple of days later he phoned to let me know the time and nature of the King's arrival. Feisal would drive down to Wokingham in his Mercedes 300SL. Colonel Kassem, his chief of Air Staff, would follow in the first of two Mark VII Jaguars; the second one would be carrying personal staff and police. The Wokingham police were warned and they patrolled the grounds of my house while the party went on.

Feisal appeared to enjoy himself: he ate six dozen large oysters and stayed until one fifteen a.m. All my friends liked him, and what had started off as a rather formal obligation ended up as a very good party. I noticed the displeasure in Kassem's eyes when the King told us how, in order to satisfy his insatiable desire for oysters, he had planes in his Air Force fitted with sea-water tanks and then sent crews on training flights to England. 'In this way, two aims are achieved,' said Feisal, 'my air crews get the training they need, and I get my Whitstable oysters.'

I remember another occasion in London when Colonel Kassem, the present ruler of Iraq, was present. Feisal told me he had just bought a Flying Box Car and, when I asked him why, he laughed and told me that he needed it for transporting his Mercedes 300SL from Baghdad to Syria. 'The roads are not very good between Baghdad and Beirut, not good enough to allow me to drive the Mercedes fast. So when I go to Syria I fly, and my car flies also; I do not like to be without my Mercedes, that is why I have bought a Flying Box Car'. I saw Kassem's eyes flash with anger, and the members of the King's entourage exchanged the most significant glances; of all this Feisal appeared completely unaware. I remember telling Angela that something was going on behind the King's back, and that Kassem was a man to be reckoned with. 'Poor mad Kassem,' Feisal would say, 'a good officer, but slightly crazy'. Feisal never saw Kassem as the usurper of his power and authority, of that I am sure. When the end came it must have been a terrible shock for him.

Once he wrote and asked Angela and I to spend Christmas with him in his new palace in Baghdad . . . 'If it is ready in time'. I wrote back thanking him for the invitation, then added: 'If the new palace is not ready I am sure we will be comfortable in the old one'. Feisal loved my little joke and he subsequently told it, in my presence, on a number of occasions. In actual fact Angela and I did not go to Baghdad for Christmas: we felt we should be with our children at that time of the year. Feisal quite understood our reasons, and it was left that he should invite us again at a more convenient time. His assassination came before another invitation, and though he may well have had his faults – and who has not – he did not deserve to die as he did – in the hands of revolutionaries.

I see, from my diary, that I paid one more visit to a race track before the end of the year, and that by helicopter. On Boxing Day I descended, dressed as Father Christmas, on Brands Hatch. Why, I am not quite sure; the diary does not say. It does record, however: '.... roast pork and an excellent rum punch'. Clearly this was no wasted journey.

★ ★ ★

Jaguars again engaged my services as a team driver for the 1956 season. Mike Hawthorn was also in the team, and from as early as January 17th we were testing the new fuel-injection cars. Most of this testing was done at Silverstone and Mike and I used to fly up there in his plane. I bought a new D-Type from the works for my own use and sold 'OKV 1' to Jumbo Goddard, after first converting it to a true road car. We removed the fairing from behind the driver's head, fitted a full-width windscreen and a hood, put carpets on the floor, and generally speaking made the car more comfortable for everyday use. When the works at Coventry saw it they promptly announced a new model: the Jaguar XKSS.

I was driving, once again, in the G.P. of Dakar. I thought it best not to bother about the Agadir race, in view of transport difficulties, and to concentrate on Dakar. I was going to drive my older D-Type so lent the new one to Graham Whitehead. The plane in which I flew from Paris to Casablanca had undercarriage trouble and, since the Prime Minister of Morocco was on board, there was a fearful panic. Eventually the undercarriage came down and we were able to land, much to the relief of the Prime Minister and his entourage.

After our experience of the previous year, Graham and I booked into an hotel outside Dakar. This hotel, the Nigor, was comfortable and quiet. Our cars and mechanics were already in Dakar having gone out from England by boat. This year we had the new Le Mans axle ratio fitted: 2.53, and to raise the gearing still higher we were using seventeen-inch wheels at the back. The cars went well in practice, but our trouble in getting away quickly on a very high first gear was accentuated when the promoters decided to start the race on the straight that was slightly uphill. We could reach 80 mph in first gear, which meant that there was no acceleration – by racing car standards – under 40 mph. To add to our troubles the Ferraris were not only very fast, but had five-speed gearboxes as well. As in the previous year their acceleration, both away from the start and out of the corners, was superior to that of the Jaguar D-Types.

At the fall of the flag Harry Schell (3-litre Ferrari) shot off into the lead closely followed by Maurice Trintignant (3.5-litre Ferrari); these two soon opened up a gap of a few hundred yards, and for 35 laps passed and repassed one another all the way round. Their average speed was 125 mph and the crowd was on its feet with excitement. The rest of the pack was led by Perdisa (3-litre Maserati), Graham and myself. The three of us were sometimes in line – no more than three or four feet separating our cars – at speeds approaching 200 mph. It was glorious stuff: I enjoyed every minute of it. At about half way Perdisa began to fall back leaving Graham and me to duel together for a few laps until joined by Jean Behra (3-litre Maserati) who had been moving up fast. Carini spun his Ferrari, mercifully without getting in the way of another car. Behra, Graham and myself were occupying the full width of one straight while Carini's spinning Ferrari occupied the full width of the other. We passed going in opposite directions with only the grass verge between us. The Ferrari spun for over half a mile.

The next time round we saw a column of smoke and presumed there had been an accident, only to discover, as we sped down the straight, that a local steam train had stopped to see the race; Arabs hung out of the windows as if watching and waiting to see whether the pall of smoke that billowed across the track might cause a spectacular accident. We had to pass through this cloud twice before the organizers were able to make the train move on. To be blinded temporarily at nearly 200 mph is not funny. Three laps from the end my engine blew up when I was going full bore down the straight. Suddenly, I was covered in oil and moving in a cloud of steam. My surprise was only exceeded by that of Graham who was close behind me. Fortunately he was not in my slip-stream at the time. If he had been our memorial services could have been read together. I coasted into the pits leaving Graham to fight out the finish with Behra and Lucas (Ferrari) who had just joined our party. I was able to watch the finish of this thrilling race. With the entire crowd on its feet shouting for one or the other Trintignant just pipped Schell by four-fifths of a second. His average speed for the race was 198.902 kph with a fastest lap at 201.923 kph (125.47 mph). Behra was third just ahead of Lucas and Graham. Lucas and Graham appeared to dead-heat but the official verdict was in favour of Lucas by just over a second.

Harry Schell was a grand driver and a great sportsman. It was a sad loss to racing when he was killed on May 13th 1960, at the age of thirty-eight, while practising at Silverstone. Graham and I left the cars in the safe hands of Robin Freeman and Arthur Birks and flew home by way of Casablanca, Paris and London Airport. Our equipe followed by boat.

★ ★ ★

The day after my return home I was, in company with Mike Hawthorn, Ivor Bueb, Lofty England and Brian Turle of Shell, flying to New York on my way to Sebring and the twelve-hour sports car race. For some reason both Ivor and I had forgotten our overcoats, and during refuelling stops in

Iceland and Newfoundland we were frozen getting from the aircraft to the airport buildings. Mike, who had a particularly warm overcoat, thought all this very funny.

Our aircraft was the last one to get into New York before the airport became snowbound, and so heavy did the snow become that it was three days before we could get a train to Washington. There was no question of our getting a plane.

Mike and I had a very good time: we visited all the sights and a fair number of night clubs. In the Waldorf Astoria one afternoon a member of a visiting woman's convention called Mike, 'boy', and demanded to know where the convention was meeting. Mike was surprised, but then saw that his blazer had confused the woman into thinking he was an attendant. Before he could explain the woman began harranguing him so Mike said: 'Eleventh floor'. For about fifteen minutes we directed all enquiring females to the eleventh floor then took the lift up to see how things were progressing. The scene was reminiscent of the Stock Exchange during a national crisis. A male convention was already in occupation of a conference hall and was objecting to the presence of so many ladies. Since all the ladies were not attending the same female conference the situation had become rather confused. Wisely we decided to go elsewhere.

That evening Ivor joined Mike and myself on a sort of night club crawl. It was difficult to get taxis and Ivor and I – who were still without overcoats – were very cold. Mike agreed to hire his overcoat for three dollars an hour – and he made us pay up too.

Taxis were hard to get and the drivers were demanding high fares. We paid up but expected reasonable conducting in return. They had no idea how to drive on snow and ice and Mike had to hit one of them to make him take his foot off the brake, and thus allow the front wheels to play their part in avoiding a lamp post. Far from being annoyed the driver thanked Mike and insisted on going round the block once more to show him that he had learnt a lesson in car control. Then there was the driver who could not get up an incline. Mike suggested that he should try. The driver bet him our fare that he could not do it. Mike did it of course and then, with the driver as guide, drove to our destination at a speed the driver could not credit. He honoured his bet and would not take even a tip. 'A guy who can handle a car like you can ought to be driving a cab,' he told Mike.

After three days we were able to travel by train to Washington, and then fly to Miami via Philadelphia. Miami was as hot as New York had been cold and Mike's overcoat became a nuisance to him. Ivor and I both offered to carry it for him at three dollars an hour; our offer was not accepted. Briggs Cunningham, who was sponsoring the Jaguar team, met us and took us up to the country club where all the drivers were staying. He told us we would need a car and asked if we had any preference. Mike suggested a Cadillac; I said a soft top with blue bodywork would be nice; and lo and behold Briggs produced a brand new Cadillac coupe as ordered, about an hour later. Both Mike and I were somewhat embarrassed, not having expected our remarks to be taken seriously; we tried to speak to Briggs about it but it was no good; he did not know what we were talking about.

The local police were most belligerent and we got very fed up with the way they threw their weight about round the track. Coming back from Miami in the early hours we were unfortunate enough to overtake a patrol car at speed. Immediately all hell was let loose – sirens, flashing lights, and so on. Mike clearly expected less than justice if he stopped so he just put his foot down and went. Luckily the road was not straight and, for all their ostentatious aggression, not many state police drivers could follow Mike round a corner: we never saw nor heard from them again.

The race went badly for Jaguars and our four cars retired with brake trouble. We simply wore the pads away. The brakes were of new design and were undercooled in the heat of Florida. We had trouble even with the black rubber hydraulic pipe hoses in practice. Lofty cured this trouble by wrapping the hoses with tape and then painting the tape with silver paint: this ruse reflected the heat away from the rubber and all was well. This is a splendid example of the ingenuity and quick thinking of which he is capable. The race was won by Fangio and Castellotti in a Ferrari; Musso and Schell were second in another Ferrari, and a privately entered D-Type Jaguar driven by Indianapolis winners Sweikert and Ensley, was third. Mike, who was sharing his car with Desmond Titterington, made fastest practice time and looked a likely winner. Our D-Types had fuel injection and were producing 300 bhp. Ivor was driving with me, Briggs Cunningham had his one-time Le Mans partner Bennett with him, and the Americans, Johnston and Spear, completed the team.

Mike was first away from the Le Mans type start and by the fourth lap he led Stirling Moss's Aston Martin by twenty seconds. Fangio, whom I had led for ten hectic laps, was now third; Phil Hill lay fourth and I was fifth. For two hours the car ran well, but the brakes were very hot, and in misjudging my approach to the pits, when coming in to hand over to Ivor, I had to brake so hard that the pads welded themselves to the disc. When Ivor tried to drive away the car would not

228

move; he let the clutch in with a jerk and that did free the discs but, of course, we lost a lot of pad in the process. Anyway, eventually they failed completely when a hydraulic pipe fractured, and Ivor drove through field and dale before coming to a halt quite unhurt.

Mike was still leading after six hours and by dint of some brilliant driving kept the car in the race until two hours from the end when, with no brakes left, and no chance of winning, the car was withdrawn.

One thing I shall always remember about Sebring was the way they allowed aircraft to land on the runways while the race was in progress. Apart from the marker barrels, at intervals of thirty yards or so, there was nothing to stop a racing car, or a landing aircraft – should it burst a tyre – from travelling on to the wrong part of the runway. There was, therefore, always the risk of a major pile up. It was quite disconcerting when travelling down the straight at 160 mph to see an aircraft approaching you; the pilot had only to make a mistake for the consequences to be too horrible to contemplate. If the local police had spent more time in controlling the antics of private planes, and less in throwing their weight about round the pit area, they would have made a useful contribution to the proceedings.

★ ★ ★

After a week's holiday in Miami, Mike and I flew back to England in time to practise for the Goodwood Easter Meeting. This meeting had a tragic outcome so far as I was concerned for a friend of mine, Tony Dennis, crashed while driving one of my D-Types, and was killed. It appeared that in the excitement of the moment – he was being lapped by the leading cars at the time – he changed from top into first at 100 mph. The back axle locked solid; the car somersaulted, and Tony was thrown out and killed.

I took my D-Type up to Oulton Park for the British Empire Trophy but did not achieve any success. Moss drove a Cooper to victory in front of Chapman in a Lotus, Salvadori in another Cooper and Mike Hawthorn in a Lotus. I remember Mike laughing when I asked him what he was doing in a Lotus: 'Just competing with the handicappers,' he said.

If Oulton Park was the wrong place for a big car I was soon able to console myself with the fact that Montlhéry was the right place. I drove the D-Type to Paris by way of Newhaven-Dieppe, and once again won the Coupe du Paris. The track was very wet at the start of the race although the rain had stopped. The principal opposition came from the Da Silva Ramos eight-cylinder G.P. Gordini, Luigi Piotti's G.P. Maserati and Andre Guelfi's 3-litre sports Gordini. I made a good start and by the end of the first lap led by ten seconds from Da Silva Ramos. He tried very hard to catch me and spun off in the process, leaving me to coast home seventy-two seconds in front of Piotti's Maserati at an average speed of 97.46 mph. I had my usual wonderful evening in Paris and then drove the D-Type home the next day.

Graham Whitehead and I had received an invitation to drive in a sports car race at Chimay in Belgium and had accepted. Since neither Pat Whitehead nor Angela had seen the Ardennes, and since they both wanted to do so, we took them with us. The promoters of the meeting had found us a hotel which it is kinder not to name, except to say that it alluded to the fragrance of flowers. The fragrance was, alas, illusory; the odour that remained was not. We left the next morning. The race was won by Benoit Musy in a Maserati with myself second and Graham third. Unfortunately, soon after the beginning of the race two cars touched and plunged into the crowd, killing four people. I had a nasty spin on my very last lap when I hit a patch of oil; the car stayed on the road, however, and I was able to go on and finish second.

I was driving for Jaguars in the 1,000 Kilometres race at the Nurburgring the following Sunday so, after some sightseeing in the Ardennes with Pat and Graham, Angela and I drove to Germany. We stayed at an hotel inside the 'Ring itself; Mike, Lofty and the rest of the team were there and we made a jolly party. Practice was hampered by mist and I had a bad spin going into the Karussel. Mike was behind me, but, fortunately, he saw my tyre marks on the road and slowed down in time. My co-driver was Paul Frere who had rather an unhappy weekend. First he crashed our car in practice, and then, after Lofty got another one from Coventry to the 'Ring in time for the race, he had gearbox trouble and retired. I never drove in the race at all.

Mike had asked me to take some pictures of the race with his cine-camera, and I was busy filming Stirling Moss's pit stop when a German policeman hit me. He was, apparently, clearing the pit area of photographers, although no one had asked him to. I was still wearing my racing overalls so he could hardly mistake me for a photographer, and anyway people do not just walk up and hit me. I caught him by the throat, gave him a good shaking, and then threw him away. He cried blue murder and soon all his buddies came along to help him, led by an officer who began immediately to shout at me in German demanding, I gather, an explanation. All he got was one or two rather rude gestures. He ordered one of his lads to arrest me, but since the fellow had to climb over the pit counter first I gave him short shrift. The arrival of some important individual, and the fact that Lofty could speak excellent German, saved me, I think, from prison.

Stirling Moss and Jean Behra shared the winning 3-litre Maserati; Fangio and Castellotti were second in a 3-litre Ferrari. Mike's car, which he shared with Desmond Titterington, split its fuel tank and retired.

There was a wonderful party in our hotel that night during the course of which I climbed a flagpole in the grounds. I meant no harm and was merely enjoying myself when a German policeman arrived below waving a pistol in the direction of my behind. I was not quite sure what to do, but before I could make up my mind he began to shake the pole. I lost my hold and fell on top of his head, clutching a German flag which had failed to arrest my progress. Since my weight was then about fifteen stone and the length of fall perhaps thirty feet it was not surprising that the German was quite unconscious. I tip-toed away before reinforcements arrived; the flag now hangs proudly in an outhouse at my home.

CHAPTER FOURTEEN

SACKED FOR WINNING

C o-driving with Ivor Bueb I won the Rheims twelve-
hour race and in so doing had my connection with
Jaguars severed. Lofty England contended that I did not
obey pit signals, and no sooner was the race over than he
told me that I would not be driving at Le Mans. We had a
fearful row and, coming as I had, straight out of the cockpit
of a racing car, I was in no mood to suffer irate team
managers gladly. The real trouble was that when told to slow
down I had actually gone faster and faster until I had broken
the lap record at the end of a twelve-hour race when my
team were placed one, two, three and with no competitor
within striking distance.

That is how the bare facts appear, but it was not quite as
simple as that. In the first place, I had in the back of my mind
the fact that Tony Rolt and I had been robbed of certain
victory during the last twelve-hour race when our back axle
gave trouble right at the end forcing us to concede victory

to team-mates who had been well behind. Then on this particular occasion I would have literally had to slow right down just to let Paul Frere pass me; he was too far behind to do it without my help. Had Mike been driving it would have been different; he would have gone faster and, anyway, he was our number one driver. As it was he was back in his hotel resting for the French Grand Prix which was to follow this race. I missed Lofty's first slow down signal but saw the second one. I decided to lift off early and to go slower on the straight past the grandstand down to Heliopolis. Previously I had gone full chat down this straight leaving my braking for Heliopolis to the last possible moment. Far from slowing me up my new method saw me through the corner faster than ever before and my lap times improved. The earlier I lifted off the faster I went. I did not try to break any records though I did try to win. It was one of those days when everything is right. The car was wonderfully responsive and I seemed to have plenty of time to do everything. Ivor and I won at an average speed of 111.009 mph; my fastest lap was 118.13 mph.

Within two hours of my dismissal Enzo Ferrari had asked me to join his equipe and I had accepted his invitation. I did not blame Lofty for what he had done; he had to do his duty by Jaguars as he saw it; I was technically guilty of indiscipline and he was enforcing his authority as he had every right to do. For my part I had given of my best; I had finished first. If the consequence of the victory I had shared with Ivor Bueb was to be dismissal, then it was encumbent upon me to decide whether that victory was worthwhile. I have no hesitation in saying that it was; for me motor racing has always been a sport. I have tried to put much back into the game; on this occasion I took something out.

Shortly after my return home I received two letters. One

was from Lofty England, the other from Enzo Ferrari. Lofty's confirmed my dismissal; Enzo's confirmed my appointment; and so far as I was concerned that was that.

I drove my D-Type in the sports car race at Silverstone on July 14th but achieved only a spectacular spin. On the 18th, in company with Graham Whitehead, I flew to Rome, via Nice, and then motored to Bari, South of Naples, where we were both driving in the Grand Prix. My D-Type and Graham's DB3S had travelled down on his transporter in company with Arthur Birks and Robin Freeman.

I found – as soon as I began to practise – that this was no circuit for the D-Type: there were no straights, and the hefty Jaguar's solid beam axle could not negotiate the sharp corners as well as the latest Italian machines with their de Dion rear ends. On this twisty circuit the 2-litre cars were nearly as fast as the larger 3-litre cars, and it was no surprise to me when Behra and Perdisa in 2-litre Maseratis finished second and third behind Stirling Moss in a 3-litre Maserati. Graham retired with a broken gearbox but I pressed on to the end and finished sixth. Early on Portago's 3-litre Ferrari 'missed' coming out of a corner, causing my D-Type to nudge his backside. The impact closed a faring through which air passed to my brakes. This, coupled with a twisty circuit, and a temperature in the nineties, led to my discs becoming red hot and losing some of their efficiency. My car was also over-geared for the circuit; all in all I was not displeased with sixth place.

We drove our hired 1,100cc Fiat back to Rome, pausing in Cassino and Naples on the way, and then flew back to London Airport. The following day Angela and I returned to the Continent and headed for Le Mans. Indeed I had gone home only to pick her up.

We collected the caravan on route (I had left it in France after the Rheims race) and on arrival at Le Mans set up home behind the Ferrari pit. The Ferrari drivers were: Phil Hill, Trintignant, Manzon, Von Trips, Portago and myself. They were all old friends and our team spirit was splendid. Mike Hawthorn was always resting in our caravan, particularly when the Marquis de Portago was present, a fact which greatly amused Portago himself.

The Ferraris we were to drive were four-cylinder 3-litre cars with solid beam rear axles, and four-speed non-synchromesh gearboxes. They lacked the top speed of the D-Type but were just as fast on acceleration up to about 150 mph. This model under-steered very much and the drum brakes required a good firm pressure before they became effective. All the power and torque of the engine was at the top end of the scale and you kept the 'revs' between 5,500 and 7,500 when racing. The gearbox was a beauty, but the absence of syncromesh meant that one had to concentrate when changing gear; in a race as long as Le Mans the less the driver has to worry about the better. On the D-Type the syncromesh was so good that gear changing was never a problem even when one was very tired.

Portago and I were the fastest pair in practice, if one took the collective times of the two drivers in each car, and we were hopeful of doing well. Jack Fairman had taken my place in the Jaguar team which was, of course, led by Mike Hawthorn. Stirling Moss and Peter Collins were leading the Aston Martin team. It rained before the start of the race, and the Ferrari team manager asked me to drive first. I did not want to do this, feeling that I was, after all, the new boy of the team. He saw my point of view and allowed Portago to take the first stint. Portago made a good start but was involved, unfortunately, in a triple crash at the Esses when a works Jaguar, driven by Paul Frere, spun and Fairman spun his sister Jaguar in avoidance. Portago, unable to miss these two cars, wrecked the front of Fairman's car, and then rammed Frere's car broadside on. Both Jaguars and our Ferrari had to retire from the race, so not only had Jaguars kept me out of their team, they had also, indirectly, prevented me from driving a Ferrari. When Portago came into the pit his first words were: 'I have written off the Jaguar team. It's just as well you weren't driving, Duncan, or they'd have said you'd done it on purpose'. Come to think of it they might at that.

Mike Hawthorn was left, along with co-driver Ivor Bueb, to carry the flag for Jaguars; unfortunately their car was dogged with fuel injection trouble, and although their's was the fastest car still running at the end of the race they had to be content with sixth place. The race was won by the Ecurie Ecosse D-Type driven by Ron Flockhart and Ninian Sanderson.

★ ★ ★

Two weeks after Le Mans I was a member of the Ferrari team which travelled to Sweden for the Swedish Grand Prix at Kristianstad. This sports car race had taken on an added significance for it was the last of the five events counting for the World Manufacturers' Sports Car Championship. Maserati and Ferrari had each won two of the previous four races so this 1,000 kilometre (621 miles) event was in the nature of a decider. Enzo Ferrari, determined to win, sent five cars and the following drivers: Fangio, Hawthorn, Collins, Musso, Castellotti, Portago, Trintignant, Phil Hill, von Trips and Hamilton. It is noteworthy that of all the afore-mentioned, Hawthorn, Collins, Musso, Castellotti, Portago and von Trips are now dead – all killed while driving.

I lent my D-Type to Peter and Graham Whitehead; both they and the car performed well and subsequently finished fourth.

Among the five cars in our team were three of the latest twelve-cylinder 3.5-litre Testa Rossa models which were fabulous.

★ ★ ★

After Fangio had chosen the car he wanted – a twelve-cylinder – the rest of us had a go. I did several practice laps in a four-cylinder model – which differed from the Le Mans cars in that it had a five-speed gearbox – then took out a twelve-cylinder. Mike Hawthorn had warned me that lifting one's foot off the accelerator made not the slightest difference once the twelve-cylinder cars were in fifth gear. He was right, as I soon discovered. The trouble was that in the course of discovering this interesting fact I had to take to an escape road at speed, enter a backyard, pass between two adjacent cottages, crush a dustbin, kill a chicken, and demolish an outside loo. What happened was that when I lifted my foot at about 160 mph the car just went on as if in neutral. I braked hard and changed into fourth only to find that I was going too fast to take the corner at the end of the straight. I changed into third and entered the escape road – at about 100 mph – with the consequences just mentioned. The combination of a very high fifth gear and a twelve-cylinder engine with a firing stroke for every thirty degrees of crankshaft turn had taken me by surprise, in spite of

Mike's warning. Fortunately the car had suffered little damage and once a few dents had been knocked out and new wheels fitted it was back on the circuit.

These Ferraris were faster on acceleration than a D–Type and, with the de Dion back axles now fitted, had superior road holding. When accelerating away from the pit you could see the black marks your tyres were leaving behind following you up the road. The engine ran round to 8,500 rpm like an electric motor, and the gearbox, despite the absence of syncromesh, was a joy to use. The only thing I did not appreciate was the physical effort required of the driver when stopping the car: you had to use all the strength in your leg. A moderate pressure on the brake pedal did not retard the car's progress at all.

Before the race we all received the usual medical check-up. When the solemn Swedish doctor asked me what my blood group was I said: 'Whisky and Perrier'. He wrote it all down without comment, and I signed without comment, wondering what sort of a transfusion they would give me if I had an accident.

After the final practice session Portago and I understood that we would be driving a twelve-cylinder car; in the end we not only drove a four-cylinder car but shared it with Mike Hawthorn as well. The Ferrari manager changed his cars and drivers around so much that no one knew exactly what was happening. Maurice Trintignant and Phil Hill won from Peter Collins and Von Trips with Mike Hawthorn, Portago and myself third. I drove for the last two-and-three-quarter hours without any brakes and was very glad the car had a four-cylinder engine. With those four big pots I was able to use my gearbox to slow the car; it would not have been possible with a twelve-cylinder engine.

Fangio and Castellotti retired with mechanical trouble towards the end of the race; they were leading at the time. The Maserati of Stirling Moss and Jean Behra was up with the leaders for a hundred of the 153 laps; it then caught fire while refuelling and was completely gutted, and Maserati's hope of winning the Manufacturers' Championship literally went up in smoke.

We Ferrari drivers had a wonderful party that night, thanks to a crate of whisky we were able to acquire. The Swedish drink laws are peculiar, and our attempts to drink what we wanted when we wanted had been frustrated on several occasions; we resolved, therefore, when one of our party saw a case of whisky, that its acquisition, either by purchase or other means, was an absolute necessity. Mike made a perfectly straightforward offer for the stuff only to be told that it was not for sale. If it was not for sale, he asked, what was it doing under a drinks table in the main bar of the hotel? The answer was unsatisfactory so we had no alternative but to employ guile. We made a plan, and then put it into operation with the timing and speed of a commando attack force. Musso fell, apparently accidentally against the table, knocking it over. The eastern adage: 'In confusion there is gain,' turned out to be true. Mike hooked the case back to Peter Collins, who passed it to me; I passed it to Portago, who passed it to Castellotti, who ran down the passage to a library. As soon as each one of us had played his part in the operation we turned to the fallen table and helped to right it, and up to the time I left the bar the case had not been missed.

After a decent period we all gathered in the library where Castellotti had opened the bottles in readiness for the party that was to follow. At four o'clock in the morning each one of us placed a contribution in the now empty case and returned it to its former resting place under the long table in the main bar. By about four-thirty a.m. Mike and I had negotiated the stairs and had finally reached our landing. We were debating whether to tip Peter Collins out of bed or not when Sculati, our team manager, came along carrying a suitcase: he was on his way to the airport to fly home to Italy. As he went by he splashed us with some water out of the fire bucket. This gesture gave Mike a foul idea; he picked up the bucket, emptied it over my head, and then ran to his room laughing in a rather idiotic way. I stood quite still for a moment or two while the water formed a pool on the carpet beneath me. Then I saw that just above where the bucket had hung was a fire hose, and a little further down the corridor a large wheel, the turning of which would send water rushing through the hose. I felt positively evil. Carefully I connected the hose to the main. Then I unrolled it down the corridor as far as the door of Mike's room. I noticed with satisfaction that the door was not quite shut. He was still laughing. I nipped back to the wheel and turned it.

My surprise at what happened next was only exceeded by Mike's. The hose became alive, and snaked off down the corridor like a great cobra. The nozzle banged on the door as if demanding entry and then thrust everything aside and shot into Mike's room. He was about to put on his pyjama legs and had paused for a moment when he heard the knock on his door. The next moment his pyjama legs were up against the wall and he was flat on his back, bowled over by the jet of water that had suddenly entered his room. The hose went quite mad as the pressure built up and the nozzle whizzed round the room like an enraged hornet. It shot the pictures off the wall, the blankets off the bed, and managed to give Mike a couple of fourpenny ones as well. He scrambled out of the room and ran out nude down the corridor to the wheel and, using all his strength, he was a big fellow, jammed it full on. By now everything was out of hand: water was running from his room both up and down the corridor, and angry voices were demanding what was going on. 'We must put the nozzle out of a window,' I said. He nodded and, our feud forgotten for the moment, we raced back to his bedroom. He managed to get hold of the nozzle but could not control it and found himself in the corridor with water shooting everywhere.

I could see that he would not be able to get back into his room so I tried the door of another bedroom hoping the window would be open. Unfortunately the maiden lady who was in occupation had not expected to be awakened by a nude man carrying a firehose, and she screamed so much Mike had to come out. I opened another door which turned out to be the bedroom of a friend of ours. As it happened he was not alone; neither were he and his friend sleeping. They were quite unprepared for the onslaught that followed. Mike charged in, desperately trying to control the nozzle. A jet of water whipped the bedclothes off the bed and deposited its occupants on the floor. Mike pressed on and finally dropped the nozzle out of the window. He then picked up a sheet, wrapped it round his body, and, looking rather like a Roman senator, walked majestically back to his room. I said something like, 'excuse us', to the couple on the floor, and then ran off to see if I could find a means of turning the wheel the other way. I found a small fireman's axe fastened to the wall near the end of the corridor and, with one or two well-timed blows, succeeded in freeing the wheel enough to be able to turn it off. It was then possible to remove the hose from our friend's bedroom; he was grateful, for he was now able to shut the door.

Fortunately most of the bedrooms on our floor were occupied by members of the various equipes who accepted this accident as something that might have happened to anyone; the Swedish guests and the management did not take such a generous view, and Mike and I were grateful when the secretary of the Swedish Automobile Club turned up the next morning and negotiated a financial settlement satisfactory to all concerned.

Mike and I accepted a lift in Peter Collins's Ford Zephyr and we drove to Malmo where we caught a boat to Denmark on the first stage of the journey home. Peter and Graham Whitehead were already on board with my D-Type and a mutual friend, Bill Holt, who had been acting as unpaid unofficial pit manager. He had kept lap charts, recorded lap times, supervised refuelling and dealt with complaints just for the kick he got out of it.

Our departure was delayed by a Swede who could not back his Cadillac on to the ship until he had attempted the feat about thirty times. When he discovered that the ship was full of racing drivers, their cars and mechanics – the Maserati and Ferrari equipes were on board – he was so embarrassed that he began boasting about the performance of his Cadillac. Peter Collins became rather bored with this character and, slipping away for a moment, coupled a railway truck that the ship was carrying to the rear bumper of the Cadillac. The Cadillac, having been the last car on, was the first car off the boat. When the Swede prepared to drive away Peter cast some aspersion as to the Cadillac's ability to get off the mark quickly. The driver rose to the bait and banged his foot down. The car and the truck moved a few feet. The startled Swede looked behind and saw what he took to be a railway truck descending on his precious car. He really opened up, and with a truly dreadful tearing sound the back bumper came off the car and the Cadillac shot on to the quay. The driver did not look back; he belted away round a corner and never returned. Peter had not expected such an ending to his joke and was quite upset that he could not make any restitution.

★ ★ ★

I had a very good holiday in Brittany with Angela and the children. We took the caravan down to Kerfede and camped near Hervé and Anna Coatalen's house. The Heads joined us, and I think it would be true to say that this was one of the best family holidays we had.

I drove in all the usual British meetings and did some testing for Ferrari in Italy. I also went to Italy with Mike Hawthorn to share a Lotus with him in the Supercortemaggiore sports car race at Monza.

Mike and I flew to Milan while a mechanic took the Lotus out there on a truck. After booking into our hotel we went round to the garage where the car was billeted to see whether I could, in fact, get into it. It was a tight squeeze, but I managed it and, after Mike – who had been reduced to a state of near collapse by my contortions – had composed himself, we went back to our hotel. A lot of the boys were there and we had a good evening. The next morning we set off for Monza. I was driving a Grand Touring Ferrari Coupe lent to me by Musso, Mike was in the Lotus, and the mechanic in the truck.

Everything happened to Mike. First of all an oil pipe burst.

The oil ran on to the exhaust pipe and the car caught fire. With the aid of the crowd that gathered the fire was put out, and the mechanic – assisted by many volunteers – set about repairing the car. After an hour and a half it was drivable, and we set off, once again, for Monza, Mike leading. We had not travelled very far when the rear tyres of the Lotus screeched and the car stopped – the gearbox had seized up. We put the Lotus into the truck and carried on to the pits at Monza where we discovered that the car needed a new gearbox and propshaft. There was no prospect of repairing anything in time for the race so we went off to see our friend Sculati. He was able – as we had hoped he would be – to offer us a drive with the Ferrari team.

He put Mike with Peter Collins and myself with Taffy von Trips. Unfortunately, my Ferrari broke down while Taffy was driving and I never got a drive in the actual race. This was disappointing, for we had been the third fastest pair in practice. Mike and Peter drove splendidly and ran out comfortable winners.

That evening Mike, Peter, von Trips, Portago, Musso, Castellotti and I visited just about every night club in Milan. It is a sober thought that I am the only member of that party still alive. They all had girl friends with them, and I remember that at one stage during the evening Mike and Peter cut a cake that had been presented to them by Enzo Ferrari himself in recognition of their victory. I am a little hazy as to when this happened, but I do remember everyone clapping and patting them on the back.

Sometime round about dawn I got involved in a fearful fracas and was lucky not to be arrested. The party had broken up and I was on my way to catch a plane at Milan airport. Mike and Peter were supposed to be helping me:

Mike by carrying my luggage, Peter as an interpreter. Some fellow demanded 1,750 lire and when I asked what for he replied in English: 'For the bus'. Mike and Peter thought this very funny and suggested that I take up his offer. This was the bus that transported passengers from Milan to the airport. After inspecting the bus I told the man that I would buy it but that I must have a receipt. Peter translated all this to him, or, at any rate I thought he had done so. The man appeared puzzled by my request, but, after further discussion with Peter agreed, and allowed him to write out in English: 'I hereby acknowledge receipt of 1,750 lire being the sum demanded for the purchase of Lancia bus registration number...'. He then signed his name across an Italian stamp. I gave him the money; he gave me the receipt; and then, to his great surprise, I got into the bus and drove off while he ran down the street after me.

I made two circuits of the square near Milan Cathedral and attempted a third only to discover that the police had set up a road block. I stopped, and an excited policeman jumped up on the step by the bus's sliding door and demanded entry. I moved the lever which opened the door and prepared to receive my first passenger only to find that he was pointing a revolver at me. I moved the lever again causing the door to close on the hand that was holding the revolver. I then removed the revolver and released the hand. This gesture caused much excitement amongst the crowd that had gathered, and something akin to anger in the police. One of them was rash enough to try and climb in by an open window at the rear end of the bus and I had to push him out. He lost his hat and, when I put it on, after closing the window, the crowd appeared to become more excited and the police more angry. They tried to pull the door open, but since it was both opened and closed hydraulically they were merely wasting energy.

A rather important policeman arrived and after a short discussion with Mike and Peter he approached the bus and surveyed me appraisingly. I acknowledged his stare by raising my hat in friendly greeting; unfortunately he was not amused. He returned to Mike and Peter for further discussion and then approached again accompanied by both of them. Mike jumped up and indicated that I should open the door, which I did. 'Pack it up Duncan,' he said, 'You've gone far enough. For heaven's sake tell the old gaffer the joke's over'. Reason began to dilute the alcohol and I was conscious of qualms and minor tremors of anxiety. 'Talk yourself out of this one Duncan,' I said to myself.

The captain was charming. 'Signor 'Amilton,' he said through the gap in the door. 'Be good. It is enough. Surrender. It must not go on'.

'But it's my bus.' I tried hard to sound injured. 'It is my bus.'

He shook his head. 'No, no, no. It is not your bus. It belongs to Italian Air Lines. Be a good fellow, surrender.'

'But it is my bus.' I produced the receipt. He read it through two or three times muttering the words to himself, then he laughed.

'So your friends tell the truth. Nevertheless I must arrest you.'

Obviously he meant it so I dared my last ploy. 'Then I have no choice but to drive away.' I started the engine. 'Tell the crowd to stand back.'

He jumped up and down in alarm. 'Signor 'Amilton, do not do this thing.'

'I must,' I said, shrugging my shoulders hopelessly. 'The disgrace of being arrested is more than a gentleman can bear.

I am a man of honour; I must do the honourable thing.' I revved the engine.

'Stop,' he said, 'I know you joke.'

'It is no joke to be arrested. I have brought disgrace on my family.' I hung my head for a moment then straightened up with a jerk. 'I must do what I must do.' I let in the clutch and the bus moved forward.

'Stop. If I let you go will you leave this bus?'

My ploy had worked but I was silent for a moment.

'I give you my word,' he said.

'The word of an Italian officer is good enough for me,' I replied in an appropriate manner.

We shook hands through the gap in the door. 'Drive round the corner,' he said, 'It would be embarrassing for you to get out of the bus here.' I opened the door wide; he entered and stood beside me. The crowd moved back and I drove to the bus station where I surrendered both the bus and my receipt.

The captain kept his word and, after he, Peter, Mike and myself had had a glass of wine together in a little cafe near the bus station, he allowed me to go and catch my plane, I travelled home with a troubled conscience and a hangover that stayed with me for a week.

★ ★ ★

I returned to the Continent in October to drive, as usual, in the Coupe du Salon at Montlhéry. The race was marred that year by two fatal accidents. Benoit Musy was killed when his Maserati flew off the banking at speed and fell thirty feet into the paddock below. Musy was killed instantly. The other victim was my old friend Louis Rosier; he lingered for nearly three weeks before he finally succumbed.

His accident was a strange one. His Ferrari was first away at the start closely followed by myself. We entered the first right-hand bend at about 150 mph; then suddenly, without any warning, he was sideways across the track in front of me. I braked hard and watched him spin round, hit the bank at the side of the road, bounce up in the air and then land upside down on the track, bounce up again right in front of me, disappear as I passed underneath both car and man, and then land upside down once more. I suppose it was all over in a matter of seconds yet, in my mind's eye, I can still see it all happening as if in slow motion. Bits and pieces of his car fell all over the track, and I believe Musy's car hit the battery from Rosier's car and that the damage this did to his steering caused his death. The bonnet of the Ferrari hit my crash helmet as I passed under the car, leaving a smudge of blue paint, I slowed right down and it was a full lap before I could orientate myself, I was so upset by what I had seen. Louis was a very great friend, and a great sportsman.

Many cars had passed me but once I had pulled myself together I came through the field very quickly. By about the seventh lap I was in second place behind Musy. Going round the banking I must have taken a quick glance at my rev-counter for quite suddenly Musy had gone. One moment he was leading, the next he had disappeared, and I, who was driving behind him, did not see him go. I eventually finished in third place behind the 3-litre Maseratis of Godia and Behra. Pilette was fourth in a D-Type.

Louis Rosier was still alive but there was little hope of his surviving. I was so miserable that I went home without even bothering to take a look at the Paris Motor Show. Louis died later in the month and as I stood by his grave after the funeral service was over, I wondered whether the thrill and excitement of the race was worth while when it so often ended like this. One thing I am sure of, however, Louis would have been the last person to complain: he knew the possible consequences of his chosen life. Nevertheless, for those of us who knew him, the season had ended on a very sad note.

I went back home and, by concentrating on my business interests and family problems, forgot all about motor racing for a while. By Christmas good spirits and optimism had returned and, when I received a seasonal card from Lofty England wishing me a Happy Christmas and a Prosperous New Year, I felt like a man who has seen his name in the personal column of a newspaper: 'All is forgiven Duncan. Come home'. That was the message I read into his card; I immediately sent him one back and now viewed the coming racing season as one I would enjoy.

CHAPTER FIFTEEN

RACING THE '3.8D'

Early in January I went up to Jaguars at Coventry and bought one of the 1956 works cars – identical to the car I had driven when winning at Rheims. The factory were not racing in 1957 and so were prepared to sell some of their team cars to certain friends. Ecurie Ecosse bought two. These long-nosed cars were faster in terms of maximum speed than the shorter-nosed D-Types of 1955. The car, as purchased, was fitted with the 3.4-litre engine; but it was agreed that the factory would fit one of the new 3.8-litre engines in the car prior to Le Mans. This 3.8-litre was a development of the 3.4litre engine and, apart from the increased capacity, it had the new and very expensive '35-40'-degree angled cylinder head. I drove the car home from Coventry as usual.

Towards the latter part of January I went to Enton Hall, near Godalming, to lose some weight as a prelude to the start of my training programme for 1957. My visit was a great success and I came away a stone lighter.

The Dakar G.P. had been cancelled, so Graham Whitehead and I arranged to go to the French Riviera instead. It was our intention, while down there, to rent two villas for the summer season so that our families could enjoy their holidays in the peace and quiet of a private house, beach and garden.

After crossing the Channel we drove, in my blue XK140 drop-head coupe, to Paris, where we spent the night. We began our evening with a few drinks in Fred Payne's bar in the Rue Pigalle, then ate an excellent dinner at La Pompadour near the Arc de Triumph. Dinner over, we visited various clubs we knew, and then, at about one-thirty in the morning when we were thinking of going back to our hotel, we could not find the car. We were in Montmartre, not the best place in which to be lost at that time in the morning. Graham insisted that we had left the car outside No. 16 Rue de la something or other and when – with the aid of a passer-by – we found the address, it did look like the house as I remembered it. We had both had quite a lot to drink, and without thinking too much, demanded of the poor Frenchman who, wearing only a nightshirt, eventually answered the door: '*Ou est le Jaguar bleu?*' His bewilderment quickly changed to anger, and he let fly a broadside of abuse, objecting, apparently, to being wakened with such an absurd question. We walked away up the street leaving him still noisy.

After a while we came upon another No. 16 and this time both of us were certain it was the house we were looking for. We knocked for quite five minutes before a light went on and the door was opened. Graham had blurted out: '*Ou est le Jaguar bleu?*' before we realized that it was the same man, in the same nightshirt. He went quite beserk. Screaming with rage he took up a broom and struck out. I ducked; Graham did not, with the result that he stopped one on his head. Now it was his turn to be angry: he snatched the broom from the Frenchman and gave him one back. The fellow panicked, and ran down the street in his nightshirt with Graham on his heels, both of them shouting at the tops of their voices. At that moment a girl appeared in a rather transparent nightdress and demanded to know what was going on. I took her to be one of the ladies of Montmartre and gave her a friendly smack on the backside. She screamed so loudly for the police that lights went on in every window in the street. I recoiled into the middle of the road just as Graham and the Frenchman completed their first lap of the block. The Frenchman shot through his front door, as if to answer the call of his mate, while Graham and I made ourselves scarce.

We wandered round Montmartre all night without finding the car. We fortified ourselves with cups of coffee in the dimly lit all-night cafes, and enquired of various people whether or not they had seen a blue Jaguar, but all to no avail. Then, at about seven a.m. we saw, on emerging from a cafe, our car parked in the street outside. The doors were locked and I still had the keys in my pocket; the radiator was cold. We never solved the mystery. Neither for that matter, did the Frenchman and his wife; I have often wondered what they made of it all.

We drove down to the Riviera and rented two villas near Ventimiglia. In the course of conversation with the owner of the villa I rented (a Commander Martin) we discovered that he had served as a midshipman with Graham's father.

Back at home I took delivery of a 3.4-litre Jaguar saloon which I intended to drive in production car races during the coming season. This car, the registration number of which was 'VDU 385', was somewhat modified by the works. There were heavy anti-roll bars front and rear, the shock absorbers were special, an extra leaf was added to each of the rear springs, and a Powr-Lok limited slip differential was fitted. The engine was a normal 3.4-litre modified as follows: a C-Type head with high-lift camshafts and two 2-inch SU carburettors (1.75-inch are fitted with standard camshafts), 9:1 compression ratio and leadbronze bearings. A racing clutch transmitted the power through a close-ratio gearbox to a 3.54 axle. The overdrive was locked out for racing. The battery was placed in the boot to improve weight distribution and racing tyres were fitted. The exhaust system was standard save that twin straight-through silencers reduced back pressure slightly. Under normal conditions this car would accelerate from zero to 100 mph in around twenty-two seconds, and the top speed was about 130 mph. Very comfortable tight bucket seats were an attractive feature of the car. Mike Hawthorn took delivery also of a similar 3.4 'VDU 881'. Later he added disc brakes to his car, the engine was modified to the extent that a three carburettor inlet manifold was fitted and he lowered his final-drive ratio to 4.09. This car was capable of a fifteen second standing quarter mile. It was the car in which he had his tragic accident.

★ ★ ★

I began the season's racing at Oulton Park in an H.M.W.-Jaguar. I borrowed this car from George Abecassis because I thought the de Dion rear would be a help on this circuit. Unfortunately I got stuck behind a driver who was much slower on the corners than myself, but who had a car every bit as fast as mine on the straights. After a very frustrating drive, during which I was repeatedly baulked, I finished sixth. To be fair to the driver concerned he did not appreciate how slow he was on the corners, and he presumed – because of his acceleration on the straight – that he was holding his own. The race was won by Archie Scott-Brown in the 3.4-litre Lister-Jaguar from Roy Salvadori in an Aston Martin DBR1 and Noel Cunningham-Reid in an Aston Martin DB3S.

At Goodwood, on Easter Monday, I drove my old short-nosed D-Type to fourth place in the Sussex Trophy. I had decided to save the long-nosed car for Le Mans. Archie Scott-Brown and the Lister-Jaguar won yet again from Roy Salvadori and Tony Brooks, both in Aston Martins. It was now obvious to everyone that Archie and the Lister-Jaguar were going to be practically invincible in 'unlimited' events that season.

During the next few weeks it was my misfortune to lose two more good friends and to witness several bad accidents. It all began at Spa in Belgium, during practice for the sports car G.P. I was driving my short-nosed D-Type on the fast uphill twisty part of the circuit, when young Max Trimble, who was in front of me in his D-Type, lost control. The car hit a bank, flew into the air, and crashed into a field at the side of the track. I stopped off the road and ran back to him. He was pinned underneath the car with terrible leg injuries. Fortunately he was unconscious. It took the ambulance men over an hour to free him.

I returned to the pit to be greeted by Angela with the news that my dear friend 'Fon' de Portago and his navigator 'Gunnar' Nelson had been killed, along with several spectators, in the Mille Miglia. The following day, in the production car race that preceded the sports car race, the driver of a Porsche was killed when his car left the road and ran into a house. Then, to add to my discomfort, the race was run in rain and hail. Due to a mechanic's illness my car had arrived late for practice and with only one set of tyres – tyres on which it had been driven out to Spa from England. These tyres had done a considerable mileage and it had not been my intention to race on them again, but in the circumstances I had no choice, and I cannot say I enjoyed the drive. I promised Angela that I would not take any unnecessary risks and I kept my promise, that is if lapping at 100 mph in a hailstorm on bald tyres is not taking risks. Tony Brooks won in an Aston Martin DBR1 at an average speed of 103.95 mph – a wonderful performance in the conditions prevailing at the time. Roy Salvadori was second in another DBR1 and Henry Taylor third in a D-Type. I finished fifth and was glad when it was all over.

Angela and I drove home in my XK140 and, whereas we had been happy to picnic in the Ardennes on our way to Spa, we now wanted only to get home.

After a week in England, during which the axle ratio of the D-Type was changed, Angela and I returned to the Continent and drove the XK140 down to St. Etienne near Lyons; Robin Freeman drove the D-Type. After booking in at our hotel I went down to take a look at the circuit. Peter and Graham Whitehead were there and we all crammed into the XK and drove round a couple of times. We did not like what we saw and decided to tell the promoters so. The most dangerous thing about the circuit was that at one point two roads in use during the race were separated only by a small hedge. You came down a hill at something like 100mph while on the other side of the hedge someone was going up the straight at a speed of 150 mph. A skid, a burst tyre, or a locked brake, and a head-on collision must result. The promoters clearly thought our fears were exaggerated, and anyway it was too late for them to do anything. They did, however, open up an escape road at the end of one of the straights, at our suggestion.

I made fastest time in practice and occupied the pole position at the start of the race. The start was actually delayed by more protests from drivers about, amongst other things, the positioning of straw bales. Some of these had been placed in certain positions to prevent nonpaying customers from seeing the race; they also prevented drivers seeing the road ahead and affected their lines into the corners. The protest was upheld and they were moved.

I made a good start, and had a lead of some fifty yards over Ron Flockhart, in an Ecurie Ecosse D-Type, at the end of the first lap. The car was running beautifully and I was able to maintain my lead. Then, suddenly, on about the fifth lap, I had to stop when the track became completely blocked after a multiple pile-up caused by the driver of a Ferrari. Straw bales were scattered all over the road, and in the excitement of the moment I jumped out of the car and cleared a passage through the bales. Before I could get back in my car Ron Flockhart had nipped through the hole I had made and was away. I settled down in second place about 150 yards behind him quite happy to see how the race would develop. Soon we began to lap the tail-enders and I was really keeping my eyes open, for the field was spread over the entire circuit. When you came down the hill you could see cars flashing by in the opposite direction on the other side of the hedge. Flockart had lapped the Ferrari of Carini and I was about to do the same when Carini – in racing parlance – 'dropped it'. He flew through the hedge and hit another Ferrari driven by young Baretto head on. Both drivers were killed instantly. A few seconds later, I drove up the hill and saw the mess on the road; I felt sick, and all enthusiasm for racing left me. 'Not two more,' I thought, 'not two more'. I did not know Baretto well, but Piero Carini and I had been friends for years. When Jock Lawrence's D-Type came up behind me I waved him on and contented myself with third place. So Jaguars finished 1, 2, 3; but it did not seem to matter very much when two young men had died.

★ ★ ★

I invited Masten Gregory, the American driver from Kansas, to share my D-Type with me at Le Mans. He was a happy choice and we got on well together. The factory had fitted the new 3.8-litre engine and the car was very fast. Although my car was a private entry, Jaguars gave me such support that Masten and I had all the advantages of team drivers without any of the disadvantages. Lofty England was there with his great experience and technical know-how at our disposal. Jaguar's best and most experienced racing mechanic, Len Hayden, was also in my pit, and I had full support from all the accessory manufacturers.

Robin Freeman drove the car from Byfleet to Le Mans by way of Lydd-Le Touquet; a truck carried all the spares; and the caravan was there as usual. The car was garaged in the Pernod factory and for some reason my friends thought this funny.

The car went splendidly in practice and I reached 186 mph on the Mulsanne Straight. I found also that I could take the

curve on the straight without lifting my foot. Both Masten
and I lapped at around 4 minutes 8 seconds; five seconds
quicker than the fastest metallic blue Ecurie Ecosse 3.8-litre
D-Type. Although the Mike Hawthorn/Luigi Musso 4-litre
Ferrari lapped at around 4 minutes 1 second, with a best lap
of 3 minutes 59.2 seconds, and the 4.5-litre Maserati of Moss
returned 3 minutes 58.1 seconds, with reserve driver Fangio
at the wheel, we were quite sure these cars would never last
twenty-four hours of racing – and we were right. Fangio did
not drive in the race: he never liked Le Mans and agreed to
drive only if one of the Maserati drivers became unfit. This
was probably the only time a reserve driver has returned the
fastest practice lap before a major race.

In view of the fact that Masten had flown over from the
United States solely to race with me at Le Mans, I insisted
that he drive first. I remembered my experience of the
previous year when Portago had shunted the Jaguars, and in
so doing had denied me a drive. I did not want Masten to
risk an experience similar to mine.

Peter Collins led at the end of the first lap in one of the 4-
litre Ferraris, but his motor soon succumbed, and after three
laps he was out. Mike Hawthorn took over, and in half an
hour built up a twenty second advantage over Stirling Moss
in the big Maserati. Masten lay around about seventh or
eighth refusing to join in the initial Grand Prix. Moss was
soon in trouble and, after a lengthy pit stop, he managed only
one more lap before he retired. Behra in another Maserati
also retired. On his twenty-seventh lap Mike Hawthorn
established the lap record which stood for years: 126.4 mph.
Soon, however, he was in trouble also; and though the car
kept going for some time it eventually broke down shortly
after he had handed over to Luigi Musso.

Masten came in at seven-thirty p.m. and I went off; the car was running beautifully. I lapped steadily for over two hours and then, while doing about 180 mph on the Mulsanne straight, my lights went out. I had just taken my line for the curve; how I got round that corner I do not know. I kept my foot down and let my memory and instinct do the rest. My speed was so great that braking was out of the question, and to have lifted my foot off the throttle would have been disastrous: the torque reversal at such speed would have sent me off the road. Fortunately, after negotiating the bend, I saw a pair of rear lights ahead, and I followed them round to the pits. The bulbs were changed and all was well again. Why the others failed is still a mystery.

I went off and drove for another hour before handing over to Masten. No sooner was he away than his lights failed also. He came in; the bulbs were changed once more; and this time they lasted till dawn. But our troubles were only beginning. Masten came in to say there was a glow in the cockpit and he reckoned there must be a fire somewhere. Neither Len Hayden nor Robin Freeman could find anything wrong so I went off to do a trial lap. There certainly was a glow in the cockpit, near the passenger's seat, but when driving at racing speeds in the dark you cannot examine the passenger's seat. I waited until I was round Mulsanne corner (a bottom gear corner) and then, before opening up, took a good look to my left. The floor of the car was a mass of flames and I guessed rightly that the exhaust pipe had fractured and the escaping flames had burnt through the floor. I opened up – to get back to the pit as soon as possible – and when I did so the flames rose to shoulder height. This was not funny; for apart from anything else there was a forty-gallon petrol tank behind me. When I got out of the car someone pointed to the left shoulder of my sweater; it was badly singed.

The mechanics found that the exhaust pipe had fractured and could not be repaired. They decided, therefore, that if they could not stop the flames coming out of the pipe they could at least stop them getting into the car. They came upon a piece of bullet-proof steel, cut it to size with a hacksaw, and bolted it to the floor of the car. How they had come upon it remained unsaid in the original text. Suffice to say that Sunday morning dawned upon a rather drafty police armoured car, parked unattended behind the pits!

This ruse worked perfectly and we did not have any more trouble for the rest of the twenty-four hours. Unfortunately we had lost over an hour and a quarter and no longer had any chance of winning. We were the last car in the race. But undaunted we set about our task to such effect that we eventually finished sixth, less than one lap behind the Ferrari of Lewis-Evans and Severi. Despite our long pit stop our average speed showed that we had been, while running, the fastest car on the circuit. The race was a triumph for Jaguars: they took the first four places. The result was:

1st, Jaguar. Flockart/Bueb.

2nd, Jaguar. Sanderson/Lawrence.

3rd, Jaguar. Mary/Lucas.

4th, Jaguar. Frere/Rousselle.

5th, Ferrari. Lewis-Evans/Severi.

6th, Jaguar. Hamilton/Gregory.

The first two cars were entered by Ecurie Ecosse. The winner's average speed – a new record for the race – 113.85 mph.

We tried desperately to overtake the Ferrari and would have done so had the race lasted a little longer. Due to a misunderstanding I believed that the Ferrari and I were on the same lap and, making a great effort, I caught and passed it right on the line only to discover that it was a lap ahead. Some very stupid over-excited Scotsmen ran on to the road and had it not been for the fact that my disc brakes were still in perfect working order many of them would have been killed.

Everyone in my equipe had played their part splendidly, and it was a great pity misfortune befell us when it did. But then that is all a part of motor racing; the unexpected is something a driver must learn to live with.

One rather amusing incident took place in the caravan during the race. Angela asked a young man, who had dropped in for a drink, which team he was with. 'None, ma'am,' he said, 'I guess I'm just having a good looksee.' Thinking he was a scrounger, and not knowing that I had asked him to look in for a drink whenever he felt like it, she determined to make him earn his supper. She gave him a broom and told him to sweep out the caravan. He then helped with the washing up and, after a time, was making himself really useful. When I came in and introduced him to her she was most amused: he was Lance Reventlow, Barbara Hutton's son, one of the richest young men in America.

★ ★ ★

It was becoming difficult to find Continental events in which to drive the 3.8: the promoters were favouring smaller-capacity races in the belief that they were safer. I had to content myself with drives in the principal British meetings at Silverstone, Aintree and Goodwood. In July, Aintree staged the European Grand Prix and a British car won for the first time since 1923! The car was, of course, a Vanwall, driven first by Tony Brooks and then by Stirling

Moss when his own car became sick. Tony was recuperating from an accident and had, very sportingly, told Stirling that should he, Stirling, have any trouble with his car he would be happy to let him take over his own. That was exactly what did happen, and Stirling went on to record Tony Vandervell's team's first Grand Prix victory.

I drove the 3.8 in the sports car race that preceded the G.P. The track was very wet (it dried out for the G.P.) and I had a wonderful time sliding the corners. Archie Scott-Brown and his Lister-Jaguar won from Roy Salvadori's Aston Martin DBR1. I was third.

A drama, of which the excited crowd was unaware, was played out in the B.A.R.C. stand when the General Secretary, H. J. Morgan, sat on the record of the British national anthem. It did not seem too serious an accident at first, for Behra's Maserati was leading Mike Hawthorn's Ferrari; and Stirling's Vanwall, although catching them, was too far behind to have much chance of winning. Then suddenly the Maserati was out of the race, and the Ferrari had to come in to change a wheel when a tyre was punctured in running over pieces of metal shed by the retiring Maserati. As the Vanwall took over the lead a party of anxious officials left Aintree and rushed to Liverpool in search of a replacement record. Fortunately they found one, and the appropriate honours were duly applied.

That evening Tony and Lois Rolt, Rob Walker, James and Audrey Tilling, Angela and I celebrated Britain's first post-war victory in a *Grande Epreuve* in the Grosvenor hotel in Chester, where we were staying. This victory was the beginning of a new era in Grand Prix racing. We had had the drivers for some time – now we had the cars.

The following weekend the American Mackay-Frazer was

killed at Rheims, and another friend was gone. Earlier in the year Eugenio Castellotti had been killed while testing at Modena, and a pattern that was to run through to the following season had begun.

When a friend of mine, Major Mickie Boyd, asked me if I would like to join Captain Michael Boyle and himself in *Vanity 1,* for the Fastnet yacht race I was more than happy to accept. The prospect of a few restful days at sea was delightful. John Goddard, to whom I had sold my first D-Type, was also invited along.

Vanity 1 was a twelve metre yacht of thirty-eight tons, and very sea-worthy; so the fact that a gale was blowing when we left the Solent did not concern me at all. By the time we reached the Needles, however, I was very concerned. All sail had gone, leaving us with bare poles; the engine was useless; it was dark; and we were being driven before the gale. It was rather like sitting in a racing car, at speed, without brakes or steering wheel. After some hours of this unpleasantness, during which people made helpful remarks such as: 'we must be near the Isle of Wight', or 'are those the Nab races?' a naval tug crossed our bows. We hailed the watch and asked if they could take a line. They appreciated our plight, took our line, and towed us into Portsmouth harbour.

A few days later my son, Adrian, was nearly drowned off Salcombe. I had hired an old converted ship's lifeboat, which was fitted with a motor, in order to watch a small dinghy race in which Mary Lyons, Sir William's younger daughter, was competing. Adrian had asked if he could sit in a dinghy the lifeboat was towing, and I had said he could. We sailed out to a suitable vantage point and watched the race. Suddenly Caroline said: 'Where's Adrian?' Angela and I looked round and saw that both Adrian and the dinghy were missing. The painter was taut so I guessed the dinghy had sunk. I threw the boat out of gear and jumped into the water. The dinghy was about five feet below the surface with Adrian trapped under one of its seats.

I had no idea how long he might have been there, and fished him out as quickly as possible. He was terribly limp until I got his head above water, but then he lashed out and gave me a black eye. It was some time before he recovered completely, but even so he was in better shape that evening than either Angela or myself. Apparently he had stood up in the nose of the dinghy and it had turned over, trapping him underneath. He had swallowed a lot of water, and it was just as well that Caroline had missed him when she did. The black eye he had given me developed into a real beauty, and for a fortnight it stayed with me as if determined to remind me of my carelessness.

★ ★ ★

The *Daily Express* International Silverstone meeting was held in September this year and not in May as usual. The reason for the postponement was the petrol rationing that had followed the Suez crisis and its probable effect on the 'gate'. It was at this meeting that someone at last succeeded in finishing in front of Archie Scott-Brown and his Lister-Jaguar; Roy Salvadori was the man; the car was a 3.7-litre Aston Martin.

I drove my short-nosed D-Type, and was well placed when, on my fifth lap, I used too much power coming out of Becketts; I slid off sideways and damaged the front of the car. It would have been possible to repair it but in a race as short as this one (fifteen laps) it was not worthwhile, so I retired. The big race of the day, the International *Daily Express* Trophy was a triumph for the B.R.M. team – they took the first three places. The drivers were: Jean Behra, Harry Schell and Ron Flockhart, the winner's speed: 99.5 mph.

Mike Hawthorn and I drove our 3.4 Jaguars in the production car race and took the first two places. Mike's average speed was 82.19, mine was 81.73 mph. Ivor Bueb was third in another of the 3.4 saloons.

Mike and I discovered in practice that we could really throw these Jaguar saloons about. We found also that the drum brakes were not equal to the task of repeatedly slowing the cars from 130 mph to 70 mph at the end of the straight. Our method, therefore, was to take the corner without braking at all; for we had learnt in practice that it was possible – provided you were going fast enough – to turn the wheel sharply and let the scrubbing of the front tyres bring the speed down by some 30mph. This manoeuvre required a light touch, and it was possible only so long as your nerve held out. It is not necessary to indulge in such capers in a disc-braked 3.4, which is probably a very good thing.

The experience Jaguars gained in races such as these showed that disc brakes were a 'must' for these fast cars. Nevertheless, it would be wrong to condemn their drum brakes out of hand. These would give a good emergency stop from as high as 100 mph and were entirely adequate at touring speeds of 75-80 mph. The work a drum brake does in slowing a car from 120 mph to, say, 70 mph is out of all proportion to the work it does when bringing a car down from 60 mph to zero. Disc brakes are a logical engineering development: as the performance of touring cars improves, so must their braking systems. By pioneering disc brakes on their sports-racing cars Jaguars made a major contribution to road safety.

I had a very nasty experience in practice when having a minor dice with Mike. I passed him going into Stowe and nearly lost it in the process. Mike flashed his headlamps as if to say: 'Have a care'. I laughed and pressed on. Then Mike began flashing continuously and thinking that I was perhaps holding him up I waved him on. He drew alongside, pointed to the rear of my car and gave me the thumbs down sign. We both drove into the pits where I discovered that my near side rear wheel was held on by one nut. If I had not passed Mike he would not have been in a position to see what was happening and next time round the wheel would have come off.

The B.A.R.C. September meeting at Goodwood provided some of the best racing of the season. The Formula 2 race for the Woodcote Cup was – up to that time – the fastest race ever run at Goodwood; Roy Salvadori won in a works Cooper at 94.43 mph. The race in which I was interested was the twenty-one lap Goodwood Trophy for unlimited capacity sports cars. I was driving my 3.8 and achieved second fastest practice time. Archie Scott-Brown and his Lister-Jaguar were fastest in practice and his car was on pole position when we lined up for the Le Mans-type start. I knew my only hope of beating Archie lay in making a superb getaway, so when the flag fell I ran for my life, leapt into the car, pressed the button, and shot off with my foot hard down. The car performed the most extraordinary convolutions and I found myself facing the chicane with excited officials and photographers scattering in all directions. By the time I turned round again the field had gone and Archie was out of sight. 1 spent the entire race passing other cars and eventually finished fifth. *Autosport* wrote: 'Duncan Hamilton motored mightily to career through the field and into fifth place after his mishap at the start – and his progress was also much to the detriment of the chicane area'. Archie won as he pleased, finishing over half a minute in front of the Tojeiro-Jaguar of Jack Brabham. Henry Taylor was third in a D-Type.

I did not race in the Coupe du Salon in October: the new 3-litre limit precluded my D-Types. The following season we had a 3-litre Jaguar engine; it was not available in 1957. I was very proud to receive from the French Government the *Medaille d'Or de L'Education Physique et des Sports,* and with it a charming complimentary letter from the French Prime Minister. The letter informed me that the award had been made in recognition of my services to motor sport and my contributions to British prestige at Le Mans. I had always enjoyed myself in France, both racing and having fun; that *La Belle France* should add a medal to all the pleasure she had given me appeared almost unfair.

CHAPTER SIXTEEN

THE FINAL SEASON

E arly in 1958 I spent a fortnight at Enton Hall dieting. I lost a stone in weight and felt all the better for it. Some friends of mine, who were of more meagre proportions than myself, had tried to suggest that I lose this stone only to improve the power-to-weight ratio of my racing cars. I denied this; but it is interesting to consider what effect the weight of the driver has on, say, a Formula 1 car. Designers go to fantastic lengths to save a few pounds weight when constructing a chassis; why not go all the way and employ drivers the size and weight of jockeys. After all there is little point in building an all-aluminium engine and saving perhaps fifty pounds in weight if the car is to be driven by a man weighing sixteen stone. This is not altogether serious; but there is many a true word spoken in jest.

In February, Angela and I drove down to Nice in my XK150. We visited Le Mans on the way, and took note of such alterations as had, or were being, made for the race in

June. The French roads were free of traffic at that time of the year and we achieved high average speeds. The weather also was good and we enjoyed ourselves. My luck in the casino was such that I covered all our expenses.

At the end of March I drove in my first club meeting. Eric Brown, the then secretary of the Jaguar Drivers' Club, asked me if I would come to their meeting at Brands Hatch and bring a D-Type along. I was only too happy to do this and I went so far as to drive an XK140 as well. I did not appreciate the fact that he had entered me as a competitor in three classes and I was very embarrassed when I learnt that I had won some silverware.

The first International meeting was at Goodwood on Easter Monday. I drove my D-Type with a 3.4-litre engine and finished third in the Sussex Trophy behind Stirling Moss in an Aston Martin DBR2, and Peter Collins in a then very new 2-litre V6 Ferrari. Archie Scott-Brown in a 3.8-litre Lister-Jaguar had a splendid dice with Stirling in the early stages, but after a few laps mechanical trouble caused his retirement and from then on Stirling was on his own. Peter's Ferrari was fantastically fast for a 2-litre.

I knew I was going quickly because there was no one behind me; and with Graham Whitehead's Aston Martin DB3S, the 3-litre V12 *Testa Rossa* Ferraris of Mairesse and Bianchi, Peter Whitehead's Lister-Jaguar, and an assortment of Aston Martins and D-Types in the field, it was obvious that they could not all be travelling slowly. At about half distance I had observed that Peter's car was slowing and I really went after him. It was all to no avail, however, though I was catching up fast at the end.

Mike Hawthorn won the principal race of the day, the Formula 1 Glover Trophy, in a new G.P. Ferrari. Stirling

Moss stalled his Cooper on the line and was last away from the start. He came up through the field very quickly, but he could not catch Mike's Ferrari, and eventually his engine blew up. Jean Behra clouted the chicane when the brakes on his B.R.M. failed but fortunately without serious injury to himself. Once Moss and Behra had gone the race became very processional and Mike won by thirty-six seconds from Jack Brabham's Cooper.

The following weekend saw everyone up at Oulton Park for the British Empire Trophy. The race, according to Mike Hawthorn, who attended only to watch, was very dull. Stirling Moss won in a 3.9-litre Aston Martin from Tony Brooks in a sister car; Archie Scott-Brown, in Bruce Halford's Lister-Jaguar, was third, and I was fourth in my D-Type. Archie's own car, a 3.8-litre Lister-Jaguar, which everyone expected to push the Aston Martins, had mechanical trouble in its heat and did not qualify for the final. Bruce Halford, who had driven very well in his heat and qualified for the final, very sportingly lent his car to Archie. Bruce's car had the 3.4-litre engine fitted and was not tailored for someone as short in the leg as Archie, who could hardly reach the pedals. That he was able to finish third is a measure of his enormous ability.

Archie and I had a spill together in the enclosure when the table we were sitting on collapsed under our weight and deposited us on the floor. Archie thought it was terribly funny, and one of my last memories of him is of our sitting there laughing at one another. A few days later he was dead: he succumbed to the severe burns he received when his Lister-Jaguar crashed at Spa in Belgium. It was typical of him that he was leading the race at the time. Everyone liked Archie. It is a British characteristic to admire those who triumph over adversity, and Archie, who had been born with a withered arm, no right hand, and short legs had certainly done that. Sportsmen everywhere mourned him.

He had driven in one major race in England before going to Spa, and that was at Silverstone in the B.R.D.C. organized, *Daily Express* sponsored, International meeting. He drove his 3.8-litre Lister-Jaguar as usual but was pipped by Masten Gregory in another 3.8-litre Lister-Jaguar. Mike Hawthorn was third in a V.6 3-litre Ferrari. Mike's car was faster down the straights than the 3.8s but it could not touch them on the corners. Only a driver of Mike's class could have driven the car at all. I gathered that the Ferrari had an experimental chassis; I know that Mike's comments on the car's handling did not please the designer – who was present – at all. I drove my D-Type, but spun off at Becketts when baulked by a slower car and damaged the steering too badly to go on racing.

The production car race was won by Mike in his 3.4 Jaguar saloon. His car was miles faster than any of the other 3.4s, but Mike told me he would give the crowd a race. It was typical of him that he did just that, winning by one second from Tommy Sopwith in another 3.4.

The Trophy race was won by Peter Collins in a G.P. Ferrari. Although Peter led for the first five laps, once Jean Behra's B.R.M. had passed him it looked as if the British car would win. The B.R.M. was faster on the corners, and had enough steam to stay in front on the straight. Nothing is certain in motor racing, however, and a stone broke a glass in Behra's goggles and cut his eye, causing him to come into the pits for new goggles and medical attention. This stop dropped him to tenth place and he was out of it so far as winning was concerned, though he drove well to finish fourth. Salvadori was second in a works Cooper and Masten Gregory third in another B.R.M.

I went back to Silverstone a fortnight later – once again at the request of Eric Brown – and drove my D-Type, with the 3.8-litre engine, for the last time on a race track. The race was a relay race for the David Brown Trophy and it was won by a team of M.Gs. I spent most of the day looking at Jaguar Drivers Club members' engines and enjoyed myself very much.

The following Wednesday I took my D-Type up to the factory to have the new 3-litre engine fitted for Le Mans. Everyone up there was wonderfully helpful and nothing was too much trouble. I lunched with Lofty England who suggested that Ivor Bueb would be a good man to rope in as co-driver; he told me also a great deal about the new engine which, in Le Mans tune, peaked at 7,000 rpm. The 3.4 and 3.8-litre Jaguar engines had given their maximum output at around 5,800 rpm and we never ran them over 6,000 rpm; I felt it was going to be interesting to drive the car with this new engine and another 1,000 rpm. When racing a 3.4 or 3.8-litre D-Type you drove in a rev range of 4,500 to 5,800; with the new engine it was to be in the rev range of 5,500 to 7,000.

The day after my lunch with Lofty, Angela and I went to a party given by Gerald Lascelles at Fort Belvedere. David Brown was there and he questioned me closely about the new Jaguar engine. I told him about as much as he told me about his Aston Martins, which was precisely nothing.

Whitsun Monday saw me back at Goodwood for an enjoyable and successful day's racing. The main event was the twenty-one lap Whitsun Trophy and but for a boob on the part of my pit I would have won. My best D-Type was up at the works and I was driving another one fitted with a 3.4-litre engine which I had in my stable. Graham Whitehead and Bruce Halford had Lister-Jaguars and their cars were faster than mine in practice as was only to be expected. Not only were they lighter than the D-Type but their independent rear ends saw them round the corners quicker.

A Le Mans start was used, and Graham's car was left behind when it refused to respond to the button. Halford led for a while until he left the course at St Mary's and let me into the lead ahead of John Dalton in a DB3S Aston Martin. Meanwhile, Graham was going through the field very quickly. By the eleventh lap Halford was chasing me hard and though I held him off for a while he passed me again on the sixteenth lap only to retire a few moments later with a deranged throttle control. There was no one behind me, and since my pit did not give me any signal I presumed the race was in my pocket and eased up. Graham Whitehead actually picked up seven seconds on me on the eighteenth lap and, by the time I saw him in my mirror it was too late. He passed me on the nineteenth lap and won. With less than four laps to go my lead had been nine seconds and, although the Lister-Jaguar was a faster car than the D-Type, it was not fast enough to concede nine seconds in four laps.

John Coombs had asked me if I would drive a disc brake 3.4-litre Jaguar saloon of his in the production car race. The car was modified like the one I had raced the previous year at Silverstone and it went very quickly. I made a good start, led into the first corner, and was never pressed for the entire race. My winning average was 78.95 mph and I finished seventeen seconds in front of Tommy Sopwith in another 3.4. It was amazing how one could throw this saloon about and, during the final practice session on the Saturday afternoon, I had the greatest fun dicing with Bill Moss in my old E.R.A. *Remus.*

That was a 1.5-litre supercharged racing car and in its day was one of the fastest E.R.A.s built. It could not live with the 3.4 on a corner, and though Moss would pass me down the straight I would regain the lead at the next corner. The explanation was the Jaguar's superior suspension. Indeed, Moss's average speed of 82.14 mph when winning the race for historic racing cars was only 3.19 mph faster than my winning time in the 3.4. Since both of us won easily the times are comparable. When you consider that the E.R.A. was a stark racing car, and the 3.4 a comfortable four-seater saloon, fitted with all modern motoring conveniences, the comparison is interesting.

I had the chance to make another comparison a few days later when I went to the M.I.R.A. proving ground at Linley and drove my D-Type with its new 3-litre engine. I was delighted with the result of the test; the new engine was sweet all the way round the dial and the car handled perfectly. I was really looking forward to Le Mans.

★ ★ ★

I took my equipe to Le Mans a full week before the race, and once again Jaguars gave me full support. Both Ivor Bueb and I were pleased with the car in practice; not only was the engine all one could wish, but the new Dunlop R5 racing tyres were a really big improvement on their predecessors. We both found that with these tyres we could take the curve under the Dunlop bridge flat out, a thing neither of us had been able to do before.

On race day I asked Ivor if he would take the first drive.

He made a good start and was always well placed. Stirling Moss, in an Aston Martin, made his usual brilliant start and was away and under the Dunlop bridge before anyone else had really got going. Behind him went Tony Brooks, Graham Whitehead and Roy Salvadori, all in Aston Martins. Then came Ivor, followed by Mike Hawthorn's Ferrari and Bruce Halford's Lister-Jaguar. Mike soon moved up to second place but could not do anything about Stirling who was going very, very fast – too fast perhaps!

Both the Ecurie Ecosse Jaguars retired with piston trouble, and Cliff Allison's Lotus, which had gone very quickly in practice and was thought to be a likely Index of Performance winner, withdrew with an overheated engine. Stirling built up an advantage of one minute thirty-five seconds in just over two hours, and then blew up, leaving Mike in the lead. Mike handed over to Peter Collins, but after only a few laps Peter brought the Ferrari in for a long pit stop and the Von Trips/Seidel Ferrari took over the lead. Storm clouds had been gathering for some time and now the rain really came down slowing most of the cars to touring speeds. A lot of mud ran on to the road, particularly in front of the Dunlop bridge.

With every car coming in to refuel and change drivers the positions of the various contestants became confused, but as soon as all changes had taken place I found that I was third behind the Ferraris of Seidel and Phil Hill. Cars were crashing all around the circuit, and Jean Brousselet, better known by his pseudonym of Mary, was killed when his Jaguar crashed and an American-driven Ferrari ran into his car and over him. I nearly joined this pile up and, had it not been for a Frenchman who threw his hat on the road in front of me, I would have done so. I guessed the significance of his gesture and slowed enough to be able to miss the crashed cars round the corner. This Frenchman – and I have never been able to find out who he was – saved my life.

When I handed over to Ivor at about ten p.m. we were lying second behind the Hill/Gendebien Ferrari. By midnight Ivor was in the lead driving brilliantly. The Ferrari got the lead back and by four a.m., half way, led us by over two minutes; there was, however, a long way to go, and both Ivor and I knew that our disc brakes would pay dividends in the concluding stages: so long as we could keep the Ferrari in sight we had nothing to worry about. Dawn came and passed, more cars retired, and the race went on. At around midday, with twenty hours of racing behind us, we lay just one lap behind the Ferrari, and nine laps ahead of the third car, the Aston Martin of Peter and Graham Whitehead. I was crowding on the pace because it was now that I wanted Hill and Gendebien to use their drum brakes to the full in order to maintain their lead. There was every chance that their brakes would not last, particularly if the rain stopped. Suddenly I drove into a cloudburst. A Panhard saloon had stopped, not only in the middle of the storm, but in the middle of the road. I tried to miss him, but in doing so got a wheel on the grass and the car spun. For a moment I was conscious of trying to steer the car while travelling backwards and then all went blank. I woke up briefly in the ambulance and a woman said: '*vous n'êtes pas mort*'. Then I passed out again.

Apparently the Panhard had suddenly misted up, and the driver, unable to see, had stopped. He was a very lucky man still to be alive. I have been told that my car hit a bank and somersaulted, falling eventually across a ditch full of water. I fell out of the car and into the water and, but for the presence of two Frenchmen who were sheltering from the storm, I would have been drowned. On the other hand, had my cockpit not fallen across the ditch, I would have been crushed to death under the falling car. It was an incredibly lucky escape.

For years I, and many other drivers, had been complaining of the danger of letting inexperienced drivers and cars of widely differing speed potential on the Le Mans circuit together. Now I was a victim of the likely circumstance I had been predicting. An experienced racing driver would never have stopped his car as the driver of that Panhard did; and if he had stopped it would have been off the road. If you ask: 'But what if he could not see?' My reply is 'What did Masten Gregory and I do when the D-Type's head lamps went out at 180 mph?'

We got round to the pits without endangering another car. The experienced driver will do something positive; he will never stop in the middle of the road in a car that is still in running order. If you have crashed or the car is undrivable it is another matter. In this case a man stopped because he could not see very well and I was very nearly killed.

After our departure the Hill/Gendebien Ferrari toured round to win by over 100 miles from Peter and Graham Whitehead's Aston Martin. A trio of Porsches led by Behra and Herrmann, took the next three places.

I woke up in the maternity ward of Le Mans Hospital feeling very unwell. My head was throbbing, and my legs were so painful I felt sure they must be broken. A doctor assured me that I was suffering only from very severe bruising and, though I was pleased to receive this information, the knowledge that my legs were only bruised did not make them any the less painful. Angela was allowed to see me, so was Lofty England, and a little later several other friends as well; I did my best to appear cheerful, and even posed for the press photographers, but I felt awful for several days.

Apart from the incredible French predisposition to carry the comedian's 'where shall I put it?' to its logical conclusion, I was comfortable in hospital. Though no sooner was I as much at ease as my injuries allowed than a cheerful nun would appear and assault me with a thermometer. I got my own back one day when the Mother Superior gave me a banana. Her startled: *'Non, non, non, monsieur 'amilton, c'est pour manger,'* is something I shall always remember.

While I was in hospital another old friend, Luigi Musso, was killed at Rheims during the French G.P. and Italy's last driver of real class had gone. His death brought home to me the fact that I was incredibly lucky to be alive; it also made me aware of the truism that no one can go on being lucky forever. Musso had had a very lucky escape at Spa only a few weeks previously, now he was dead.

Angela drove me home to Wokingham in Lofty England's 3.4 Jaguar: he had very kindly left the car behind for this purpose. The passenger seat was removed so that I could sit in the back without bending my legs. After some time at home I felt well enough to go up to Silverstone for the British G.P. Peter Collins drove a wonderful race and won with something to spare.

A week later Sir William Lyons gave a twenty-first birthday party for his daughter, Mary. Angela and I went up to Coventry with Mike Hawthorn; we met Tony and Lois Rolt and many other friends and had a very amusing weekend. The party was terrific, and I was glad that my recent injuries gave me a good excuse for not getting up from my chair until I felt able so to do.

Towards the end of July I began to drive again. My right leg was not as badly injured as the left and I found that I could drive my Rolls-Royce, which had automatic transmission, without too much difficulty. I drove up to London one day and lunched with two friends, Tony Samuel and Leopold Ullstein. After lunch I was driving down Norfolk Street on my way to the Embankment when I saw an old friend whom I believed to be dead. I stopped the car and hailed him.

'Nobby Clark?' I enquired.

'Duncan Hamilton,' he replied.

'I thought you went down in the *Glorious*,' I said.

He laughed 'No I was blown on to a destroyer before *Glorious* went down, but because of wireless silence and one thing and another I was reported missing believed killed.'

'Well we can't talk here,' I said, 'let's go down to H.M.S. *President* for a drink.' H.M.S. *President* is moored not far from Cleopatra's Needle on the Embankment. He got into the passenger seat and we drove down to and parked on the Embankment. We got out of the car; he on to the pavement, I on to the road. I was about to shut the driver's door when I saw a bus bearing down on me. I pressed myself against the car and the bus smartly removed the seat of my pants and the door of the Rolls. I was, not unnaturally, shaken and when the driver and conductor of the bus began to blame me for the accident I became very annoyed. The conductor claimed to have witnessed everything, though since he admitted to being on his platform at the relevant time it was difficult to see how he could have seen the bus removing the seat of my pants without losing his nose on the roof of the Rolls. Anyway he made his claim and gave his particulars to a policeman who arrived on the scene. I gave the policeman the details he required and exchanged information with the driver. I then mentioned that I had a witness, and explained that the witness had been my passenger. By now the driver of the bus was very cocky and he demanded particulars, as did the patient and good-humoured policeman.

'Name?' asked the policeman.

'Commander Clark,' Nobby replied.

'Address?'

'Berkeley House, Berkeley Square, W.1.'

'Occupation?'

'Inspector of Accidents, Ministry of Transport.'

I laughed so much that I dropped one of the two crutches with which I was obliged to walk and fell down. Here was a man I had not seen for eighteen years; a man about whom I knew nothing. I had given him a lift so that we could have a quiet drink together and a chat about things past and present. I had, through no fault of my own, an accident, and this man turned out to be perhaps the most qualified and experienced witness in the United Kingdom.

London Transport did not contest my claim. They put a new door on the Rolls, and a new seat in my trousers, and I have a feeling that the driver of that bus never took anything for granted again.

In August I took Angela and the children down to Devon on holiday and while we were there Tim Seccombe telephoned to say that Peter Collins had been killed in the German G.P. It took all the pleasure out of my holiday; only two weeks before I had been congratulating Peter after his win in the British G.P. and now he too was gone. Poor Peter, one of the gayest and most likeable characters who ever graced a race meeting. Peter, Mike Hawthorn and myself had had some wonderful times together, and for Mike and myself no meeting was ever quite the same again.

In September I drove in my last big race: the Tourist Trophy at Goodwood. I shared my D-Type with Peter Blond and we finished sixth. We made a good pair: he had a broken toe, I was still walking with two sticks.

The race was a triumph for Aston Martin who took the first three places. The drivers were Stirling Moss/Tony Brooks; Roy Salvadori/Jack Brabham; Carroll Shelby/Stuart Lewis-Evans.

During practice Reg Parnell asked me if I would like a few laps in the DBRl Aston Martin. Naturally I said yes, and in the course of twenty laps I equalled the then sports car lap record. The car handled quite differently from a D-Type and I could appreciate why it had performed so well on circuits such as the Nurburgring. The traction was good, and very little steering effort was needed on a corner compared with the D-Type. The engine was rough: it lacked the turbine-like smoothness of the Jaguar engine. The brakes were good, but required much more pedal pressure than the 'assisted' discs on the D-Type. The five-speed gearbox was pleasant in use. All in all a very good and interesting specially designed sports-racing car. I do not think it could have been driven on the road as one could drive a D-Type but, on the Nurburgring, in a race, it was superb.

Two more fine drivers were to die before the end of the year: Peter Whitehead and Stuart Lewis-Evans. Peter, like myself, was one of the few private owners still racing; his death, in the Tour de France, after so many years in the sport, was tragic. After all the racing he had done, fate was unkind to kill him in a rally.

Lewis-Evans died from burns received when his Vanwall crashed in the Moroccan G.P. This was the last Grand Prix of the season; the race that gave Mike Hawthorn the World Championship.

When Mike came back from Africa he told me that he intended to retire, and then he added: 'You'd do well to do the same Duncan, you can't go on having shunts forever'. I had been considering the question of retirement for some time and Mike's decision helped me to make up my mind. In the first place the D-Type was now somewhat passé, and there was no other British car coming along in which a private owner could hope to compete against the world's sports cars. After my long association with Jaguars I did not really want to drive another make.

I had hoped Sir William Lyons would release his E-Type; if he had done so I might not have retired when I did. The small-capacity sports cars did not interest me; they were capable of fast lap times and handled well, but they could not have the maximum speed of the larger capacity sports cars, and could not, therefore, give the thrill and enjoyment which to me was inseparable from real road racing. I would have liked to see the capacity of Formula 1 cars going up not down. Anyone who saw the pre-war Mercedes-Benz and Auto Union Grand Prix cars will know what I mean from a spectator's point of view – you knew you were watching racing cars. Anyone who has driven a 4.5-litre Ferrari or Lago-Talbot of the immediate post-war era knows what I mean from a driver's point of view – you knew you were driving a racing car. The modern small-capacity space-framed cars were wonderful examples of the designer's art; but both to drive, and to watch, they were but shallow imitations of the real thing.

On Friday, December 19th 1958, Mike Hawthorn, his girlfriend Jean Howath, Angela and myself had dinner together at the Ivy Restaurant in London. We uncorked a bottle of champagne, shook hands, and drank to a mutually long and happy retirement. A month later Mike was dead, killed when his car skidded on the Portsmouth road and hit a tree. I had an appointment with him that afternoon to discuss details of a pending sporting business venture of ours; with his death the venture never came to fruition. Instead of meeting him in his office as arranged, I went to Guildford Mortuary and formally identified him; it was almost the saddest moment in my life.

★ ★ ★

In April 1959, I gave a small dinner party at the Royal Thames Yacht Club and formally announced my retirement from active motor racing. Sir William Lyons was kind enough to come along and his warm remarks meant much to me. Lofty England, Bill Heynes, Tony Rolt, Reg Parnell, Mike Couper, John Eason-Gibson, Joe Wright, Brian Turle, Dick Jeffrey, Donald Healey and Gregor Grant were present and I believe we all enjoyed our evening together.

During the next two years my business and family occupied most of my time. My new hobby was yachting, and this pursuit, although much less exciting than motor racing, was equally interesting. I sailed *Joya*, a fifteen-ton yacht, during 1959; and in 1960 I progressed to something more ambitious in thirty-eight ton *Valmara*. It was for me the start of a whole new chapter, and a highly enjoyable one too...

CHAPTER SEVENTEEN

REFLECTIONS

Looking back today – at a range of thirty years – on *Touch Wood*, it's interesting to observe how fashions have changed in the way motor racing stories are now told. Today such a story might be more a tale of intrigue and high-finance in negotiating with devious team chiefs and high-rolling sponsors, of petty likes and dislikes within the enclosed world of modern motor racing. But it simply wasn't a sport played that way during the 1950s. We were essentially sportsmen paying our own way most of the time to participate in a game we thoroughly enjoyed. Looking back at some of the circuits we used to race on, I am often asked if we had any conception of danger? No – I don't suppose we did. Motor racing was really a simple extension of everyday road driving. It wasn't the totally different specialised science it has become today. So, in simple straightforward 'it will hurt if you hit it terms', it didn't really occur to us that we should not accept racing past ditches and trees and walls and telegraph poles, since most of us were accustomed to driving pretty quickly on everyday roads in any case.

Another very potent factor which contributed to this attitude was of course that many of us – particularly in the late-'40s and early-'50s, counted ourselves damned lucky to have got away with six years of wartime activities, when every morning one awoke seemed like a bonus. I certainly felt that. It was quite a pronounced sensation when you were, for example, encased in a floating aerodrome – an aircraft carrier – on the way to Russia... In comparison with being shot at and threatened and subject to the arguable reliability of all kinds of flying machine, motor racing was incredibly, unutterably SAFE... Looking back now I really consider the Zandvoort G.P. of 1948 to have been my first real race, in the Maserati 6CM. When Reg Parnell spun on the last lap – as related in Chapter Six – and I slowed down and waved him on to finish ahead of me I vividly remember Tony Rolt saying 'Blimey, you're kind!'

Later, in the *Daily Express* Trophy at Silverstone when I drove my Lago-Talbot in the pouring rain, Reg led in the ThinWall Special with me right up his jumper and the Alfa 158s of Fangio & Co struggling behind with water cascading into their supercharger intakes. Reg spun at Club and in the water I avoided him but slowed and waved him on, falling in behind him again. I suppose to a modern readership this might sound rather odd behaviour since it was meant to be 'A Motor Race', but it really came as second nature at the time. Most of us were reasonably courteous men and it was a genuine sport.

During those early years when we were running foreign-built cars there was the ever-present complication of potentially falling foul of H.M. Customs & Excise. At one stage we invested in a Maserati 4CLT, which I believe I only drove once. The car was actually loaned to us by the Italian private entrant Enrico Platé on the basis that we paid so much for its use and were aware that eventually it would have to return to Italy.

Now there was at that time a certain Mr Bird of the Customs & Excise who was quite interested in motor racing and certain cars. He had a small son who wielded a Kodak Box Brownie camera and used to photograph the racing cars and, as Mr Bird was bright enough to spot the differences between one car and another, he developed a very good grasp of what was going on and who was driving which car, and when.

Now I have never smoked in my life but I got so excited during an eight-hour Customs & Excise interview concerning importation of a foreign racing car and whether or not His Majesty was owed duty on same, that I smoked two whole packets. Ultimately Mr Bird declared 'You are clearly not making a profit out of this activity. We look upon you as proper sportsmen. . .'and then he added darkly ' . . . not like the others...'.

I saw him out of his car and passed the time of day, and we came to quite an amicable arrangement regarding further business. In that particular case we both signed a paper to the effect that, while I did in fact – for paperwork purposes – own that car, I would thereupon ensure that it was sent back out of the country a bit quick! That was the start of quite a long and friendly relationship between Mr Bird and his department and I ... and I think in general we always played pretty fair with one another. I was always entirely truthful with him, though occasionally I might choose my words with reasonable care.

The car I really loved was the 4 1/2-litre GP Lago-Talbot. I just loved the look of those things. At Silverstone in 1951 I just hung around the Talbot pits like a schoolboy, hoping for a word which might lead to a drive. Tony Lago said 'Hallo' and that broke the ice and after some discussion I asked if I could sit in one.

That rather broke the spell, because I found I simply couldn't fit behind the steering wheel! The driving position was incredibly confined, with the steering wheel in one's chest – it was pure pre-war and most unnatural for me, because I liked to drive more straight-armed style, and I'm a large chap anyway although Louis Rosier and Yves Giraud-Cabantous – neither of whom were exactly midgets – both fitted in.

But for all their size and undoubted weight, those Lago-Talbots were quite well-balanced cars and you could drift them like mad, and the brakes weren't too bad either. At the British Grand Prix at Silverstone, Johnny Claes, who I knew well, was driving his yellow, Belgian-liveried car. He was a funny fellow – he ran his jazz band of course but his family was also quite wealthy, in the Kaolin business in Brussels, and he was separated from his wife and lived in a gorgeous flat in the centre of the city. Anyway, at Silverstone he spun off at Abbey Curve and his Lago-Talbot came whirling round through the straw bales by the farm and nearly killed Angela and Lois Rolt; he covered them both with straw. I told him not to do it again! His was a twin-plug car and Tony Lago told him Duncan Hamilton might want it. With Tony's approval and some measure of support that became my car and of course I had it maintained and prepared for me by my dear old friend Louis Giron, who was another Belgian, living in my lodge in Wokingham, Berkshire.

The only trouble I had with the car was that its offset transmission casings would split. But I had a lot of fun with it. For Rouen, Tony Lago sent me a telegram asking me to drive a new car with twin-plug head '*special pour vous . . .*'. I said 'Yes of course I would'. He said that the finance was all arranged, but instead I crashed my Jaguar C-Type in the Oporto G.P., broke my ribs, fractured a vertebra in my neck and busted my jaw!

After I had driven the Lago in all the Grands Prix, including Nurburgring, and decided it was time it should go, I tried desperately to sell it but there wasn't a single nibble.

Eventually, I had left the car in store at a 'garage' behind a house on the front at Dieppe in France, because although I was free to drive it when and wherever I wanted, owing to the eagle eyes of Mr Bird and his boy's Box Brownie I couldn't keep it in England.

In fact the lady on the front at Dieppe owned a hotel and all those houses and hotels there had quite large cellars with access through doors at the back and through a hatch in the pavement at the front – the classical 'coal 'ole' in fact. So I asked her 'Do you mind if I leave a Lago-Talbot in your coal-hole?' and there it went!

Every Christmas thereafter I sent her roses. The car had been thoroughly greased-up so it should not corrode too much, years passed, and eventually I more or less forgot about the car in the coal 'ole.. .

Then out of the blue a letter arrived from a chap named Freeman in Australia, who offered me £750 Australian for it. We had a Labour Government at the time so I was desperately keen to rip his arm off at such an offer. He specified the car should be in running order and fitted with all new tyres, and I agreed immediately. All I had to do then was to retrieve the car and load it into a south-bound ship.

I called my friend John Marshall and told him 'We've got to get the Lago back to London Docks and off to Australia!' So we rushed straight off to Dieppe – and couldn't find the house!

It was hopeless – a terrible, silly, situation. I remembered that it had faced the sea with a big lawn in front, but there were rows of the damned things, all looking much like that. Eventually I convinced myself we had found the right house and I knocked the door and breezily told the lady who opened it 'I've come to collect my Lago-Talbot'. Her expression hardly changed, she uttered not a word but simply shut the door in my face! Perhaps it wasn't the right house after all.

We consulted Mr Locker, the RAC rep at Dieppe who had been there since the 1920s, but he couldn't remember which house it was either. We finally concluded that the house owner had died, but after a few brandies Johnny said 'Let's go round the back and have a look'. So we stole round the back of the row of houses to see if anything there might jog our memories. We had a Vanguard van ready to tow the Talbot and one coal hole door seemed to ring bells so we opened it. The cellar was full of coke, but Johnny was convinced this was the place and he grabbed a shovel which lay there and began digging. It was an extraordinary scene, and after an hour we found the tops of the tyres and the Lago emerged. We eventually attached a tow rope to it and after two hours digging drew it out. We blew off as much of the coal-dust as we could, tipped in five gallons of fuel and towed it off behind the Vanguard, and after all its years of storage it fired up and blew coal-dust all over Dieppe. I drove it down to the ferry, where we found RAC Port Officer Locker waving a Union Jack!

The car was on the boat on its way to Australia when another letter arrived from Freeman saying he could only send £7 10s a month, payable by banker's draft. I wrote back saying I'll accept it but could you please pay rather larger instalments – and he did eventually, I can't remember receiving the correct amount.

Of course my Jaguars formed the backbone of my racing career. I really liked the C-Types, and my D-Types became the most extensively developed cars of their type ever to be raced.

I think Lofty England of Jaguar first decided I could drive a bit when my works Healey Silverstone beat all the expensive factory Aston Martins in the Production Car Race at Silverstone as described in Chapter Seven. Despite its rather sober appearance, never ever under-estimate the Healey Silverstone! That car handled wonderfully well. I could drive it flat around Stowe Corner – I could perhaps have used a higher axle ratio – but its independent front suspension was superb while the rear end's only problem was that it allowed the tyres to rub the bodywork and the inside rear wheel tended to lift and spin in tighter corners.

I really felt that day that I could fix them all, and I did, and Lofty came over afterwards and said '. . . you went well in that thing' and asked me to drive for them. I wasn't really very keen on sports car racing, but I had a contract with Shell which was compatible with Jaguar and so that particular relationship began.

A severely limiting factor on all cars at that time was the fact the available tyres were always too narrow and too hard. The manufacturers were only interested in wear, nothing else mattered, and I made myself unpopular by insisting 'I want adhesion'. I used to let down the pressures to achieve it, and Freeman of Dunlop would throw up his hands in horror. I used to threaten him, saying I would go to Englebert instead, but we got on well really and I never left Dunlop. They always provided free tyres for me, and I sold a 3.4 Jaguar which I had had to Freeman. I really had more faith in Dunlop than I would ever admit to them. They seldom let me down, although in the terrible heat at Dakar for example, where my D was genuinely exceeding 200 mph, we had to buff our tyres down to half the tread thickness and even then they split. The first time in fact cost me the race.

I was always happier than most to race in the wet, and also in the dark, which subsequently bore fruit of course at Le Mans. The slicker conditions became, the more I enjoyed myself. One certainly used to see an awful number of bad decisions being made by those about me... I really objected to some of the silly errors perpetrated, particularly those of the French goon in his misted-up Panhard who caused me to crash at 160mph while lying second at Le Mans in '58, sending me spinning three times in the air and falling out as the car crashed down on top of me. I really didn't appreciate that, and looking back today I still don't. Some times when similar – but less consequential – incidents occurred in front of me I would often get out of the car very angry at the end of a 4 1/2-hour driving spell.

The Sarthe was always unique for its weather and you could always tell when rain was in the offing there amongst the pine forests because the air would take on a kind of bitter taste, there'd be a scent to it almost of smelling salts as you charged round in your open cockpit. Then down would come the rain, and up from the road and the verges and the pine forest floor would come the mist.

After Sir William Lyons had decided to withdraw from racing with his Jaguar factory team after Le Mans 1956, he was very good to me. He said 'We're very happy over what you've done for us,' and was most helpful with almost anything I wanted.

I had seven D-Types from him in all – first the aluminium front subframe 1954 car 'OKV 1' – then two more after that.

There was a stage when the factory couldn't sell them for love nor money. Fortunately the factory caught fire!

We made what was in effect the first road-going XKSS out of 'OKV 1' and sold it to Jumbo Goddard at Chobham.

The idea was to cut out the centre structural beam within the cockpit to provide a conventional wide-open affair, and then add a practical-sized windscreen and proper hood and habitable gear. I telephoned Lofty about cutting out the beam and he said ask Munger Heynes who said I couldn't do it, the car would fold in half. From my own engineering knowledge I didn't believe it would, so I said 'Cut it out anyway' and my chaps cut it out and it provided a nice open cockpit and 'OKV 1' thus became in effect the first XKSS, followed by a dozen or so others built complete with bumpers by the factory as Sir William thought it would be a good idea.

You couldn't at that time get things like windscreens made in England, short of investing a fortune in a one-off. A fellow in Bracknell made a brass screen surround for us and we adopted the rear window from the Studebaker which fitted the D perfectly.

Jumbo Goddard was another ex-Naval chap. He'd been at Scapa during the war, and our mutual friend Jack Howey had bought my pale-green C-Type earlier – 'MDU 214' – and he wood-panelled it, and had the steering wheel from a gullwing Mercedes-Benz fitted.

Jumbo also wanted a magneto on 'OKV 1' because he didn't trust reliance upon a battery for starting, and he specified a starting handle instead poking through the car's nose. I told him in no uncertain terms not to mess it about any more, but he was certainly a great enthusiast even if some of his preferences did seem rather eccentric.

Eventually, each of my racing D-Types sold for more than £3,500 each which was excellent money at the time – more than Jaguar's could realise for them. But of course my cars were quite special by the time we had finished with them. I had quite a lot of good chaps who worked for me on the cars. One Dutchman was very good, Fredricus Gorelius Boelens, and then Robin Freeman BSc came along later, very bright, very young, quite impossible of course, and someone who would not be told a thing. We got on and argued like a house on fire, and Robin and I did all sorts of things, he really was a good chap at his job and soon started his own business.

I had twice had blown head gaskets and I said 'I've got to see inside the head before I race' so Robin invented an inspectorscope which is now used in jets and in the medical world.

Pat Griffith of Coopers Mechanical Joints was ex-Fleet Air Arm and he came to Hyeres in the South of France when he crashed his Aston DB3. He subsequently made me our special gaskets free of charge. They never failed.

I also became increasingly fed up with Vandervell's ThinWall bearings because our oil temperature was always too high on the Jaguars. Another school chum was

Chairman of Glacier bearings and when I told him some of our problems he responded by making special new bearings for me on the strength of winning the Jaguar contract, which unfortunately did not happen.

We had more special Borg pistons made for us in Paris – and because the standard D-Type starter was in light alloy and prone to shearing and cracking, as it once did on the start line in Lisbon, which could have cost us Le Mans – all my cars had starting motor castings all in bronze and they never gave any trouble.

Those bronze starter motor castings were made for us by Martins Almeida – the Jaguar agent in Portugal – in just 24 hours and they only cost £12. We did try to succeed.

With our Glacier bearings and special head gaskets and other tweaks our Jaguars had real strength and real stamina and that was really why they shone during that period. A lot was written about the success of such standard cars, but mine were anything but standard. Munger Heynes was super but one could never talk figures to him. I had big carburetters fitted and generally fiddled about with everything. I did a separate deal with Lodge Plugs who made what I really wanted, with platinum electrodes – more expensive of course, but in my recollection faultless.

We had also used sodium-filled valves on the C-Type – the thicker stem demanding different valve guides – and where the standard Jaguar valve cost around 7-shillings, my sodium-filled valves cost nearer £12... But they contributed a great deal to our success.

Because there was good money to be earned in racing extensively around Europe, and in North Africa too – I had at one stage cars based in Scandinavia, Europe and Morocco – because you couldn't fly cars around so much nor so easily in those days and so I placed those three cars in these strategic places.

Ecurie Ecosse obviously did terribly well with their ex-works cars. They really made the best of a very difficult job, but the only time I was really beaten by Ecosse was at St Etienne, in France, by Ron Flockhart who passed me while I was stopping to sort out the Carini/Baretto head-on collision which had killed both drivers. I had previously taken pole position by almost 2 seconds in the rain, so I was rather miffed by that.

While still driving for the Jaguar works team, I did a lot of disc-brake testing at M.I.R.A. near Nuneaton. We used to call these 'Earth-moving Days' because without warning those early disc-brakes would simply go away – rather like Formula 1 car wings falling off in later years. Happy days.

Obviously the original *Touch Wood* text reveals a great deal about my friendship with Mike Hawthorn, ten years my junior, but a kindred character and a very great racing driver. I would have liked to have had Mike on my side in the war – he was that kind of chap. He was also in my experience a good engineer and aviator. We were in so many ways kindred spirits.

We were very frank with each other whatever the subject. When we drove together Mike was always ready to ask if any particular corner would be taken in a certain manner or if some tweak on a car might be possible and I would give him my honest opinion. Often where driving was concerned I would tell him that I was too old to do it now, but it can be done – and he'd go out and do it, probably even better.

The Longnose D-Type at Le Mans pulled 197mph in 1955 and Mike and I were the only two who could take the Mulsanne kink flat out in the wet. In discussing this, it became a case of 'Are you going to kid me or not?'.

And I confided in Mike that 'I go into it flat and about three-quarters of the way through the head takes over and I ease my foot about half an inch off the throttle'. And Mike said 'Put it there! That's exactly what I do!'.

After giving up motor racing, life could have been dull in comparison, but it really did not. I flung myself energetically into the motor business and into sailing. In 1959 I bought *Joya* a 40-foot Bermuda-rigged sloop – and from her graduated to *Valmara* a 60-foot Bermudan cutter in which we covered most of the south-west coast of England and all the French ports we could get into.

In 1962, we took the family and some friends, and went west-about. I hoped that with luck and a high tide we would get into Salcombe where Sir William and Lady Lyons of Jaguar had a house at Bolt Head. We hit the bar as we came in, but floated clear and moored-up by the town where Sir William came down to inspect the yacht and have a good look at the engine rooms.

He then invited us all up to Bolt House. On the face of the cliff were two World War Two gun emplacements, one below the other, about 200 yards apart. He had had the tops of them removed, the gun aperture filled in and converted them into swimming pools. The sea water was pumped by electricity all the way up to a waterfall in the garden which streamed down to both pools.

One of his house guests was Sir Frank Whittle, the inventor of the jet engine, who joined us at the pool and the conversation, of course, was all aeroplanes, engines and cars. I always regarded that morning as Adrian's first lesson on engineering – you could not have wished for better lecturers!

The following day, with 'good weather' forecast, the Lyons joined us for a day's sailing, but after lunch the sun went in, the sea started to get rough, the wind backed 180-degrees and was rising steadily.

Sir William and Lady Lyons had never sailed in a yacht of this size and as everyone was finding it hard to move about, they decided the best and safest place was on the floor of the saloon. With Adrian, Sid – my hand – and I on the helm, we got on with the sailing but there was no way we could get back into Salcombe with a heavy sea and a rising force 8 gale. The only option was to sail down to Dartmouth where we stayed the night and our very relieved guests returned home by car.

I greatly admired both Sir William and his wife for their fortitude and later received a very kind letter from him – nonetheless saying he was not going to sea again for a very long time!

I kept *Valmara* for five years and we had many happy times in her but, with a view to warmer climes, I forthwith headed for the Mediterranean in my E-Type Jaguar with James Tilling and bought *Cynara*, a beautiful classic 120-ton gaff-rigged ketch which I had coveted for some time. We had a permanent crew of three hands and a chef – and we kept her moored in Monaco. She was very spacious and we sailed extensively in the Mediterranean and were even chartered for film making when we had an entertaining few days with Tony Curtis, Zsa Zsa Gabor and Warren Mitchell – long before Alf Garnett. During the Monaco Grand Prix period we would have many parties on board and around 1965 Adrian did his best to drown Graham Hill while towing him on water skis, and Gregor Grant – founding editor of *'Autosport'* magazine – toppled cheerfully overboard after spending some time consuming Cointreau in a half-pint glass.

On another occasion, Prince Rainier invited all the

members of the *Club des Anciens Pilotes* – an association of
retired racing drivers – and our wives to the palace for a
reception. David Niven, another guest, was talking to Fangio
and he suggested we should see the cars in the dungeon but
first we should inspect the Prince's idea of HiFi. We set forth
along a lengthy, carpeted corridor overhung by enormous
chandeliers and flanked by sentries in 18th Century uniform
guarding each of the massive mahogany doors. From one of
these doors issued the sound of music and as we entered we
were greeted by the amazing spectacle of a 40-piece
orchestra complete with conductor standing on his dais
complete with white tie and tails.

David then asked if we would like to see 'a bit of Africa' so
off we went to another room with an even more bizarre
revelation as we found ourselves in tropical heat surrounded by
palm trees, monkeys and squawking parrots. There we settled
into deck chairs and were served drinks by a palace retainer.

Our next venture was to ride down in a lift to the
dungeon which housed a beautifully kept collection of
vintage and classic cars, including several Bugattis. There was
also a London Taxi with the interior beautifully upholstered
in petit point which had been used by the Prince and
Princess, I believe, during their honeymoon. While I was
scanning the cars, the Prince arrived and asked me what I
thought of them and I was able to tell him that his 1927
Buick road wheels should not be painted black but that the
spokes should be scraped and varnished as they were made
of oak. This was put in hand forthwith.

The Mediterranean is a lovely region for sailing but can be
dangerous and we had many cruises to Italy, North Africa
and Greece and the surrounding islands. For fitting out each
winter we had to go to Italian ports and the workers – who

started at 5am each day – were all potential opera singers going full chat throughout.

After one holiday with our children, Adrian and Caroline, on board, Adrian left us to join the Sugar Line – a subsidiary of Tate & Lyle – as a supernumery officer and he went off round the world for two years in the Merchant Navy.

On the business front, Duncan Hamilton Ltd operated from my original premises within what would have been earshot of the old Brooklands Track at Byfleet. Naturally, we sold Jaguars until in 1969 we closed the Byfleet branch to concentrate our activities upon Bagshot, where we still remain today. During this period, Adrian was playing an ever more active role in the business, although looking back today, he recalls one of his greatest triumphs at the time as turning down Paul Hawkins' offer to sell him the ex-works D-Type Jaguar 'OKV 3' for £3,000 on the grounds that he knew the rugged Australian racing driver had paid only £1,500 for it and was greedily demanding excessive profit. Times change... it would cost over a million pounds today.

Adrian is now Managing Director of Duncan Hamilton & Company while I eventually retired from active full-time participation in my business in 1971. Adrian had begun to deal in what are known today as classic and historic cars around 1968, and for 14 years I owned and ran a Ford GT40 of my own – the ex-Girling brake development car, which served to keep me fully in touch with modern high-performance car capabilities. Adrian raced the GT40 a couple of times, and we also ran a Cosworth FVA engined Ford Escort in the British Saloon Car Championship, driven for us by John Hine, Mike Hailwood and occasionally Adrian, with some success. And in the early 1980s we bought not only '2

CPG' but also the Le Mans-winning C-Type of 1953 which we have retained.

I still feel that the nicest days in motor sport were just before World War Two and during the '50s and '60s. When I retired, I spent twenty years on the British Racing Drivers' Club committee and was fortunate to be able to enjoy Earl Howe's Presidency. He was a truly great sportsman with vast experience as a driver and he also kept our enthusiasm in order when it was necessary.

The B.R.D.C. at the Silverstone circuit has changed very much, like everything else, but in this case for the good and for the advancement of the sport. I well remember the day in the Mikado Room at the Savoy Hotel when, as a representative of the B.R.D.C., I signed the contract to purchase the Silverstone site from the Air Ministry, with my old friend Mike Couper of pre-war Brooklands fame.

Angela and I moved to Somerset twenty years ago, where our friends from all over come and stay with us, and I still go to Le Mans and to the Grand Prix races whenever possible.

We still have our family of Springer Spaniels whose line goes right back to when we first married 45 years ago. We have both had our 70th birthday parties, which were great fun, but sadly so many faces were missing – the years roll by quickly now, but we have been very fortunate and have many happy memories.

RACE-BY-RACE INDEX